Educational Communications and Technology: Issues and Innovations

Series Editors
J. Michael Spector
M. J. Bishop
Dirk Ifenthaler
Allan Yuen

This book series, published collaboratively between the AECT (Association for Educational Communications and Technology) and Springer, represents the best and most cutting edge research in the field of educational communications and technology. The mission of the series is to document scholarship and best practices in the creation, use, and management of technologies for effective teaching and learning in a wide range of settings. The publication goal is the rapid dissemination of the latest and best research and development findings in the broad area of educational information science and technology. As such, the volumes will be representative of the latest research findings and developments in the field. Volumes will be published on a variety of topics, including:

- Learning Analytics
- Distance Education
- Mobile Learning Technologies
- Formative Feedback for Complex Learning
- Personalized Learning and Instruction
- Instructional Design
- Virtual tutoring

Additionally, the series will publish the bi-annual AECT symposium volumes, the Educational Media and Technology Yearbooks, and the extremely prestigious and well known, Handbook of Research on Educational Communications and Technology. Currently in its 4th volume, this large and well respected Handbook will serve as an anchor for the series and a completely updated version is anticipated to publish once every 5 years.

The intended audience for Educational Communications and Technology: Issues and Innovations is researchers, graduate students and professional practitioners working in the general area of educational information science and technology; this includes but is not limited to academics in colleges of education and information studies, educational researchers, instructional designers, media specialists, teachers, technology coordinators and integrators, and training professionals.

More information about this series at http://www.springer.com/series/11824

Thomas D. Parsons • Lin Lin
Deborah Cockerham

Editors

Mind, Brain and Technology

Learning in the Age of Emerging
Technologies

 Springer

Editors
Thomas D. Parsons
College of Information
University of North Texas
Computational Neuropsychology
and Simulation
Denton, TX, USA

Lin Lin
Department of Learning Technologies
University of North Texas
Denton, TX, USA

Deborah Cockerham
Department of Learning Technologies
Fort Worth Museum of Science and History
University of North Texas
Fort Worth, TX, USA

ISSN 2625-0004   ISSN 2625-0012   (electronic)
Educational Communications and Technology: Issues and Innovations
ISBN 978-3-030-02630-1   ISBN 978-3-030-02631-8   (eBook)
https://doi.org/10.1007/978-3-030-02631-8

Library of Congress Control Number: 2018963223

This Springer imprint is published by the registered company Springer Nature Switzerland AG
The registered company address is: Gewerbestrasse 11, 6330 Cham, Switzerland

This book is dedicated to my family, mentors, co-editors, and students—my greatest gifts.
Thomas D. Parsons, PhD

To my co-editors, mentors, and colleagues, and to my family, especially my husband Bill, for sharing this journey with me.
Lin Lin, EdD

Special thanks to my co-editors for sharing this adventure, to my family for their encouragement, and to my husband, Ken, for his inspiration.
Deborah Cockerham, PhD Candidate

Foreword

Technology as Culture[1]

Many aspects of the brain are common to all humans and are shaped by genes we share. Genes, however, come in various forms and our individuality is influenced by the form of gene we inherit and their expression. Moreover, the brains of individual humans are also shaped by the culture that the individual experiences. In infancy culture is mainly conveyed through caregivers. This volume proposes that a major element of the cultural experience of modern children and adults is the technology to which they are exposed. This could, over time, make for a common worldwide cultural influence. If this view is correct, the smartphone and its technological successors might rival the genome as an influence of what it is to be human.

The first three chapters of this volume lay out the case for understanding how the brain is shaped by technology in early life. Chapter 1 provides the reciprocal links between cognition and the brain by reviewing work in modern cognitive neuroscience. While Chap. 3 provides the relation to education in the field of educational neuroscience. Chapter 2 lays out the importance of the elements of critical thinking including collaboration, communication, creativity, and contemplation. Although these skills are discussed in cognitive and educational studies, we have a very limited understanding of how the brain carries out or learns these high level skills.

A critical issue raised by the second set of chapters is whether we are capable of designing an educational system that can take advantage of this universal cultural to improve the learning of our children. Our record to date is not a cause for optimism, but the chapters provide hope. For example, careful monitoring of the direction of gaze (Chap. 6) can provide critical information on whether the person is orienting

[1] The author thanks the editors for the opportunity to comment on their volume. My comments are guided both by their work and by the current direction of my own research, which has been examining the cellular and molecular changes in brain circuits during learning. I am grateful to the Office of Naval Research for their continued support of this work under grants ONR grant N00014-17-1-2824 and N00014-15-1-2148 to the University of Oregon. Special thanks to my longtime collaborator Mary K. Rothbart for her help in this foreword.

to the task, while monitoring other physiological response may help maintain alertness and applying critical thinking (Chaps. 5 and 7). Chapters 4 and 8 raise the issue of whether virtual reality can be used to enhance social relations and create an environment for learning at home and in school.

Whether technology produces a common worldwide culture may depend on how policies and practices are shaped in various societies. As Facebook extends to nearly a universal social experience for the world's youth, we are seeing various efforts to shape and control its influence. The third part of this volume considers whether neuroscience can influence these choices (Chap. 9), in a manner that provides an ethical framework for policy (Chap. 11) and allows policy to screen out irrelevant background sounds (Chap. 10).

So far the influence of neuroscience has been felt most strongly in the very early stages of learning. In learning to read the study of brain areas through neuroimaging has revealed an important lesson for phasing phonics with the visual experience of reading to develop a fluid skill. Understanding of the brain's development of a number line has supported the use of games to improve early arithmetic, and cognitive tutors for more advanced algebra learning are being linked to brain systems. As we understand more about the expert brain, the opportunity for understanding how to teach critical thinking may expand.

In some quarters technology is viewed as a menace to the formation of our ability to maintain focus and sustain effort. However, this volume tries to point the way where technology can enhance learning experiences when it is incorporated and used with the support of discoveries in neuroscience and learning science.

Eugene, OR, USA   Michael Posner Z

Contents

Contributors

Pavlo D. Antonenko University of Florida, Gainesville, FL, USA

Jeremy Bailenson Department of Communication, Stanford University, Stanford, CA, USA

Zhengsi Chang University of Texas at Dallas, Denton, TX, USA

Deborah Cockerham Department of Learning Technologies, Fort Worth Museum of Science and History, University of North Texas, Fort Worth, TX, USA

Sidney K. D'Mello Institute of Cognitive Science, University of Colorado, Boulder, Boulder, CO, USA

Unai Diaz-Orueta Maynooth University, Maynooth, County Kildare, Ireland

Tyler Duffield Oregon Health & Science University, Portland, OR, USA

Sabrina A. Huang Department of Communication, Stanford University, Stanford, CA, USA

Andreja Istenic Starcic Faculty of Education, University of Primorska, Koper, Slovenia

University of Ljubljana, Ljubljana, Slovenia

H. Chad Lane Department of Educational Psychology, College of Education, University of Illinois, Urbana-Champaign, Champaign, IL, USA

Nancy W. Y. Law Faculty of Education, The University of Hong Kong, Pokfulam, Hong Kong

Lin Lin University of North Texas, Denton, TX, USA

William Mark Lipsmeyer Zoic Studios, LA, Culver City, CA, USA

Timothy McMahan University of Texas at Dallas, Richardson, TX, USA

Thomas D. Parsons College of Information, University of North Texas, Computational Neuropsychology and Simulation, Denton, TX, USA

Mike Schellen University of North Texas, Denton, TX, USA

Jonathan Michael Spector Department of Learning Technologies, College of Information, University of North Texas, Denton, TX, USA

Haley W. C. Tsang Faculty of Education, The University of Hong Kong, Pokfulam, Hong Kong

Part I
Introduction: Mind, Brain, and Learning Technologies

Chapter 1
Rethinking Learning in the Rapid Developments of Neuroscience, Learning Technologies, and Learning Sciences

Lin Lin, Thomas D. Parsons, and Deborah Cockerham

> *"If we teach today's students as we taught yesterday's, we rob them of tomorrow."*
>
> —*John Dewey*

Abstract In this chapter, we discuss the purpose of this book and provide an overview of evolving discussions on the definitions of human learning, the processes of learning, and the methods to assess learning based on new advances and discoveries in learning sciences, learning technologies, and neurosciences.

Introduction

As technology becomes increasingly integrated into our society, cultural expectations and needs are changing. Social understanding, family roles, organizational skills, and daily activities are all adapting to the advances of ever-present technology, resulting in changes in human brains, emotions, and behaviors. An understanding of the impact

L. Lin (✉)
University of North Texas, Denton, TX, USA
e-mail: Lin.Lin@unt.edu

T. D. Parsons
College of Information, University of North Texas, Computational
Neuropsychology and Simulation, Denton, TX, USA
e-mail: Thomas.Parsons@unt.edu; https://cns.unt.edu/

D. Cockerham
Department of Learning Technologies, Fort Worth Museum of Science and History,
University of North Texas, Fort Worth, TX, USA
e-mail: deborahcockerham@my.unt.edu

© Association for Educational Communications and Technology 2019
T. D. Parsons et al. (eds.), *Mind, Brain and Technology*, Educational
Communications and Technology: Issues and Innovations,
https://doi.org/10.1007/978-3-030-02631-8_1

of technology upon our learning and lives is essential if we are to educate children adequately for the future and plan for meaningful learning environments for them.

The purpose of this book is to provide an overview of some changes from a wide variety of perspectives. Designed for students in the fields and interdisciplinary areas of psychology, neuroscience, technology, computer science, and education, this book provides insights for researchers, professionals, educators, and anyone interested in the integration of mind, brain and technology in learning. The book guides readers to explore alternatives, generate new ideas, and develop constructive plans both for teaching, learning, and for future educational needs.

For over 2000 years, philosophers and scientists have used various technologies to understand and enhance human learning in terms of what, where, when, how, and why a person learns. Historically, research using learning technologies has been limited to behavioral observations, but many questions have extended beyond observable phenomenon: When is memory the same as or different from learning? What helps people learn, will or interest? What associations and technologies help people learn? What is the role of prior knowledge? What do people learn better on their own, and what with learning technologies? The rise of technology has increased the complexity of these issues, as technological innovations bring access to new methods of learning and interactions. At the same time, specialized new technologies are also providing new insights directly into the processes of learning, as scientists investigate learning within the brain.

This chapter will begin with an overview of early learning theorists and their contributions to the understanding of learning. Following this foundational work, we discuss opportunities to extend learning through new technologies. The chapter concludes with a look at neural correlates of learning, social and technological connections of learning, and student learning skills in a digital age.

Evolutions of Learning Theories from a Historical Perspective

Ancient Greek reflections on technology (i.e., *techne*) can be found in the thesis that technology learns from or imitates nature (Plato, Laws). Discussions of how people learn date back to Plato (428–347 BC) and earlier. Plato proposed the question: How does an individual learn something new when the topic is brand new to that person? (Phillips & Soltis, 2009). As is known of the *Theory of Recollection* or *Platonic epistemology* (Silverman, 2014), Plato answered his own question by stating that knowledge (i.e., *episteme*) is present at birth and that all information learned by a person is merely a recollection of something the soul has already learned previously. Plato described learning as a passive process, and his theory has elicited more questions in terms of how an individual gained the knowledge in the first place. It is important to note that while Plato differentiated between techne and episteme, he also viewed them as having connections.

In the days of Aristotle (384–322 BC), the ability to read and write was primarily limited to the wealthy and elite. Memory was an important skill for transfer of knowledge, and one upon which Aristotle focused his studies. Aristotle's view of learning, known today as associationism, embraced the idea that humans learn through cognitively linking concepts (e.g., "sun" brings up images of "bright"; "soft" might inspire thoughts of the opposite concept, "hard"). According to Aristotle, associations between concepts were based upon three principles: contiguity (nearness in time and space), frequency (events often experienced together), and similarity (Gluck, Mercado, & Myers, 2008). Plato and Aristotle's philosophies are learning played important roles in some of the dominant learning theories discussed below. Like Plato, Aristotle distinguished (and identified associations) between techne and episteme. For Aristotle, technology imitates nature and, in some cases, completes what nature cannot (physics).

Behaviorism. John Watson (1878–1958) and Edward Thorndike (1874–1949) extended Aristotle's association model, asserting that the primary goal of learning is for a student to respond correctly to a stimulus (e.g., teacher's question). B. F. Skinner (1904–1990), influenced by these theorists and the physical stimulus-response ideas of I. E. Pavlov (1839–1936), connected learning with rewards and external behavior. To behaviorists such as these, learning involved response to a stimulus (Posner & Rothbart, 2007). Skinner's investigations of positive reinforcement were primarily focused on providing positive reinforcement for "correct" responses of on rats and pigeons. Based on his findings, he defined learning as the production of desired behaviors, and denied any influence of mental processes. Learning would be visible when appropriate reinforcement was provided to the student, with an emphasis on reward over punishment as small steps of progress are made (Bransford, Brown, & Cocking, 2000; Gluck, Mercado, & Myers, 2008). BrainPop and ClassDojo are examples of learning technologies that employ both gamification and behaviorism.

Cognitivism. Jean-Jacques Rousseau (1712–1778) suggested that a child's learning should occur naturally, without constant instruction from his elders, and advocated that the child should take the lead. Jean Piaget (1896–1980) built upon this foundation, focusing upon the child's understanding of the world around him as the basis of his learning. According to Piaget, discrepancies between knowledge and discoveries lead students to adjust their understanding and increase their learning. Learning might not be observable, since mental processes such as memory, language, problem-solving, and concept formation are the goal (Ertmer & Newby, 1993). Piaget focused on cognitive development, stating that language follows the knowledge and understanding acquired through cognitive development. Computer games (online and offline) like Quizlet are examples of cognitivism. Such games typically proffer previous knowledge schema in a different way, which produces disequilibrium and a desire to adapt and learn the new information to continue.

Constructivism. Lev Vygotsky (1896–1934) also emphasized the importance of scaffolding new knowledge and understanding upon previous knowledge and beliefs. However, in contrast to Piaget, he hypothesized that learning occurs as meaning is created from experience, and each learner builds his own interpretation of the world. Vygotsky's concept of the zone of proximal development (ZPD) suggested that the amount of external instructional support should be adapted to the needs of the student. Since learning resides within the student, the importance of personal meaning and understanding lead to increased student agency and learning. Many other theories arise in this camp including Gardner's theory of multiple intelligences, in which Gardner suggests that different kinds of intelligence exist in human beings (1983). An example of constructivism in technology can be found in Google Apps for Education, which allows for student-led collaborative opportunities online. Moreover, students can work together collaboratively on group blogs (Blogspot), group presentations (Sliderocket), and webpages (Google Sites).

Connectivism. As technology has become increasingly ubiquitous in modern society, learning needs have changed. George Siemens (2005), in his theory of connectivism, proposed that the digital age is creating new approaches to learning. No longer is learning limited to what is happening within an individual, but it has become a social and cultural phenomenon requiring the ability to manipulate fast changes in information. Critical thinking skills such as synthesis and concept integration, along with the ability to identify connections and patterns, are basic to this learning theory. In addition, the theory suggests that learning may occur in non-human devices; that maintaining accurate, up-to-date information should be central to learning activities; and that decision-making is in itself a learning process (Siemens, 2005). Massive open online courses (MOOCs) comes from connectivist theory (cMOOC). MOOCs utilize open software and systems across the Internet to facilitate learning and sharing.

Schwartz, Tsang, and Blair (2016) presented 26 approaches to help people learn, and they discussed how these approaches would work and when to use them. For instance, elaboration, generation, and excitement help one better remember what ones to remember and what one wants to learn, while hands-on, contrasting cases, and visulization help discoveries. Schwartz et al. (2016) highlighted important components of learning, which include understanding, memory, motivation, expertise, study skills, sense of inclusion, problem-solving, collaboraiton, and discovery.

Extensions of Learning Through Technologies

Learning is commonly discussed as a cognitive process through which humans acquire knowledge or skills. Yet it is a multidimensional activity comprised of numerous sub-processes, including attention, memory, prediction, pattern recognition, reasoning, decision-making, spatial cognition, and social cognition (Bruner, Goodnow, & Austin, 1986). Because the hierarchy of these sub-processes is mediated by context, learning may be defined differently in different situations. For example, a culture that is highly dependent upon oral history and instruction may see learning as memory (Wineburg, 2001). A piano teacher might define learning as repetition (Maynard, 2006), and an elementary math teacher may consider learning to be pattern recognition (Papic, Mulligan, & Mitchelmore, 2011). Each of these elements plays a role in learning, but none independently defines the learning process.

The definition of learning becomes more elusive with the use of networked computing and communications technologies. In addition to traditional classrooms and methods, learning can take place through simulations, remote laboratories, visualization technologies, games, virtual communities, digital libraries, and mixed realities. New technologies have changed the traditional educational boundaries of time, space, and informational access (Borgman et al., 2008). Virtual and augmented reality support new educational possibilities that allow a student to move beyond his immediate environment (Bainbridge, 2007; Parsons, Carlew, Magtoto, & Stonecipher, 2017; Parsons, Gagglioli, & Riva, 2017; Parsons, Riva, et al., 2017). Social media extends the social experience of learning, as online networks parallel those of offline social networks (Dunbar, 2016; Parsons, 2017; Parsons, Gagglioli, et al., 2017). Students have new opportunities to learn in ways otherwise not possible, developing creative pursuits, decision-making, and social learning, and critical thinking skills (Roschelle, Martin, Ahn, & Schank, 2017). Learning has become a complex, continually evolving group of skills that can be applied in a variety of settings.

Technology can provide flexible learning environments and increase learning equity for individuals with special needs. Adjustable screen and font size, along with text-to-speech capabilities, can help individuals with vision difficulties read the text, and can boost the reading skills and understanding of students with specific reading disabilities. The National Education Technology Plan (U.S. Department of Education, 2017b) promotes equity of access to learning, and provides principles and examples that underscore learning specifications set by Congress in the 2015 Every Student Succeeds Act (U.S. Department of Education, 2017a).

As innovative technologies create new learning opportunities, the skills needed to be an efficient learner are changing (Trilling & Fadel, 2009). Nowhere is this more obvious than in the previous century's focus on memorizing facts. The abundance of information that is available at the touch of a button has replaced our need to remember information with a need to sift through and prioritize information quickly. However, the availability of knowledge from multiple technologies may in effect complicate the learning process.

Understanding Learning Through Neuroimaging Technologies

To understand why learning has become more complex than ever, we start with the concept that human learning involves change (Green & Bavelier, 2008). The change takes place through a sequence of patterns and predictions, as the human brain constantly watches for patterns, makes predictions, and then checks to see if the predictions are being met (Bar, 2007; Parsons, 2017). When predictions are violated, dopamine appears to be activated in the substantia nigra and the ventral tegmental areas of the brain, leading to a sense of reward (Hollerman & Schultz, 1998). The association of learning with reward fuels the human desire to learn; and, as learning opportunities are extended and available through multiple technologies, the desire to learn may lead to media multitasking. The prevalent mobile technologies have been labeled multitasking facilitators that support even more multitasking (Pea et al., 2012). Yet, as we seek the rewards of multitasking, we may work against ourselves. Multitasking may interfere with learning (Uncapher et al., 2017), and continued learning while multitasking may change our brain and learning (Poldrack & Foerde, 2007). Although some report on the negative impacts of media multitasking (Ophir, Nass, & Wagner, 2009), others find that media multitaskers perform better on multisensory integration tasks (Lui & Wong, 2012). Lin (2009) has argued the attentional style of media multitaskers may not emphasize attending to the information that is presented as static stimuli (as in the Ophir et al., 2009 study). Instead, media multitaskers may have a greater breadth of attention that inclines them to pay attention to a larger scope of information instead of a specific piece of information. Novel approaches to assessing the impacts of multitasking are needed to clear up inconsistencies in the literature (Lin & Parsons, 2018).

Neuroimaging technology provides insight into the neural underpinnings of specific activities. Studies by Small, Moody, Siddharth, and Bookheimer (2009) suggested that individuals who use technology regularly might use different neural circuits when searching the Internet than when reading text. The authors concluded that decision-making and critical thinking may be impacted by these changes. Other research (Kanai, Bahrami, Roylance, & Rees, 2011) found correlations between the size of online friendship networks and neural areas that are associated with social perception and associative memory: the right superior temporal sulcus, the left middle temporal gyrus, and the entorhinal cortex.

Over the past 50 years, neuroimaging techniques have allowed scientists to move beyond observations of behavior or the mind to observations of cognitive activation in the brain, providing new insights into behaviors and neural correlates that appear to underlie learning. Studies related to both mind and brain have indicated basic principles that are involved in the process of learning.

A human's perceptions and understanding of the world are built on patterns. Sensory input is registered as patterns of perceptions, and may be preserved either as unisensory or as multisensory perceptions. In multisensory patterns, each sense will be preserved independently: the visual patterns that are observed in a friend's facial features and the auditory patterns heard in her voice may be recorded simultaneously, but they may be stored for individual access (Hawkins & Blakeslee, 2004). The brain continuously searches for patterns, and is well adept at discovering them even in the midst of chaos and disorder (Hawkins & Blakeslee, 2004; Kelso, 1997, p. 3). Patterns, or relations between items or events, are stored for access when humans encounter new situations.

As the cortex searches its store of patterns, the neocortex predicts what it expects to see, hear, and feel. When the expectations are violated, learning takes place. Prediction is a primary task of the neocortex (Hawkins & Blakeslee, 2004), and the human drive to predict has been described as a "powerful tool for learning" (Elman, 2009, cited in Misyak, Christiansen, & Bruce Tomblin, 2010).

Advances in technology have fuelled the development of more accurate neuroimaging capabilities, leading to improved scientific understanding of neural functioning. Over the past decade, neuroimaging technology capacities have expanded from the controlled lab environments of the twentieth century to portable neuroimaging devices (Engin, Dalbastı, Güldüren, Davaslı, & Engin, 2007; McMahan, Parberry, & Parsons, 2015; Parsons, McMahan, & Parberry, in press), social neuroscience experiences (Parsons, 2015; Parsons, Gagglioli, et al., 2017; Schilbach, Eickhoff, Rotarska-Jagiela, Fink, & Vogeley, 2008), and virtual reality (Parsons, 2015, 2017; Parsons & Phillips, 2016). The capacity to merge neuropsychological assessments with real-life experiences has supported a more detailed and accurate understanding of neural functioning during learning (Parsons, 2016; Parsons, Carlew, et al., 2017; Parsons & Kane, 2017).

Connecting Learning with Social and Technological Networks

To foster the inclusion of research advances from the neurosciences, Parsons (2017) presented a brain-based cyberpsychology framework that can be applied to cyberlearning via (1) the neurocognitive, affective, and social aspects of students interacting with technology; and (2) affective computing aspects of students interacting with devices/systems that incorporate computation. As such, a brain-based cyberlearning approach investigates both the ways in which educators and students make use of devices and the neurocognitive processes, motivations, intentions, behavioral outcomes, and effects of online and offline use of technology.

Parsons (2015, 2017) argues that past conceptualizations that separate emotion from cognition are wrongheaded and not well supported by scientific findings. He draws upon Antonio Damasio's, Tranel, and Damasio's (1991) Somatic Marker Hypothesis to note the interconnectedness of the two realms. Damasio's et al. (1991) Somatic Marker Hypothesis proposes that emotions may be evidenced in somatic (body) markers, such as rapid heart rate with anxiety or nausea with disgust.

Mills, Wu, and D'Mello (2017) suggested that optimal emotional states may vary according to task. When task performance of adults experiencing either positive or negative affect states was assessed, researchers found that the sad group of participants outperformed the happy group on tests of deep reasoning. These findings emphasize the role of emotions in attention and motivation, which are intricately involved in the learning process (Immordino-Yang, 2016, p. 87).

Humans live in a social world, and social processing is intertwined with emotion. As a result, social context highly impacts learning capacity. While Giacomo Rizzolatti and Vittorio Gallese (as well as some of their colleagues) in Italy (di Pellegrino, Fadiga, Fogassi, Gallese, & Rizzolatti, 1992; Gallese, Fadiga, Fogassi, & Rizzolatti, 1996) observed the brains of monkeys and noted that particular cells activated both when a monkey performed an action and when the monkey viewed another monkey performing the same action. This resulted in the discovery of "mirror neurons." Research has emerged linking these neurons appeared to abilities such as empathy and the perception of another's intentions (Iacoboni et al., 2005; Ramachandran, 2000; Ramachandran & Oberman, 2006). New fMRI studies involving multiple participants (Konvalinka & Roepstorff, 2012) are producing insights into the neuroscience of socialization. Research findings suggest a large-scale brain network (anterior insula, anterior cingulate cortex, and inferior frontal cortex) activates both when one experiences emotions and when observing another person experiencing an emotion.

Although social media and messaging can be distractions when an individual seeks knowledge through technology, social connections remain an important component of learning. Social interaction is an important factor in cognitive development (Vygotsky, 1978), and the social processes of observation, imitation, and modeling are fundamental to learning (Bandura, 1978). Emotion plays an important role in motivation to learn, decision-making, and problem-solving (Damasio et al., 1991; Immordino-Yang & Damasio, 2007; Parsons, 2017). Because emotions are deeply bonded with social processing (Immordino-Yang, 2017), social and emotional connections have a strong influence on human learning (Immordino-Yang, 2008; Oberman, Pineda, & Ramachandran, 2007, cited in Immordino-Yang & Gotlieb, 2017).

Student Learning Skills in a Digital Age

The skills required for effective learning assume different priorities in learning in a technology immersive environment. When learning with technologies, easy access to continuously updated information minimizes the need for memory work, but requires skill in sifting through information and determining which material is relevant and factual. In addition, the student must know how to access quality informational sources and must self-monitor in order to limit interruptions from social messages, advertisements, online entertainment, and other distractions.

Scaffolding and prior knowledge. Both Piaget and Kamii (1978) and Vygotsky (1978) espoused the view that new knowledge must be constructed from existing knowledge, and that connections with past experience and knowledge can strengthen learning. A variety of technological programs and websites support scaffolding and links to prior knowledge through easily accessible examples and illustrations, tools that support the development of graphic organizers, and opportunities to learn, review, and expand concepts. These tools provide models for the learners, help students visualize the goal to be accomplished, and build a more solid learning foundation (Alber, 2011).

Digital students and agency. Technology provides new opportunities for learners to assume control of their own learning. Whereas traditional students often depended upon an instructor to share knowledge with them, digital students can access a plethora of information from their smartphones, computers, or other technological devices. Throughout the twentieth century, learning theorists have promoted the need for learners to manipulate objects, engage in discussion, and experience schema in order to build mental models of the world (Dewey, 1938; Piaget, 1964; Vygotsky, 1986). Digital learners build knowledge as they observe and interact with virtual and real-time phenomena, build social networks, and make connections between new ideas and prior understandings.

Critical thinking skills. A student in today's digital world does not require the support of a physical classroom in order to learn. Through technology, she has anytime, anywhere access to an abundance of information, including homework, tutoring, and classroom materials. She can explore unlimited environments virtually, and can manipulate objects within the environments. Through interacting with her virtual world, she can explore destinations around the globe, determine how the contents of a cell fit together, and create new ways to travel. Her learning goal will not primarily be to acquire knowledge, but rather to problem-solve and respond creatively to the challenges and needs of a dynamic world.

When students think critically, they are actively engaged in analysis, synthesis, problem-solving, evaluation, and reflection (Mansbach, 2015). The ability to self-regulate reinforces a student's ability to use these processes independently (Tilus, 2012). Instructors in today's schools must use strategies and technological tools that can support growth in each of these skill areas.

Learning Technologies and the Extended Mind

In Parsons (2017) book on cyberpsychology and the brain, he argued that an additional component for our understanding of cognitive, affective, and social processes for cyberlearning is the notion that technology extends the minds cognitive processes. Daniel Dennett (1996, pp. 134–135) has argued that our remarkable cognitive abilities are less a factor of our large frontal lobes than they are an evolutionary offspring of our capacity for extending our cognitive processes into the environment with which we interact. Hence, our enhanced intelligence is due to

> our habit of offloading as much as possible of our cognitive tasks into the environment itself—extruding our minds (that is, our mental projects and activities) into the surrounding world, where a host of peripheral devices we construct can store, process and re-represent our meanings, streamlining, enhancing, and protecting the processes of transformation that are our thinking. This widespread practice of off-loading releases us from the limitations of our animal brains.

This idea is reflected in Clark and Chalmers (1998) development of an "extended mind" theory, in which human cognitive processing consists of complex feedback (including feedforward and feed-around) loops among brain, body, and the external world. Clark and Chalmers argue that a parity-stance should be applied to our considerations of the internal and external mind:

> If, as we confront some task, a part of the world functions as a process which, were it to go on in the head, we would have no hesitation in recognizing as part of the cognitive process, then that part of the world is (so we claim) part of the cognitive process (Clark & Chalmers, 1998, p. 8).

Following the "extended mind" approach, cognitive processes are understood as going beyond the brain to software and hardware. Moreover, cognition can be viewed as something being processed by a system that is coupled with the environment (Clark & Chalmers, 1998). In a forward to Clark's (2008) book *Supersizing the Mind*, Chalmers explains how his iPhone has become an extension of his mind:

> A month ago, I bought an iPhone. The iPhone has already taken over some of the central functions of my brain. It has replaced part of my memory, storing phone numbers and addresses that I once would have taxed my brain with. It harbors my desires: I call up a memo with the names of my favorite dishes when I need to order at a local restaurant. I use it to calculate, when I need to figure out bills and tips. It is a tremendous resource in an argument, with Google ever present to help settle disputes. I make plans with it, using its calendar to help determine what I can and can't do in the coming months. I even daydream on the iPhone, idly calling up words and images when my concentration slips. (p. 1)

The point that Chalmers is making is that smart technologies may, under some circumstances, act as a person's cognitive states and beliefs even though they are external to the physical boundaries of the person's brain.

Parsons (2017; in press; see also Chap. 8 in this book) describes the learning technologies of the extended mind in terms of extended cognitive systems that include both brain-based cognitive processes and technologies like tablets, iPads, and smartphones that serve to accomplish functions that would otherwise be attained via the action of brain-based cognitive processes acting internally to the student. In this learning technology of the extended mind, the student's cognitive processes are understood as going beyond wetware (i.e., student's brain) to educational software and hardware. This perspective allows for an understanding of the child's cognition as processed in a system coupled with the child's environment.

How should learning technology extended cognitive systems (i.e., a student performing cognitive processes with learning technologies) be educated and assessed? Heersmink and Knight (2018) argue that educators should teach children to participate in responsible practices of technology use by reverse engineering the cognitive integration, illustrating the steps over which that integration was established, and develop the approaches toward those technologies. This also reflects Wheeler's (2011) reflection on the education of coupled assemblages between the student and technologies of the extended mind. For Wheeler, this focus is entirely in line with the objective of providing the student's brain with the competences necessary for efficient involvements in such assemblages. Wheeler contends that we should aim to educate extended cognitive systems and permit students to utilize technology when they carry out exams.

This approach is reflected in many of the chapters in this book. While most do not explicitly argue for learning technologies of the extended mind, there is an implicit association between students and the cognitive processes that occur while using educational technologies, being immersed in virtual environments, and being evaluated via technologies. As you read through these chapters, we invite you to consider the possibilities of learning technologies that extend students' minds.

References

Alber, R. (2011). Six scaffolding strategies to use with your students. *Edutopia*. Retrieved August 16, 2018, from https://www.edutopia.org/blog/scaffolding-lessons-six-strategies-rebecca-alber.

Bainbridge, W. S. (2007). The scientific research potential of virtual worlds. *Science, 317*(5837), 472–476.

Bandura, A. (1978). Social learning theory of aggression. *Journal of Communication, 28*(3), 12–29.

Bar, M. (2007). The proactive brain: Using analogies and associations to generate predictions. *Trends in Cognitive Sciences, 11*(7), 280–289.

Borgman, C. L., Abelson, H., Dirks, L., Johnson, R., Koedinger, K. R., Linn, M. C., et al. (2008). *Fostering learning in the networked world: The cyberlearning opportunity and challenge, a 21st century agenda for the National Science Foundation*. Report of the NSF task force on cyberlearning, 59.

Bransford, J. D., Brown, A. L., & Cocking, R. R. (Eds.). (2000). *How people learn: Brain, mind, experience and school* (pp. 3–23). Washington DC: National Academy Press.

Bruner, J., Goodnow, J., & Austin, G. (1986). *A study of thinking (Social science classics series)* (2nd ed.). New York: Transaction Publishers.

Clark, A. (2008). *Supersizing the mind: Embodiment, action, and cognitive extension*. New York: Oxford University Press.

Clark, A., & Chalmers, D. (1998). The extended mind. *Analysis, 58*(1), 7–19.

Damasio, A. R., Tranel, D., & Damasio, H. C. (1991). Ch. 11: Somatic markers and the guidance of behaviour: Theory and preliminary testing. In: H. S. Levin, H. M. Eisenberg, & A. L. Benton (Eds.), *Frontal lobe function and dysfunction* (pp. 217–229). Oxford: Oxford University Press.

Dennett, D. C. (1996). *Kinds of minds*. New York: Basic Books.

Dewey, J. (1938). *Experience & education*. New York: Kappa Delta Pi.

Di Pellegrino, G., Fadiga, L., Fogassi, L., Gallese, V., & Rizzolatti, G. (1992). Understanding motor events: A neurophysiological study. *Experimental Brain Research, 91*(1), 176–180.

Dunbar, R. I. (2016). Do online social media cut through the constraints that limit the size of offline social networks? *Royal Society Open Science, 3*(1), 150292.

Elman, J. L. (2009). On the meaning of words and dinosaur bones: Lexical knowledge without a lexicon. *Cognitive Science, 33*, 547–582.

Engin, M., Dalbastı, T., Güldüren, M., Davaslı, E., & Engin, E. Z. (2007). A prototype portable system for EEG measurements. *Measurement, 40*(9), 936–942.

Ertmer, P. A., & Newby, T. J. (1993). Behaviorism, cognitivism, constructivism: Comparing critical features from an instructional design perspective. *Performance Improvement Quarterly, 6*(4), 50–72.

Gallese, V., Fadiga, L., Fogassi, L., & Rizzolatti, G. (1996). Action recognition in the premotor cortex. *Brain, 119*(2), 593–609.

Gardner, H. (1983). *Frames of mind: The theory of multiple intelligences*. New York: Basic Books.

Gluck, M. A., Mercado, E., & Myers, C. E. (2008). *Learning and memory: From brain to behavior*. New York: Worth Publishers.

Green, C. S., & Bavelier, D. (2008). Exercising your brain: A review of human brain plasticity and training-induced learning. *Psychology and Aging, 23*(4), 692.

Hawkins, J., & Blakeslee, S. (2004). *On intelligence*. New York: Times Books.

Heersmink, R., & Knight, S. (2018). Distributed learning: Educating and assessing extended cognitive systems. *Philosophical Psychology, 31*(6), 969–990.

Hollerman, J. R., & Schultz, W. (1998). Dopamine neurons report an error in the temporal prediction of reward during learning. *Nature Neuroscience, 1*(4), 304.

Iacoboni, M., Molnar-Szakacs, I., Gallese, V., Buccino, G., Mazziotta, J. C., & Rizzolatti, G. (2005). Grasping the intentions of others with one's own mirror neuron system. *PLoS Biology, 3*(3), e79.

Immordino-Yang, M. H., & Damasio, A. (2007). We feel, therefore we learn: The relevance of affective and social neuroscience to education. *Mind, Brain, and Education, 1*(1), 3–10.

Immordino-Yang, M. H. (2008). The smoke around mirror neurons: Goals as sociocultural and emotional organizers of perception and action in learning. *Mind, Brain, and Education, 2*(2), 67–73.

Immordino-Yang, M. H. (2016). Emotion, sociality, and the brain's default mode network: Insights for educational practice and policy. *Policy Insights from the Behavioral and Brain Sciences, 3*(2), 211–219.

Immordino-Yang, M. H., & Gotlieb, R. (2017). Embodied brains, social minds, cultural meaning. *American Educational Research Journal, 54*(1_suppl), 344S–367S.

Kanai, R., Feilden, T., Firth, C., & Rees, G. (2011). Political orientations are correlated with brain structure in young adults. *Current Biology, 21*(8), 677–680.

Kelso, J. S. (1997). *Dynamic patterns: The self-organization of brain and behavior*. Cambridge: MIT Press.

Konvalinka, I., & Roepstorff, A. (2012). The two-brain approach: How can mutually interacting brains teach us something about social interaction? *Frontiers in Human Neuroscience, 6*, 215.

Lin, L. (2009). Breadth-biased versus focused cognitive control in media multitasking behaviors. *Proceedings of the National Academy of Sciences of the United States of America (PNAS), 106*(37), 15521–15522.

Lin, L., & Parsons, T. D. (2018). Ecologically valid assessments of attention and learning engagement in media multitaskers. *TechTrends, 62*(5), 518–524.

Lui, K. F., & Wong, A. C. (2012). Does media multitasking always hurt? A positive correlation between multitasking and multisensory integration. *Psychonomic Bulletin & Review, 19*(4), 647–653.

Mansbach, J. (2015). *Using technology to develop students' critical thinking skills*. Northwestern School of Professional Learning: Distance learning. Retrieved August 16, 2018, from https://dl.sps.northwestern.edu/blog/2015/09/using-technology-to-develop-students-critical-thinking-skills/.

Maynard, L. (2006). The role of repetition in the practice sessions of artist teachers and their students. *Bulletin of the Council for Research in Music Education, 167*, 61–72.

McMahan, T., Parberry, I., & Parsons, T. D. (2015). Modality specific assessment of video game player's experience using the Emotiv. *Entertainment Computing, 7*, 1–6.

Mills, C., Graesser, A., Risko, E. F., & D'Mello, S. K. (2017). Cognitive coupling during reading. *Journal of Experimental Psychology: General, 146*(6), 872–883.

Misyak, J. B., Christiansen, M. H., & Bruce Tomblin, J. (2010). Sequential expectations: The role of prediction-based learning in language. *Topics in Cognitive Science, 2*(1), 138–153.

Oberman, L. M., Pineda, J. A., & Ramachandran, V. S. (2007). The human mirror neuron system: A link between action observation and social skills. *Social Cognitive and Affective Neuroscience, 2*(1), 62–66.

Ophir, E., Nass, C., & Wagner, A. D. (2009). Cognitive control in media multitaskers. *Proceedings of the National Academy of Sciences, 106*(37), 15583–15587.

Papic, M., Mulligan, J., & Mitchelmore, M. (2011). Assessing the development of pre-schoolers' mathematical patterning. *Journal for Research in Mathematics Education, 42*(3), 237–268.

Parsons, T. D. (2015). Virtual reality for enhanced ecological validity and experimental control in the clinical, affective, and social neurosciences. *Frontiers in Human Neuroscience, 9*, 660.

Parsons, T. D. (2016). *Clinical neuropsychology and technology: What's new and how we can use it*. New York: Springer.

Parsons, T. D. (2017). *Cyberpsychology and the brain: The interaction of neuroscience and affective computing*. Cambridge: Cambridge University Press.

Parsons, T. D. (in press). *Ethical challenges in digital psychology and cyberpsychology*. Cambridge: Cambridge University Press.

Parsons, T. D., Carlew, A. R., Magtoto, J., & Stonecipher, K. (2017). The potential of function-led virtual environments for ecologically valid measures of executive function in experimental and clinical neuropsychology. *Neuropsychological Rehabilitation, 37*(5), 777–807.

Parsons, T. D., Gagglioli, A., & Riva, G. (2017). Virtual environments in social neuroscience. *Brain Sciences, 7*(42), 1–21.

Parsons, T. D., & Kane, R. L. (2017). Computational neuropsychology: Current and future prospects for interfacing neuropsychology and technology. In R. Kane & T. D. Parsons (Eds.), *The role of technology in clinical neuropsychology* (pp. 471–482). Oxford: Oxford University Press.

Parsons, T. D., McMahan, T., & Parberry, I. (in press). Neurogaming-based classification of player experience using consumer-grade electroencephalography. *IEEE Transactions on Affective Computing.*

Parsons, T. D., & Phillips, A. (2016). Virtual reality for psychological assessment in clinical practice. *Practice Innovations, 1*, 197–217.

Parsons, T. D., Riva, G., Parsons, S., Mantovani, F., Newbutt, N., Lin, L., et al. (2017). Virtual reality in pediatric psychology: Benefits, challenges, and future directions. *Pediatrics, 140*, 86–91.

Pea, R., Nass, C., Meheula, L., Rance, M., Kumar, A., Bamford, H., et al. (2012). Media use, face-to-face communication, media multitasking, and social well-being among 8- to 12-year-old girls. *Developmental Psychology, 48*(2), 327–336.

Phillips, D. C., & Soltis, J. F. (2009). *Perspectives on learning. Thinking about education* (5th ed.). New York: Teachers College Press.

Piaget, J. (1964). Part I: Cognitive development in children: Piaget development and learning. *Journal of Research in Science Teaching, 2*(3), 176–186.

Piaget, J., & Kamii, C. (1978). What is psychology? *American Psychologist, 33*(7), 648–652.

Poldrack, R. A., & Foerde, K. (2007). Category learning and the memory systems debate. *Neuroscience and Biobehavioral Reviews, 32*, 197–205.

Posner, M. I., & Rothbart, M. K. (2007). Research on attention networks as a model for the integration of psychological science. *Annual Review of Psychology, 58*(1), 1–23.

Ramachandran, V. S. (2000). *Mirror neurons and imitation learning as the driving force behind "the great leap forward" in human evolution, Edge Website article.* Retrieved from http://www.edge.org/3rd_culture/ramachandran/ramachandran_p1.html.

Ramachandran, V. S., & Oberman, L. M. (2006). Broken mirrors: A theory of autism. *Scientific American, 295*(5), 62–69.

Roschelle, J., Ahn, J., Asbell-Clark, J., Berland, M., Chase, C., Enyedy, N., et al. (2017). *Cyberlearning Community Report: The state of cyberlearning and the future of learning with technology.* Menlo Park, CA: SRI International.

Schilbach, L., Eickhoff, S. B., Rotarska-Jagiela, A., Fink, G. R., & Vogeley, K. (2008). Minds at rest? Social cognition as the default mode of cognizing and its putative relationship to the "default system" of the brain. *Consciousness and Cognition, 17*(2), 457–467.

Schwartz, D. L., Tsang, J. T., & Blair, K. P. (2016). *The ABCs of how we learn: 26 scientifically proven approaches, how they work, and when to use them.* New York: W. W. Norton.

Siemens, G. (2005). Connectivism: A learning theory for the digital age. *International Journal of Instructional Technology and Distance Learning, 2*(1), 3–10.

Silverman, A. (2014). Plato's middle period metaphysics and epistemology. In E. N. Zalta (Ed.), *The Stanford encyclopedia of philosophy.*

Small, G. W., Moody, T. D., Siddarth, P., & Bookheimer, S. Y. (2009). Your brain on google: Patterns of cerebral activation during internet searching. *The American Journal of Geriatric Psychiatry, 17*(2), 116–126.

Tilus, G. (2012). *Six critical thinking skills you need to master now.* Rasmussen College Blogs. Retrieved January 14, 2018, from http://www.rasmussen.edu/student-life/blogs/main/critical-thinking-skills-you-need-to-master-now/.

Trilling, B., & Fadel, C. (2009). *21st century skills: Learning for life in our times.* San Francisco: Wiley.

U.S. Department of Education. (2017a). *Every Student Succeeds Act.* U.S. Department of Education. Retrieved January 14, 2018, from https://www.ed.gov/esea.

U.S. Department of Education. (2017b). *Reimagining the role of technology in education: National Education Technology Plan Update.* Retrieved January 14, 2018, from https://tech.ed.gov/netp/.

Uncapher, M. R., Lin, L., Rosen, L. D., Kirkorian, H. L., Baron, N. S., Bailey, K., et al. (2017). Media multitasking and cognitive, psychological, neural, and learning differences. *Pediatrics, 140*(Supplement 2), S62–S66.

Vygotsky, L. S. (1978). Interaction between Learning and Development. In M. Cole, V. John-Steiner, S. Scribner, & E. Souberman (Eds.), *Mind in society: The development of higher psychological processes*. Cambridge: Harvard University Press.

Vygotsky, L. S. (1986). *Thought and language* (Abridged from 1934; A. Kozulin, Trans.). Cambridge: MIT Press.

Wheeler, M. (2011). Thinking beyond the brain: Educating and building, from the standpoint of extended cognition. *Computational Cultures, 1*.

Wineburg, S. (2001). *Historical thinking and other unnatural acts: Charting the future of teaching the past*. Philadelphia: Temple University Press.

Lin Lin is a Professor of Learning Technologies at the University of North Texas (UNT). Lin's research looks into interactions between mind, brain, and technology in smart learning environments. Specially, she has conducted research on (1) media multitasking; (2) learning in online/blended/virtual reality environments; and (3) computer-supported collaborative learning (CSCL). Lin is the Editor-in-Chief for the development section of *Educational Technology Research and Development*, one of the most respected journals in the field. She is also Associate Editor for the *International Journal of Smart Technology and Learning* (IJSmartTL) as well as serving on the several other journal editorial boards. Lin has played leadership roles in several professional organizations (e.g., AECT and AERA). Lin has been invited as an honorary professor at several universities overseas. Lin serves as Director for Texas Center for Educational Technology, and Co-director on the Joint-Lab on Big Data, Little Devices, and Lifelong Learning.

Thomas D. Parsons is Director of the NetDragon Digital Research Centre and the Computational Neuropsychology and Simulation (CNS) laboratory at the University of North Texas. His work integrates neuropsychology, psychophysiology, and simulation technologies for novel assessment, modeling, and training of neurocognitive and affective processes. He is a leading scientist in this area and he has been PI of 17 funded projects during his career and an investigator on an additional 13 funded projects (over $15 million in funding). In addition to his patents for eHarmony.com's Matching System (U.S. Patent Nos. 2004/6735568; 2014/0180942 A1), he has invented and validated virtual reality-based assessments (including the Virtual School Environment) of attention; spatial abilities; memory; and executive functions. He uses neural networks and machine learning to model mechanisms underlying reinforcement learning, decision-making, working memory, and inhibitory control. In addition to his five books, he has over 200 publications in peer-reviewed journals and book chapters. His contributions to neuropsychology were recognized when he received the 2013 National Academy of Neuropsychology Early Career Achievement award. In 2014, he was awarded Fellow status in the National Academy of Neuropsychology.

Deborah Cockerham, Managing Director of the Research and Learning Center at the Fort Worth Museum of Science and History, also serves as Visiting Research Scholar at Texas Christian University's Center for Science Communication. In these roles, she works to strengthen interdisciplinary communication and build connections between research scientists and the public, and has supported multiple research university collaborations in public education and communication. In earlier work as a learning disabilities specialist, she taught children and adolescents with a variety of learning and attentional differences. Her work with students who have attention deficit hyperactivity (ADHD) and/or autism spectrum disorder (ASD) has focused on social learning, based on connections between communication skills and the fine arts. Cockerham's research takes place at the intersection of learning technologies, psychology, education, and communication. Recent investigations include EEG studies on ASD interpretation of nonverbal emotional cues, and behavioral studies focused on media multitasking and mobile technology. She is a graduate of the University of Texas at Arlington's Masters of Mind, Brain, and Education. Through her work and studies, Cockerham focuses on developing community-based collaborations that build skills for lifelong learning.

Chapter 2
Complexity, Inquiry Critical Thinking, and Technology: A Holistic and Developmental Approach

Jonathan Michael Spector

Abstract Among the skill and competency areas being addressed in national education plans and by prominent educators are collaboration, communication, creativity, and critical thinking. In this chapter, a fifth C is added to that list—namely, contemplation. The argument to be presented in this chapter involves two assumptions: (a) technologies can play an important role in developing these competencies, and (b) to be effective in developing the five C's, a holistic and developmental approach seems appropriate. Given those assumptions, the solution approach here is that a learner should be considered as a whole person and not simply a cognitive processor. Moreover, promoting effective learning involves developing stable and persistent changes in what a person knows and can do. Consequently, developing habits of inquiry and reasoning takes time and is not likely to happen in one unit of instruction, nor in one course. The earlier those habits are developed, the more likely they are to persist and to be applied to multiple domains of inquiry.

Introduction

Imagine the following scenario, which is based on a composite of interviews with electronics maintenance technicians in the Air Force. A recent graduate of an electronics technical training school is working with an experienced technician troubleshooting the electronics on an F-16 fighter jet aircraft based on a troubled report that has been received after a flight training mission. The senior master sergeant (the experienced technician) immediately examines the cable housing for radar system. The assisting inexperience airman asks, "Why did you immediately start examining that cable housing unit? The protocol I was taught in electronics school was to first perform a diagnostic that would rule out about half of the likely causes of the

J. M. Spector (✉)
Department of Learning Technologies, College of Information, University of North Texas, Denton, TX, USA
e-mail: mike.spector@unt.edu; https://sites.google.com/site/jmspector007/

© Association for Educational Communications and Technology 2019   17
T. D. Parsons et al. (eds.), *Mind, Brain and Technology*, Educational Communications and Technology: Issues and Innovations,
https://doi.org/10.1007/978-3-030-02631-8_2

problem that was reported." The senior master sergeant replies, "I know F-16s and I also know this particular plane. Loose cable housing is a recurrent problem on this plane, which is why I started here."

Such exchanges are not uncommon and lead some to the conclusion that schooling is wrongheaded or ill-conceived as it is not often connected with real-world problems. The conclusion reflects an assumption that expertise and knowledge are domain specific, and, as a consequence, that learning and instruction need to be focused on authentic problems and meaningful tasks (Brown, Collins, & Duguid, 1988; Charness & Tuffiash, 2008; Collins, Brown, & Newman, 1989). While there is evidence to support the notion of meaningful tasks and domain-specific expertise, the studies in support of those conclusions are most often conducted with adult learners and do not take into account early learning and knowledge development.

The issue addressed in this chapter involves the impact of early learning and knowledge development on subsequent learning and development. While acknowledging that authentic learning is significant, one is not thereby committed to embracing a domain-specific approach to early learning. Merrill's (2002, 2013) *First Principles of Learning* emphasize the notion of using meaningful problems and four treatment stages, which are popularly presented as follows: (1) tell learners relevant information, (2) ask learners if they understand and ask them to demonstrate some understanding, (3) show learners how to apply new knowledge, and (4) have learners demonstrate the application of new knowledge on a variety of problem-solving tasks. This is a robust framework that has been shown to work using more elaborated frameworks such as cognitive apprenticeship (Collins et al., 1989). It is somewhat robust and can be applied to a wide variety of learners and learning tasks if one adds a fifth stage—namely, "rinse and repeat," using a popular term suggested by a student.

In elaborating what tasks are meaningful prior to college, an impressive coalition involving the National Research Council, the National Science Teachers Association, and the American Association for the Advancement of Science, and Achieve (a nonprofit education organization) developed the Next Generation Science Standards (NGSS; see https://www.nextgenscience.org/) that are meant to integrate engineering and science throughout K-12 curricula. These new standards recognize the complexity of scientific reasoning and the value of Merrill's fourth DO component mentioned above. They also represent a step or two away from a strict domain-specific orientation.

The National Technology Leadership Coalition (NTLC; see http://www.ntlcoalition.org/) and the Smithsonian Institution's educational outreach program have examined and responded to the NGSS standards. NTLC came to the conclusion that many of the NGSS standards are not easily supported in schools without substantial training and professional development of teachers. The Smithsonian was involved in the NTLC studies and responded with a number of education kits aimed at helping developing teaching support and expertise.

The impact of NGSS and associated efforts in developing stable and persistent changes in what a person knows and can do remains to be seen. The remainder of this chapter is aimed at challenging strong domain specificity arguments and in developing a theory- and research-based framework for the development of inquiry and critical thinking skills using technology that is likely to persist and be applicable in multiple domains.

Theory and Empirical Foundations

The point of departure for the underlying theoretical and empirical foundations for the framework to be presented is based on the notion of a holistic view of a learner (Spector, 2016; Spector & Park, 2018). The basic view of a person presented in those and other works is that a person is an integrated set of cognitive, physical, and affective attributes which are interrelated and which interact over time to create an individual's personality, habits, and thoughts. A holistic account of learning involves that embodied notion of being a person as well as a perspective that recognizes changes and development. This is not a new concept of personhood in the education and educational technology literature. One can easily find parts of this view in early Chinese and Greek writings (see Spector & Ren, 2015). Moreover, the notion of a person being more than a cognitive processor is widely accepted by psychologists (e.g., Rogers, 1965) just as many medical professionals see a person as more than a collection of physical attributes (McNamara & Boudreau, 2011).

It is commonly accepted that moods change and can affect learning and performance (Brand, 2012; Brand, Reimer, & Opwis, 2007; Spector & Park, 2018). It is also acknowledged that cognition is a dynamic construct and difficult to measure without considering non-cognitive factors (Ifenthaler, Kinshuk, Isaias, Sampson, & Spector, 2011; Ifenthaler, Masduki, & Seel, 2011). In addition, physical and other learner differences are acknowledged to have an impact on learning (Felder & Brent, 2005). Research on individual differences that impact learning should be considered when designing instruction (Bransford, Brown, & Cocking, 2000; Jonassen & Grabowski, 1993). Moreover, the cognitive science construct of mental models is influenced by a number of factors, including learning challenges such as autism and the influence of parents, teachers, peers, and others (Heijltjes, van Gog, Leppink, & Paas, 2014).

The above referenced research and many other studies suggest that communication skills, collaboration, and the ability to be creative all have an impact on learning. Moreover, those influencing factors involve skills, attitudes and habits that exist or are formed (or not) early in an individual's life. As a consequence, when developing instructional strategies and learning activities aimed at promoting inquiry and critical thinking skills, it seems appropriate to initiate that process early in an individual's life.

The situation is further complicated when the focus is on learning to confront and resolve complex problems. Complex problems arise in many domains of inquiry as well as in everyday life. Much of the effort to develop complex problem-solving skills has focused on college students and adults within a particular domain. However, focusing on adults overlooks habits and attitudes formed early in an individual's life, and, in addition, ignores the reality that many of the complex problems that an individual is likely to confront cross over common domain boundaries, which is already acknowledged in the NGSS standards to some extent.

One remaining foundational factor related to an individual learning to deal with complex problems involves habits that influence behavior and decision-making. Dietrich Dörner (1996), a German psychologist, has investigated human failure in solving complex factors. Dörner argues that what makes a problem are (a) many interrelated factors, (b) non-linear relationships among factors, (c) delayed effects of a decision or action, and (d) uncertainty with regard to aspects of the problem situation. Given those factors, there is a tendency for a person to only focus on a familiar part of a complex problem. In addition, people tend to misunderstand exponential relationships and to expect immediate results of an action or decision. In short, many adults have already developed a habit of simplifying and focusing without due consideration of alternative perspectives or a careful examination of assumptions and biases that influence decision-making.

Developing Inquiry and Critical Thinking Skills

Critical thinking is typically associated with concepts and language, which involve purposeful and reflective judgement and logical reasoning (Butler, Pentoney, & Bong, 2017; Halpern, 2014; Ku, Ho, Hau, & Lai, 2014). However, it is not realistic to only consider cognition within a conceptual and language-based approach or in an analysis of critical thinking skills. A more holistic approach that includes biases, dispositions, moods, preferences, and other factors is likely to be more insightful and provide both teachers and learners with useful feedback to improve critical thinking skills. In other words, it is perhaps best to consider critical thinking as an embodied and situated skill that involves both cognitive and non-cognitive factors (Bransford et al., 2000).

Critical thinking is often discussed and analyzed along with problem-solving and decision-making. This seems natural in that critical thinking skills are often required and found useful in solving challenging problems and in making difficult decisions. However, problem-solving and decision-making skills are more domain specific than are the broader critical thinking skills which can be developed in many domains and are probably best developed in a maturing mind (i.e., early adolescence) that is not so engaged in highly domain-specific learning enterprises. This is probably the most contentious ascertainment in this chapter and the one least well supported with empirical evidence.

Critical thinking is also often discussed and analyzed along with creativity, which is perhaps even broader and more difficult to define and operationalize than critical thinking. This is also somewhat natural because challenging problems and difficult decisions often require an innovative approach that goes beyond one's previous experience, training, and learning. In one sense, nearly everyone is creative in that as a person acquires a native language that person begins to use words and phrases in ways that have not entered that person's prior experience. Moreover, people naturally create internal representations (sometimes called mental models) to make sense of the things they experience. Since everyone is creating mental representations to make sense of and react to their experiences (according to mainstream cognitive psychology), everyone could be considered creative. On the other hand, a different account of creativity involves an ability not merely to create something not previously experienced or in one's cognitive repertoire but the ability to change the problem-solving space in a way that the originator of the problem did not envision. In any case, creativity, like critical thinking, arguably spans multiple domains although it might be especially in only a few of the enterprises in which a person engages. One implication of this notion is that formulaic responses to problems may not encourage the development of critical thinking skills. To support this implication, an emphasis on formative feedback is critical in early learning. This involves both positive and challenging feedback, as well as eliciting how and what a learner was thinking (Dwyer, Hogan, & Stewart, 2014; Ku et al., 2014; Milrad, Spector, & Davidsen, 2003; Tiruneh, de Cock, Spector, Gu, & Elen, 2017).

A Nine-Phase Developmental Framework

The above research literature suggests a developmental framework for the development of inquiry and critical thinking skills aimed at primary and secondary school students. The framework begins with the formation of habits of mind with the initial habit of asking questions, followed by having questions. The developmental process proceeds in stages that emphasize exploring answers and explanations. The teacher or teaching system should first model the process—reminiscent of Merrill's Show the application of knowledge and principles phase of instruction. The teacher or teaching systems should not focus on right or wrong in response to students, but, rather, should focus on understanding why a student responded in a particular way and encouraging the student to explore that response or explanation. The goal is not to get an answer right or wrong. It is to understand why something makes sense and what alternatives might exist. Throughout the process, the five C's are developed: communication, collaboration, critical thinking, creativity, and contemplation. Contemplation is generally referred to as self-regulation and meta-cognition in many of the works already cited (see Spector & Park, 2018). Table 2.1 presents the nine phases associated with this framework.

Similar frameworks can be found in some of the works already cited (e.g., Ku et al., 2014; Merrill, 2002, 2013; Milrad et al., 2003; Paul & Elder, 2010; Tiruneh et al., 2017). The point of having nine phasesand calling this a developmental and holistic approach is to emphasize these key ideas: (a) inquiry and critical thinking skills are not likely to be mastered in one course. Years of practice are involved; (b) both cognitive and non-cognitive factors need to be taken into consideration; and (c) formative feedback and stimulating encouragement should be provided throughout the process.

Roles for Technology

Since technology was addressed in the title of this chapter, it is legitimate to ask how technologies might be used to support such a framework. There are many possible ways to use various technologies to help develop inquiry and critical thinking skills

Table 2.1 Nine phases for developing inquiry and critical thinking skills

Development phase	Skills being developed
1. Inquiry and puzzlement	Observing oddities, answering questions, asking questions
2. Exploration and forming explanations	*Finding relevant factors, creating explanations*
3. Evidence and hypothesis testing	Confirming and disconfirming evidence and predicting outcomes
4. Influence and causality	Differentiating coincidence, correlation and causality
5. Explanation and communication	Explaining reasons for beliefs and the quality of evidence to others
6. Coherence and consistency	Identifying inconsistencies and contradictions
7. Assumptions and biases	Recognizing unstated assumptions and identifying biases
8. Perspectives and alternatives	Considering multiple points of view
9. Reflection and refinement	Monitoring progress, adjusting to new evidence, and contemplating processes

(see, for example, http://www.educationworld.com/a_lesson/worksheets/critical_thinking/3-5/). Two specific technologies are the focus of this section: games and conversational interfaces.

A meta-analysis by Wouters, van Nimwegen, van Oostendorp, and van der Spek (2013) shows that games can have a positive impact on learning. Other studies suggest that games with goals that are well aligned with specific learning goals are more likely to have a positive impact on measured learning (Tobias, Fletcher, & Wind, 2014). The logic behind this impact seems to be that given appropriate background knowledge and information and relevant prior experience exists, that time spent on learning with formative feedback (in this case from a game), learning outcomes are likely to be positive. Games often are able to stimulate interest and engagement, resulting in more time being spent in and outside a classroom setting on a learning task. As a consequence, game-based applications to support each of the nine phases indicated above is likely to be productive, especially for young learners.

As a reminder, this framework does not encourage just getting a correct answer. The fundamental of this approach is to encourage exploration, explanation, reasoning, communication with others, collaborating on innovative solution approaches and reflecting on the quality and efficacy of each step along the way. Given those areas of emphasis in the nine phases, and the engagement factor of game-based applications, the second technology likely to be effective is a conversational interface. Having an application talk to learn in a positive and encouraging manner is required in order to encourage exploration, explanation, and the other areas being emphasized. Natural language processing has advanced and can be used in game-based applications. Children are already interacting with devices such as Alexa, Echo, Google Home, and Siri. These technologies are gaining use among children, modelled by parents who want to encourage their children to ask questions and explore explanations (McTear, Callejas, & Griol, 2016).

Concluding Remarks

An effort to implement and evaluate this framework is underway as a collaboration with three universities and NetDragon. One of the universities involved (East China Normal University) has settled on the notion that a game is needed to assess the progressive development of inquiry and critical thinking skills and has a prototype under development and testing. A second university (Beijing Normal University) has a postdoctoral researcher working with the other university (University of North Texas) on the project.

This effort represents a serious effort to take serious games seriously. In other words, measuring outcomes and efficacy is built around the framework and instruments already validated pertinent to that framework. In addition, the effort addresses both cognitive and non-cognitive aspects of inquiry and critical thinking. Finally, the effort embraces a multiyear developmental approach, unlike most efforts to date, to develop inquiry and critical thinking skills.

Given the need for informed, thoughtful and responsible citizens and the increasing complexity of problems that people encounter, it is imperative to take seriously the development of inquiry and critical thinking skills in young children. In a sense, this effort and the associated framework is a return to the ideas and lessons of John Dewey (1910, 1938). It is not too late to take those ideas and lessons into the twenty-first century.

Acknowledgements Support from a yumber of colleagues at NetDragon, East China Normal University, Beijing Normal University and the University of North Texas have contributed many ideas reflected in this chapter.

References

Brand, S. (2012). Mood and learning. In N. M. Seel (Ed.), *Encyclopedia of the sciences of learning* (pp. 132–211). Boston: Springer. https://doi.org/10.1007/978-1-4419-1428-6_40

Brand, S., Reimer, T., & Opwis, K. (2007). How do we learn in a negative mood? Effects of a negative mood on transfer and learning. *Learning and Instruction, 17*, 1–16.

Bransford, J. D., Brown, A. L., & Cocking, R. R. (Eds.). (2000). *How people learn: Brain, mind, experience and school* (expanded ed.). Washington, DC: National Research Council. Retrieved from https://www.nap.edu/read/9853/chapter/1.

Brown, J. S., Collins, A., & Duguid, P. (1988). *Situated cognition and the culture of learning* (Report No. IRL 88-0008). Palo Alto, CA: Institute for Research on Learning.

Butler, H. A., Pentoney, C., & Bong, M. P. (2017). Predicting real-world outcomes: Critical thinking ability is a better predictor of life decisions than intelligence. *Thinking Skills and Creativity, 25*, 38–46.

Charness, N., & Tuffiash, M. (2008). The role of expertise research and human factors in capturing, explaining and producing superior performance. *Human Factors, 50*(3), 427–432.

Collins, A., Brown, J. S., & Newman, S. E. (1989). Cognitive apprenticeship: Teaching the craft of reading, writing, and mathematics. In L. B. Resnick (Ed.), *Knowing, learning, and instruction: Essays in honor of Robert Glaser* (pp. 453–493). Hillsdale, NJ: Lawrence Erlbaum Associates.

Dewey, J. (1910). *How we think*. Boston: D. C. Heath.

Dewey, J. (1938). *Experience and education*. New York: Kappa Delta Pi.

Dörner, D. (1996). *The logic of failure: Recognizing and avoiding effort in complex situations* (R. Kimber & R. Kimber, Trans.). Cambridge, MA: Perseus Books.

Dwyer, C. P., Hogan, M. J., & Stewart, I. (2014). An integrated critical thinking framework for the 21st century. *Thinking Skills and Creativity, 12*, 43–52.

Felder, R. M., & Brent, R. (2005). Understanding student differences. *Journal of Engineering Education, 94*(1), 57–72.

Halpern, D. F. (2014). *Critical thinking across the curriculum: A brief edition of thought & knowledge*. New York: Routledge.

Heijltjes, A., Van Gog, T., Leppink, J., & Paas, F. (2014). Improving critical thinking: Effects of dispositions and instructions on economics students' reasoning skills. *Learning and Instruction, 29*, 31–42.

Ifenthaler, D., Kinshuk, Isaias, P., Sampson, D. G., & Spector, J. M. (Eds.). (2011). *Multiple perspectives on problem solving and learning in the digital age*. New York: Springer.

Ifenthaler, D., Masduki, I., & Seel, N. M. (2011). The mystery of cognitive structure and how we can detect it. Tracking the development of cognitive structures over time. *Instructional Science, 39*(1), 41–61. https://doi.org/10.1007/s11251-009-9097-6

Jonassen, D. H., & Grabowski, B. L. (1993). *Handbook of individual differences, learning, and instruction*. New York: Routledge.

Ku, K. Y. L., Ho, I. T., Hau, K. T., & Lai, C. M. (2014). Integrating direct and inquiry-based instruction in the teaching of critical thinking: An intervention study. *Instructional Science, 42*(2), 251–269.

McNamara, H., & Boudreau, J. D. (2011). Teaching whole person care in medical school. In T. A. Hutchinson (Ed.), *Whole person care* (pp. 183–200). New York: Springer.

McTear, M., Callejas, Z., & Griol, D. (2016). *The conversational interface: Talking to smart devices*. New York: Springer.

Merrill, M. D. (2002). First principles of instruction. *Educational Technology Research & Development, 50*(3), 1042–1629.

Merrill, M. D. (2013). *First principles of instruction: Identifying and designing effective, efficient and engaging instruction*. San Francisco: Pfeiffer.

Milrad, M., Spector, J. M., & Davidsen, P. I. (2003). Model facilitated learning. In S. Naidu (Ed.), *Learning and teaching with technology: Principles and practices* (pp. 13–27). London: Kogan Page.

Paul, R., & Elder, L. (2010). *The miniature guide to critical thinking: Concepts and tools*. Dillon Beach: Foundation for Critical Thinking Press. Retrieved from https://www.criticalthinking.org/files/Concepts_Tools.pdf.

Rogers, C. R. (1965). The place of the person in the new world of the behavioral sciences. In F. T. Stevens (Ed.), *Humanistic viewpoints in psychology: A book of readings* (pp. 387–407). New York: McGraw-Hill.

Spector, J. M. (2016). *Foundations of educational technology: Integrative approaches and interdisciplinary perspectives* (2nd ed.). New York: Routledge.

Spector, J. M., & Park, S. W. (2018). *Motivation, learning and technology: Embodied educational motivation*. New York: Routledge.

Spector, J. M., & Ren, Y. (2015). History of educational technology. In J. M. Spector (Ed.), *The SAGE encyclopedia of educational technology*. Thousand Oaks, CA: Sage.

Tiruneh, D. T., de Cock, M., Spector, J. M., Gu, X., & Elen, J. (2017). Toward a systematic and model-based approach to design learning environments for critical thinking. In J. M. Spector, B. B. Lockee, & M. D. Childress (Eds.), *Learning, design, and technology: An international compendium of theory, research, practice, and policy*. New York: Springer.

Tobias, S., Fletcher, J. D., & Wind, A. P. (2014). Game-based learning. In J. M. Spector, M. D. Merrill, J. Elen, & M. J. Bishop (Eds.), *Handbook of research on educational communications and technology* (pp. 485–503). New York: Springer.

Wouters, P., van Nimwegen, C., van Oostendorp, H., & van der Spek, E. D. (2013). A meta-analysis of the cognitive and motivational effects of serious games. *Journal of Educational Psychology, 105*(2), 249–265.

Jonathan Michael Spector is a Professor and Former Chair of Learning Technologies at the University of North Texas. He was previously Professor of Educational Psychology and Instructional Technology at the University of Georgia, Associate Director of the Learning Systems Institute at Florida State University, Chair of Instructional Design, Development and Evaluation at Syracuse University, and Director of the Educational Information Science and Technology Research Program at the University of Bergen. He earned a Ph.D. in Philosophy from The University of Texas at Austin. He is a visiting research professor at Beijing Normal University and at East China Normal University. His research focuses on intelligent support for instructional design, assessing learning in complex domains, developing critical thinking skills, and technology integration in education. Dr. Spector served on the International Board of Standards for Training, Performance and Instruction (*ibstpi*); he is a Past President of the Association for Educational and Communications Technology. He was an editor of *Educational Technology Research & Development* for 15 years. He edited the third and fourth editions of the *Handbook of Research on Educational Communications and Technology*, as well as the *SAGE Encyclopedia of Educational Technology*, and has more than 150 scholarly publications to his credit.

Chapter 3
Educational Neuroscience: Exploring Cognitive Processes that Underlie Learning

Pavlo D. Antonenko

Abstract This chapter reviews the most important neurotechnologies, neuroscience approaches, and empirical research using neuroscience methods and tools in education. Four specific technologies and representative studies using them are discussed in detail: eye tracking, electroencephalography, functional magnetic resonance imaging, and functional near-infrared spectroscopy. These neurotechnologies are examined as tools that offer high temporal resolution and those that provide high spatial resolution. A separate section addresses the use of neuroscience frameworks and tools that explore social cognition, focusing specifically on collaborative learning in teams. The chapter concludes with a discussion of important challenges and implications that educational researchers must keep in mind as they design empirical studies employing approaches and technologies from cognitive, social, and affective neuroscience. These implications include ensuring adequate signal-to-noise ratios, reducing the possibility of perceptual-motor confounds that may distort data of interest, and training psychophysiological signal classifiers using tasks that represent the cognitive processes involved in the experimental task. Careful task and study design and proper interpretation of physiological data in the context of cognitive and learning performance will improve the validity of educational studies conducted with EEG, fMRI, fNIRS, and eye tracking and will improve the reliability of data and generalizability of the findings.

Introduction

Learning is a complex perceptual, attentional, cognitive, affective, and social process. From the cognitive perspective, the learner must set up and maintain the learning goals, attend to the relevant information from multiple media and modalities, select the information most relevant to the learning goal, organize the information

P. D. Antonenko (✉)
University of Florida, Gainesville, FL, USA
e-mail: p.antonenko@coe.ufl.edu

© Association for Educational Communications and Technology 2019
T. D. Parsons et al. (eds.), *Mind, Brain and Technology*, Educational
Communications and Technology: Issues and Innovations,
https://doi.org/10.1007/978-3-030-02631-8_3

27

units into a meaningful representation, integrate the newly developed representations with the previously learned schemas, and develop an integrated representation of the relevant information from the multimedia presentation (Mayer, 2014; Wiley, Sanchez, & Jaeger, 2014). Affectively, it is important for the learner to respond to the ongoing demands of experience with the range of emotions to permit spontaneous reactions as well as the ability to delay impulsive reactions as needed, monitoring, evaluating, and modifying emotional responses (Koole, 2009). This has to be done in a way that is socially acceptable and that encourages collaboration with others, building upon the strengths of each individual learner and mitigating each individual's weaknesses. Because there are many perceptual, attentional, cognitive, affective, and social processes involved in the process of learning, it is reasonable to assume that individual differences in perception, attention, cognition, emotional regulation, and social competence would influence learning in the same environment differently for each individual learner.

An important problem with much of the prior research on learning is that the measures employed in studies tend to focus on the final product of the learner's interaction with the learning material and with each other, leaving the attentional, cognitive, affective, and social processes during learning almost completely unexamined. Current measures in many learning studies employ traditional tests of knowledge retention and transfer taken at the end of the learning intervention. As a result, what we learn from the empirical evidence generated by these studies are the effects on the final outcomes of the learning process but we have little sense regarding how or why the learners achieve a particular score on that test of learning. This issue is especially important in the context of the individual differences approach to understanding learning, where the core assumption is that each learner is a unique individual with a unique set of cognitive, affective, and social abilities (Plass, Kalyuga, & Leutner, 2010). Knowing more about the *process* of cognition and learning for the individual would help inform customized instruction and design of adaptive learning technologies. As a means to this end, educational neuroscience frameworks, methods, and tools can help shed light on the cognitive processing that reveals specific mechanisms that hinder or facilitate effective learning.

Cognition and Learning

Cognition has been the focus of the science of learning since the cognitive revolution in psychology (Baars, 1986; Chomsky, 1959; Hebb, 1949). Cognition is defined as the processes of knowing, including attending, remembering, and reasoning; also the content of the processes, such as concepts and memories (American Psychological Association, 2002). The American Psychological Association's definition of learning conceptualizes it as a process based on experience that results in a relatively permanent change in behavior or behavioral potential (2002). In order to be able to learn a set of skills or develop knowledge, one has to make use of a blend of cognitive functions. For example, chemistry students are expected to learn how to differentiate between different molecules using two-dimensional and three-dimensional models of those molecules. To develop this important skill, students must first rely on their visuospatial abilities such as mental rotation, mental animation, and pattern comparison. Each of these visuospatial abilities, in its turn, relies on the learner's visual attention span, visuospatial working memory capacity, inhibitory control, visuospatial processing speed, and a host of other cognitive variables. As chemistry students practice comparing molecule models and develop expertise in this task, they develop diagrammatic reasoning, that is, learned heuristics to understand and compare complex spatial representations and transformations without invoking mental images (Stieff, 2011). Diagrammatic reasoning is a different cognitive strategy than imagistic reasoning, which relies on *visuospatial* abilities, in that it requires that students develop *analytical* strategies to deal with complex representations and so some of the basic visuospatial cognitive variables such as visual attention span may be less important in cognition and learning when comparing molecule models. This example illustrates how the study of cognition may provide important insights regarding how, when, and why learning may occur for a particular individual and within a particular learning task and context.

A number of frameworks have been developed to conceptualize cognition, a complex set of processes and abilities that are not directly observable. A popular model of human cognition proposes three core cognitive structures: sensory memory, working memory, and long-term memory (Atkinson & Shiffrin, 1968; Baddeley & Hitch, 1974). Sensory register stores information acquired through sight, hearing, smell, taste, and touch as sensory images for a very brief period. Sensory images decay very quickly, after about 200–500 ms, and so sensory memory processing is mostly not registered in human consciousness. Those sensory images are then transferred into the working memory where most of the active cognitive processing is known to take place. Information is converted in working memory from sensory images into verbal and pictorial representations that are compared with the schemas in long-term memory. In other words, working memory is used as a mental "workspace" (Baars & Franklin, 2003) for temporally holding and manipulating information acquired through the senses and information retrieved from the long-term memory, which is the more permanent storage system. Working memory plays such a critical role in human cognition that it has been described as the "bottleneck" of our cognitive system (Chase & Ericsson, 1982) and equated with human consciousness (Baddeley, 2000). Information that has already been learned, that is, stored in long-term memory in the form of schemata, reduces cognitive demands on working memory because a schema can be handled in working memory as a single information element. Moreover, when a task or aspects of a task are repeatedly practiced, schemata become automated, and no longer require controlled processing (Shiffrin & Schneider, 1977), which further frees up working memory resources.

Assessment of cognitive processing has traditionally been achieved using the self-report paradigm. Self-reports of cognition often consist of one question (e.g., "Please rate the amount of mental effort invested in the task"), and the responses range from "very, very low mental effort" to "very, very high mental effort" as in the widely used mental effort scale by Paas (1992). These ratings are collected immediately after each task (e.g., Paas & Van Merriënboer, 1994; Van Gog, Paas, & Van Merriënboer,

2008), in which case they presumably reflect the cognitive dynamics for a series of individual tasks. Thus, self-reports offer limited insight into fluctuations in cognitive processing over time, unless they are applied repeatedly within a task, which disrupts the primary cognitive activity (e.g., Ayres, 2006). Even when applied multiple times during a learning experience, it is unclear whether self-reports provide a continuous measure of cognitive dynamics because they are necessarily retrospective.

Prior work indicates that self-report is often inaccurate. Working memory processes involve interaction with long-term memory schemas, which become automated with practice and may be unavailable for introspection (Feldon, 2004; Guan, Lee, Cuddihy, & Ramey, 2006). Students also tend to overestimate how well they understand, fail to recognize their own states of impasse during learning, and persist with unproductive strategies (Anderson & Beal, 1995; Gobert, Sao Pedro, Baker, Toto, & Montalvo, 2012). Karpicke and Blunt (2011) showed that while undergraduate students' metacognitive predictions identified repeated study (re-reading the chapter) as the most effective strategy to study for a test, objective measures of learning showed that retrieval practice (recall of information from the chapter) proved to be significantly more effective, even compared with the concept-mapping strategy to review for exam. In our own work, students' self-reports of their cognitive load were significantly less reliable than the electroencephalogram (EEG) data in terms of predicting successful or unsuccessful learning outcomes (Antonenko & Niederhauser, 2010; Wang et al., 2018).

Given the limitations of self-report, educational researchers have been employing measures that track changes in the psychophysiological responses of individual learners to explore cognitive function. Eye tracking, electroencephalography (EEG), functional magnetic resonance imaging (fMRI), and functional near-infrared spectroscopy (fNIRS) have all been used to study various attentional and cognitive dynamics during learning. Converging data from these sources with the more traditional measures of cognition and learning can provide a more comprehensive account of attentional and cognitive processing during a learning experience.

Eye Tracking and Distribution of Visual Attention

Eye tracking is a psychophysiological method that has recently gained much popularity among scholars of learning. The main assumption behind the use of eye tracking in educational research is the eye-mind hypothesis (Just & Carpenter, 1980), which suggests that visual attention is the proxy for mental attention and so visual attention patterns reflect cognitive strategies used by individuals. Eye tracking has been employed to study visual attention distribution in a wide variety of visual tasks from visual search (Pomplun, Reingold, & Shen, 2001), to reading (Schneps et al., 2013) to watching instructional video (Wang & Antonenko, 2017). Eye tracking has been applied in multiple usability studies to provide insights regarding the design of websites, multimedia instruction, and games (Conati, Jaques, & Muir, 2013; De Koning, Tabbers, Rikers, & Paas, 2010; Russell, 2005).

With the recent advancements of sensor technology, eye tracking has also become more affordable and less intrusive to use (Pernice & Nielsen, 2009). However, to benefit from the information provided by eye tracking, one must understand specific eye movement metrics and what they represent. Most modern eye trackers can accurately record two types of eye movements: gaze fixations and saccades (Rayner, 1998). A gaze fixation occurs when the eye focuses on a visual target for a short period of time (i.e., around 300 ms). A saccade is a rapid eye movement between two fixations and saccades range in amplitude from small movements to large ones. Researchers have examined these types of eye movement phenomena as quantified indices, such as the duration of each fixation, number of fixations, and saccade amplitude.

Eye tracking has been a useful technique in educational research, particularly in situations that require evaluation of the learner's attention distribution relative to various (often competing) information elements they see. For example, eye tracking has been employed in multimedia learning research to understand the cognitive processes learners use when using multimedia. Some of this research is summarized in a 2010 special issue of *Learning and Instruction* (Mayer, 2010). The studies reported in this special issue all employed a gaze fixation measure (time looking at relevant information) and produced important empirical and theoretical contributions. These studies helped determine that (a) a strong link exists between eye fixations and learning outcomes; (b) visual cues guide learners' visual attention (Boucheix & Lowe, 2010; De Koning et al., 2010); (c) prior knowledge guides visual attention (Canham & Hegarty, 2010; Jarodzka, Scheiter, Gerjets, & van Gog, 2010); and (d) learners who view animation and on-screen text must split their attention between graphics and printed words (Schmidt-Weigand, Kohert, & Glowalla, 2010).

Eye tracking has also been used to study the cognitive mechanisms underlying reading. Schneps and colleagues (2013) used eye movement data to determine that shorter lines facilitate reading in high school students with dyslexia. Reading using a smaller device (iPod™) compared to a bigger device (iPad™) resulted in substantial benefits, improving reading speed by 27%, reducing the number of eye fixations by 11%, and, importantly, reducing the number of regressive saccades by more than a factor of 2, with no cost to comprehension. The effects of attention modulation by the hand, and of increased letter spacing to reduce crowding, were also found to modulate oculomotor dynamics in reading. Importantly, these factors depended on individual learner characteristics, such as visual attention span, that varied within the sample.

As a research methodology to investigate allocation of attention during learning tasks, eye tracking can be both versatile and incisive (Duchowski, 2007). For example, observations of changes in pupil size can be used as an indicator of cognitive load (Guillory et al., 2014) and gaze contingent displays can be used to rapidly adapt task displays in response to attention. Chukoskie, Westerfield, and Townsend (2017) developed gaze-contingent video games that provide users visual and auditory feedback in real time from a remote eye tracker designed for in-home use. The games— *Whack the Moles*, *Shroom Digger*, and *Space Race*—require players to control the distribution of their visual attention and fixate their gaze on select objects based on the rules of the game. In *Whack the Moles*, for instance, players are to look at the moles as they appear out of the ground and use their gaze to "hit" ninja moles but avoid hitting the professor mole. Playing these games has helped individuals with autism spectrum disorder improve both the speed of attentional orienting and duration of fixation on task-relevant stimuli (Chukoskie et al., 2017). Research using eye tracking offers a unique approach to testing important learning hypotheses, particularly concerning attentional processing during learning within complex multimedia environments and relative to the individual differences among learners.

Using EEG to Explore *When* Cognitive Changes Happen

Educational researchers have long recognized that cognitive processing can be measured directly and objectively with brain activity measures (Brünken, Plass, & Leutner, 2003). Brain activity measures are widely categorized as either (a) high spatial resolution methods that track relatively slow changes in brain metabolism and blood flow, such as functional magnetic resonance imaging (fMRI) and functional near-infrared spectroscopy (fNIRS) or (b) tools that provide high temporal resolution and detect fluctuations in the electrical activity of the brain such as electroencephalography (EEG). While fMRI and fNIRS provide the advantage of high spatial resolution that allows localizing brain activity (while being temporally less sensitive), temporal methods such as EEG have the advantage of being sensitive to millisecond differences in the electrical activity of the brain and can thus provide evidence on the time course of neural processing. Most EEG systems, however, offer lower spatial resolution, making analyses of specific brain regions more challenging than when using fMRI or other metabolic imaging techniques. Thus, a major advantage of using EEG in the context of assessing cognition is that it may allow identification of temporal dynamics and cognitive events such as instantaneous load, peak load, average load, and accumulated load (e.g., Xie & Salvendy, 2000).

EEG is a popular neuroimaging technique that measures electrical activity produced by the brain via electrodes that are placed on the scalp. These measurements vary predictably in response to changing levels of cognitive stimuli (Antonenko & Niederhauser, 2010; Anderson & Bratman, 2008; Gevins & Smith, 2003; Klimesch, 2012). Unlike other neurotechnologies, which require participants to lie in a restricted position (fMRI), or to ingest hazardous materials (PET), EEG can noninvasively measure brain activity in authentic or near-authentic settings. Wireless EEG solutions (Stevens, Galloway, Wang, & Berka, 2012) appear especially promising because they offer better ecological validity by reducing the overall size of the equipment and allowing collection of data from multiple participants at the same time in an authentic context such as a classroom.

EEG hardware consists of a cap or a headset that houses anywhere from one to hundreds of electrodes that are fitted over an individual's scalp to record low-amplitude electrical activity at the surface of the skull. The EEG signal is typically measured as the voltage gradient between two electrodes. Multiple electrodes are to be placed in standard arrangements (such as the 10–20 International system, Jasper, 1958) that cover large portions of the scalp and allow investigators to observe the activity of the entire brain simultaneously.

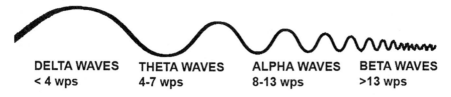

DELTA WAVES   **THETA WAVES**   **ALPHA WAVES**   **BETA WAVES**
< 4 wps   4-7 wps   8-13 wps   >13 wps

Fig. 3.1 Human brain wave frequencies (in waves per second, or Hz)

The first human EEG recording was obtained by Hans Berger in 1924. Berger's early work resulted in identifying what he referred to as "first-order waves" oscillating at a rate of 10 cycles per second or 10 Hz (now known as alpha waves) and "second-order waves" or beta waves oscillating at about 20–30 Hz. At present, it is believed that electrical activity in the brain generates at least five distinct rhythms (Basar, 2004). Figure 3.1 shows that brain waves cover a spectrum ranging from the large, slow delta and theta waves to faster (i.e., higher frequency) alpha, and beta waves (Antonenko, Paas, Grabner, & van Gog, 2010).

Alpha oscillations are widely regarded to be the predominant brain wave rhythm (Basar, 2004). Alpha waves are frequently used in experiments as a baseline when wakeful subjects are asked to close their eyes. When the eyes are opened, a suppression (sometimes referred to as "desynchronization") of alpha activity occurs, which is used as an index of an alert state of external information intake (Antonenko et al., 2010). Alpha waves can be recorded from at least 85% of humans in the 8–13 Hz frequency range and an amplitude ranging from 20 to 200 μV (Fisch, 1999). Different areas of the brain are more likely to generate particular brain waves, and alpha waves are known to be prominent in the occipital and parietal lobes (Klimesch, 1999).

Researchers have repeatedly observed that the alpha rhythm is related to many types of cognitive activity (Andreassi, 2007). For many decades, it was assumed that alpha oscillations reflect "idling" cortical tissue and thus, as cognitive activity increases, the amplitude of alpha oscillation should decrease, indicating "activation" of cortical tissue (Fisch, 1999). Although this inverse relationship is well documented for various types of mental activity, tasks, and stimuli (Andreassi, 2007), research in the cognitive neurosciences has demonstrated robust alpha enhancement in tasks that require covert (non-sensory, internal) types of cognitive activity, such as the retention interval in visual working memory tasks (Jensen, Gelfand, Kounios, & Lisman, 2002), or narrative imagery tasks (Bartsch, Hamuni, Miskovic, Lang, & Keil, 2015). Using advanced time series analyses, recent research has shown that alpha oscillations reflect the extent and time course of working memory retention, in the absence of stimulation (Anderson, Serences, Vogel, & Awh, 2014). Importantly, because of their large amplitude and robust nature, alpha oscillations are considered more promising for applied research and for real-time assessment than smaller-amplitude beta and gamma-band signals.

Researchers have repeatedly observed that alpha, theta, and gamma activity is related to the intensity of cognitive processing in a variety of task demands (Antonenko et al., 2010; Neubauer, Fink, Grabner, Christa, & Wolfgang, 2006). Klimesch and colleagues have repeatedly emphasized (Klimesch, Schack, & Sauseng, 2005; Klimesch, Doppelmayr, Hanslmayr, Christa, & Wolfgang, 2006; Klimesch, 2012) that alpha activity, especially in the higher frequency range (10–13 Hz, referred to as upper alpha), is associated with semantic information processing, in particular with searching, accessing, and retrieving information from long-term memory. Since most cognitive tasks draw on these processes, alpha event related-desynchronization (ERD/ERS; Pfurtscheller & Lopes da Silva, 2005) can be observed in a wide range of task demands (Klimesch et al., 2006). Theta activity, in contrast, has been frequently related to episodic and working memory as theta synchronization increases parametrically with working memory load and is sustained during the retention period (e.g., Jensen & Tesche, 2002).

Educational research that employed EEG as a measure of cognitive dynamics is still scarce and the studies have been very tentative (Gerjets, Walter, Rosenstiel, Bogdan, & Zander, 2014). The fine temporal resolution of EEG allowed Antonenko and Niederhauser (2010) to detect differences in the participants' cognitive processing while they were accessing hyperlinks with and without page previews. Page previews reduced brain wave activity associated with split attention and extraneous cognitive processing and improved conceptual and structural knowledge acquisition. Another study demonstrated that gifted students displayed higher alpha power (i.e., reduced cognitive processing) when learning from text, pictures, and video presentation compared to non-gifted counterparts (Gerlic & Jausovec, 1999). These differences were especially pronounced for the video format, which prompted the authors to conclude that multimedia presentations of learning content might be less effective for gifted students (although no learning performance data were reported to support this conclusion). A recent study conducted by educational researchers employed the ERD/ERS paradigm to assess working memory load during online text reading with and without hyperlinks (Scharinger, Kammerer, & Gerjets, 2015). The researchers took the effort to design a hypertext system that had the appearance of a functioning hypertext with links but the hyperlinks were not functional. This simulated link selection provision was included in the design to minimize the potential perceptual and motor differences that might confound the measurement of the actual working memory load (e.g., Gerjets et al., 2014). Consistent with prior research, reading text with hyperlinks was hypothesized to induce higher levels of working memory load. A significant main effect of task condition (with or without hyperlinks) on alpha frequency band power was found. Similar to the findings of Antonenko and Niederhauser (2010), alpha power was significantly lower in the test condition compared to the baseline condition. These results provide further evidence that the ERD/ERS paradigm is a viable EEG-based method of assessing working memory load.

Using fMRI and fNIRS to Study *Where* Cognitive Changes Happen

Unlike EEG, functional magnetic resonance imaging (fMRI) and functional near-infrared spectroscopy (fNIRS) are optical neuroimaging methods that offer a high spatial, rather than temporal, resolution to assess cognitive dynamics during various learning tasks (Anderson, Betts, Ferris, & Fincham, 2011; Ferrari & Quaresima, 2012; Hoshi, 2003; Strait & Scheutz, 2014).

The advent of fMRI in the 1990s enabled neuroscientists to "see" changes in brain activity associated with performing an experimental task. This neurotechnology requires inserting the participant into a scanner with a large, tube-shaped magnet, which creates images of the magnetic resonance signal generated by the protons of water molecules in brain cells. Task performance activates certain brain areas which leads to enhanced oxygen consumption by cells in those areas and therefore enhanced blood flow to those cells. Using fMRI, changes in the oxygenation state of hemoglobin can be registered. This is called the BOLD (blood oxygenation level dependent) response, which is the outcome measure used in most fMRI studies. The fine spatial resolution of fMRI (1–3 mm) has allowed neuroscientists to analyze brain activation patterns and link them to cognitive functions ranging from discourse comprehension (Martín-Loeches, Casado, Hernández-Tamames, & Álvarez-Linera, 2008) to mathematical problem solving (Anderson et al., 2011). Yet, despite the obvious advantages over more direct but also more invasive imaging techniques like positron emission tomography (PET), which relies on tracking radioactive tracers that have been injected into the blood stream, fMRI has certain limitations. While most fMRI scanners allow participants to be presented with different visual, auditory, and kinesthetic stimuli, and to make different actions such as pressing a button or moving a joystick, participants must remain relatively motionless, which limits the range of behaviors that can be studied. Participants also have to wear headphones to shield their ears from noise, and this noise also makes the analysis of overt verbal responses difficult, although methods have been developed to filter out the scanner noise (e.g., Jung, Prasad, Qin, & Anderson, 2005). Furthermore, the cost (starting around $300,000) and expertise required both to maintain the equipment and to collect and analyze data act as barriers to educational researchers looking to incorporate fMRI into their work.

A lower-cost non-invasive alternative to fMRI that is gaining popularity among neuroscientists is fNIRS. fNIRS uses specific wavelengths of light to provide measures of cerebral oxygenated and deoxygenated hemoglobin (Cui, Bray, Bryant, Glover, & Reiss, 2011). A positive correlation between the increase of oxygenated blood and the increase in cognitive effort has been found by several research groups (Hirshfield et al., 2009; Izzetoglu, Bunce, Onaral, Pourrezaei, & Chance, 2004; Parasuraman & Caggiano, 2005). Hirshfield et al. (2009) showed that the accuracy of fNIRS-based classification of mental workload reached 82% distinguishing two workload classes and 50% distinguishing three classes. In a similarly designed study, Girouard and associates (2010) were able to predict whether the subject was experiencing no workload, low workload, or high workload. Additionally, they were able to distinguish between mental workload on low spatial working memory tasks and high spatial working memory tasks with 70% average accuracy. In another study, Ayaz and colleagues (2012) showed that frontal cerebral oxygenation measured by fNIRS increases with working memory load. Specifically, average oxygenation changes due to task engagement at optode 2 (that is close to AF7 in the International 10–20 System, Jasper, 1958) were associated with task difficulty and increased monotonically with increasing task difficulty. This region has been implicated in several previous visuo-spatial processing studies using PET (Reuter-Lorenz et al., 2000), fMRI (Owen et al., 2005), and fNIRS (Schreppel et al., 2008). Given these findings, fNIRS appears to hold high potential for the monitoring and assessment of cognitive dynamics.

So, why is it important to understand *where* in the brain changes associated with cognitive function may be happening? One of the classic debates in literacy research and education focuses on the role of "whole language" text immersion versus the development of phonetic skills (National Reading Panel, 2000). Neuroscience research aimed at delineating the brain areas that support reading provides useful insights regarding this issue. For example, the so-called dual-route theory provides a framework for describing reading in the brain at the level of the word (Jobard, Crivello, & Tzourio-Mazoyer, 2003). Supported by dozens of fMRI studies, this theory proposes that words are first processed by the primary visual cortex and then pre-lexical processing occurs at the left occipito-temporal junction. After that, processing follows one of two complementary pathways (Jobard et al., 2003). The "assembled pathway" involves an intermediate step of converting letters and words into sounds (grapho-phonological conversion), which occurs in certain left temporal and frontal areas, including Broca's area. The discovery of this pathway suggests the importance of the phonic approach to reading instruction. In case of the second route, known as the "addressed pathway," information is transferred directly from pre-lexical processing to semantic processing (extraction of meaning), which implies the significance of using the whole language approach to reading instruction. Both pathways terminate in the left basal temporal area, the left interior frontal gyrus, and the left posterior middle gyrus, or Wernicke's area, which is known to be involved in understanding written and spoken language. These fMRI results confirm the assumptions of the dual-route framework, which helps explain different patterns of activation observed in participants during a reading task. This neuroimaging evidence is also consistent with (and partly informed) the conclusions of the US National Reading Panel (2000) and National Research Council (Snow, Burns, & Griffin, 1998) that highlight the educational benefits of a balanced approach to reading instruction, which combines whole language and phonics approaches.

Another example that highlights the importance of examining where in the brain cognitive functions are represented involves the study of the "mathematical brain." Many mathematical problems are rehearsed to such an extent in elementary school that they are stored as declarative knowledge (Goswami, 2004). This explains the language-dependent activation patterns found during drill-and-practice counting exercises and rote learning like the multiplication tables. In contrast, approximate arithmetic, or approximation of number manipulation rather than a precise arithmetic operation, was found to be language independent, rely on a sense of numerical magnitudes, and recruit bilateral areas of the parietal lobes (including a distinct parietal-premotor area) involved in visuospatial processing. Using a positron emission tomography (PET) paradigm, Zago and colleagues (2001) found that a region associated with the representation of fingers (left parieto-premotor circuit) was activated during adults' arithmetic performance. Observers note that this result may explain the importance of using finger-counting as a strategy for the acquisition of calculation skills and have important consequences for the developing brain because they partially underpin numerical manipulation skills in adults (Goswami, 2004). This conclusion was supported by an fMRI study revealing that the human cortical motor system plays an important role in the representation of numbers, and that organization of numerical knowledge is influenced by individual finger-counting habits (Tschentscher, Hauk, Fischer, & Pulvermüller, 2012). The complex interplay of the brain systems responsible for processing and storing the different types of numerical knowledge is believed to result in the development of advanced quantitative skills and mathematical intuition characteristic of experts in mathematics, statistics, and other related disciplines (Dehaene, Spelke, Stanescu, Pinel, & Tsivkin, 1999).

Using Neuroscience to Explore Social Cognition

Social neuroscience is a burgeoning area within the larger neuroscience community and the approaches and tools used by social neuroscientists may be of much interest to educational researchers. Team neurodynamics has been the focus of several recent social neuroscience studies. One such investigation analyzed neurosynchrony between team members during submarine piloting simulations (Stevens et al., 2012). In this study, EEG-derived measures of cognitive engagement were normalized and pattern classified by self-organizing artificial neural networks. Results demonstrated that neurosynchrony expression for engagement shifted across task segments and task changes. Shannon entropy measures of the neurosynchrony data stream revealed predictable decreases associated with periods when the team was stressed. In a follow-up study, Stevens and colleagues (2012) explored whether and how their neurodynamics modeling approach could contribute to the more traditional approaches to studying team function such as shared mental models (Entin & Serfaty, 1999), team cognition (Cooke, Gorman, & Kiekel, 2008), and macrocognition (Warner, Letsky, & Cowen, 2005). EEG-derived measures of engagement in a submarine piloting team task were normalized and pattern classified by self-organizing artificial neural networks and hidden Markov models. The temporal expression of these patterns was mapped onto team events and related to the frequency of team members' speech. Standardized models were created with pooled data from multiple teams to facilitate comparisons across teams and levels of expertise and to provide a framework for rapid monitoring of team performance. The neurosynchrony expression for engagement shifted across task segments and internal and external task changes. These changes occurred within seconds and were affected more by changes in the task than by the person speaking. Shannon entropy measures of the neurosynchrony data stream showed decreases associated with periods when the team was stressed and speaker entropy was high. These studies indicate that expression of neurophysiologic indicators measured by EEG may complement rather than duplicate communication metrics as measures of team cognition.

In a more traditional, tightly controlled neuroscience task paradigm, Konvalinka and colleagues (2014) studied the neurophysiologic signatures of leaders versus followers. This study employed a synchronized finger-tapping task while measuring dual-EEG from pairs of individuals who either mutually adjusted to each other (interactive condition) or followed a computer metronome (non-interactive condition). The interactive condition was characterized by a stronger suppression of alpha over frontal areas in contrast to the non-interactive condition. A multivariate analysis of two-brain activity to classify interactive versus non-interactive trials revealed asymmetric patterns of the frontal alpha suppression in each pair. Analysis of behavioral data allowed the authors to conclude that team leaders exhibited stronger frontal alpha suppression in eight out of nine pairs, possibly suggesting that leaders invested more cognitive resources in prospective planning and control.

A recent study explored the role of brain-to-brain synchrony in a highly authentic setting—that is, a high school biology classroom over an entire semester (Dikker et al., 2017). The researchers recorded brain activity from a group of 12 students as they engaged in natural classroom activities (discussion, lecture, and video viewing) and social interactions. They found that brain-to-brain synchrony between students consistently predicted class engagement and social dynamics reported by students for each class. These findings suggest that EEG-based brain-to-brain synchrony is a sensitive measure that can predict dynamic classroom interactions, and this relationship may be driven by shared attention within the group.

Antonenko (2016) employed EEG to explore team neurodynamics during cyber-enabled collaborative problem solving. Dyads worked within a cyberlearning environment to define and solve an authentic problem using either a collaboration script. One group of dyads used a social script that scaffolded role distribution for examining information resources (as either a Summarizer or Questioner), while the other group dyads employed an epistemic script that structured the problem-solving process by advising students on the sequence of steps to take while solving the problem together. For individual learners, parietal alpha desynchronization was higher in the epistemic script condition, suggesting more intense periods of cognitive activity in epistemic dyads. At the team level, epistemic dyads demonstrated higher levels of across-brain neurosynchrony evidenced by more and stronger inter-subject correlations in event-related alpha power changes. Epistemic dyads also demonstrated significantly better collaborative problem-solving performance and spent less time on the problem. Coupled with results of problem-solving efficiency and performance, this study confirms that changes in alpha power can help understand team function during an authentic learning task.

Challenges and Implications

The value of neuroscience frameworks, methods, and technologies to study attention, cognition, and learning is well established (Gazzaniga, 2009). However, the vast majority of this research is performed in tightly controlled laboratory experiments using relatively simple tasks and stimuli. There are several important reasons for this.

Reliable Neuroimaging Data Require Sufficient Signal-to-Noise Ratios

EEG, fNIRS, and fMRI measures show vast differences in their variability and reliability. The robustness and diagnostic usefulness of these neuroimaging measures is affected not only by what is measured and what computational approach is taken (regression, classification, discrimination), but more importantly by how well the paradigm is geared towards eliciting the particular event of interest. For example, it is important to remember that ERD/ERS computation common in EEG research requires averaging over time or trials to yield satisfactory reliability (Pfurtscheller & Lopes da Silva, 2005). This means that to acquire reliable EEG indices of working memory load, it is important to ensure that participants engage in the learning task multiple times (e.g., solving multiple similar math problems in the control condition and multiple similar math problems in the treatment condition).

In our own work, we have achieved this by designing tasks that make use of multiple trials. For example, a recent study examined differences regarding how effectively and efficiently a diverse group of 120 community college students compared models of molecules when these models were provided as 2D and 3D representations (Antonenko, 2016). The authentic learning task was a chirality task common when studying stereochemistry in organic chemistry courses. Specifically, the chirality task was a custom-built Matlab™ application that consisted of two blocks of 80 trials. One of the blocks contained only 3D models of molecules and the other block included only 2D models of molecules to compare. The task was designed to ensure that model dimensionality was the only difference between the molecular representations used in each block. Each trial presented participants with a pair of molecular models and participants were asked to determine whether the two models represented the same molecule or different molecules. This task paradigm allowed us to examine multiple trials and isolate the separate noise from the brain activity of interest. Specifically, parietal alpha synchronization was larger for the 2D task compared to the 3D task. Alpha desynchronizes with visual processing and then synchronizes reflecting top-down, inhibitory control processes (Klimesch, Sauseng, & Hanslmayr, 2007; Klimesch, 2012).

Perceptual-Motor Confounds May Distort Data of Interest

When designing studies and analyzing neuroimaging data, particularly EEG, it is important to exclude brain activity data that may be confounded by perceptual and motor processes associated with eye blinks, response to a change in the background color on a presentation slide, mouse and keyboard clicks, hand and finger movements associated with using a touch interface, and so on. Time windows of analysis must be selected very carefully to ensure that the presence of possible perceptual-motor confounds is minimized and that the data under analysis reflect changes in the dynamics of cognitive processing, rather than perceptual responses to changing sensory stimuli or motor responses associated with movement.

A good example of addressing this problem is the design of the study by Gerjets and colleagues (2014). The authors employed a cross-task classification paradigm with a support vector machine algorithm that was trained using two working memory tasks (reading span and numerical n-back) that were relevant to the learning tasks that participants were asked to engage in during the actual experiment (i.e., mathematical word problems presented in a simple to complex sequence for each participant). The study was carefully designed to account for potential perceptual-motor confounds such as ending windows of analysis 125 ms before each keypress during participant responses to exclude EEG data reflecting motor planning (e.g., Grabner & De Smedt, 2011).

Signal Classifiers Must Be Trained Using Tasks that Match the Experimental Task

Many studies that make use of neuroimaging data, such as the Gerjets et al. (2014) study described above, rely on signal classification algorithms that use machine learning techniques (e.g., support vector machines, artificial neural networks). These classifiers are trained using data that involve, for example, low-load data (e.g., simple mental arithmetic) and high-load data (e.g., complex mental arithmetic). The algorithm then preprocesses each data source in order to extract an array of signal features that are computed for the low-load condition and for the high-load condition. The features are then combined for the low-load condition and high-load condition as inputs to train a machine learning model (e.g., an artificial neural network) that will be able to produce an index of working memory load during the actual experimental task by comparing experimental data for each epoch of interest to the low-load array of features and high-load array of features.

The key issue with this approach is that the tasks used to train signal classifiers should be designed to match the cognitive task requirements of the study. Using the example of simple versus complex mental arithmetic for training a working memory load classifier, this means that if the experimental task does not have to do with mental arithmetic, and instead focuses, say, on visuospatial processing such as comparing molecular models, this classifier may be useless because the signal features used to train the classifier do not really apply to visuospatial processing.

This is a significant problem for educational researchers because many "turn-key" EEG and fNIRS systems designed for non-clinical applications and used by educational researchers do just that—use signal classification tasks that may not be a good match to the actual learning tasks used by researchers during their experiments. The software tools provided by turn-key neuroscience systems often include cognitive load, engagement, distraction, and boredom classifiers that are marketed as robust indicators of these respective cognitive or affective phenomena. Caution is warranted when using these classifiers, however, because the tasks used to train the classifier may not necessarily match the attentional and cognitive task characteristics of the actual experimental task. Thus, a better option would be systems that come with cognitive state classification algorithms that are trainable by the researcher to ensure proper alignment between the task used in the experiment and the task used to train the classifier.

Conclusion

Psychophysiological tools such as EEG, fMRI, fNIRS, and eye tracking can provide important insights into the cognitive processes that underlie learning alone or in groups. EEG offers a high temporal resolution to allow tracking of millisecond changes in cognitive activity and reveal the dynamics of cognitive processing. Other tools such as fMRI and fNIRS boast excellent spatial resolution and afford analysis of where in the brain changes related to the task demands may be happening. Eye tracking offers both temporal and spatial resolution and is appropriate in studies of learning that rely on effective distribution of visual attention and competing visual stimuli such as those found in most tasks within multimedia learning environments.

Despite being highly complex and involved, neuroscience measurement paradigms provide educational researchers with frameworks, methods, and tools to detect even the most subtle fluctuations in physiological activity associated with cognitive dynamics. Recent advances in hardware systems and analytical software appear very promising because they remove many of the barriers to conducting research on learning using neuroscience tools and allow collecting data from multiple participants at the same time and in authentic settings. Meticulous task and study design and proper interpretation of physiological data in the context of cognitive and learning performance will improve the validity of educational studies conducted with EEG, fMRI, fNIRS, and eye tracking and will improve the reliability of data and generalizability of the findings.

Acknowledgments This material is based upon work supported by the National Science Foundation under Grant No. #1540888.

References

American Psychological Association. (2002). Glossary of psychological terms. Cognition. Retrieved from http://www.apa.org/research/action/glossary.aspx?tab=3

Anderson, C. W., & Bratman, J. A. (2008). Translating thoughts into actions by finding patterns in brainwave. *Proceedings of the Fourteenth Yale Workshop on Adaptive and Learning Systems* (pp. 1–6). Yale University, New Haven, CT.

Anderson, D. E., Serences, J. T., Vogel, E. K., & Awh, E. (2014). Induced alpha rhythms track the content and quality of visual working memory representations with high temporal precision. *Journal of Neuroscience, 34*(22), 7587–7599.

Anderson, G., & Beal, C. R. (1995). Children's recognition of inconsistencies in science texts: Multiple measures of comprehension monitoring. *Applied Cognitive Psychology, 9*, 261–272.

Anderson, J. R., Betts, S., Ferris, J. L., & Fincham, J. M. (2011). Cognitive and metacognitive activity in mathematical problem solving: Prefrontal and parietal patterns. *Cognitive, Affective, & Behavioral Neuroscience, 11*(1), 52–67.

Andreassi, J. (2007). *Psychophysiology: Human behavior and physiological response*. Mahwah, NJ: Lawrence Erlbaum Associates.

Antonenko, P. (2016). On the same wavelength: Exploring team neurosynchrony during technology-enhanced collaborative learning. In Proceedings of the 2016 Conference of the National Association for Research in Science Teaching (p. 154), Baltimore, MD. Retrieved from: http://narst.org/annualconference/NARST_2016_Abstracts.pdf

Antonenko, P., & Niederhauser, D. (2010). The influence of leads on cognitive load and learning in a hypertext-assisted learning environment. *Computers in Human Behavior, 26*(2), 140–150.

Antonenko, P., Paas, F., Grabner, R., & van Gog, T. (2010). Using electroencephalography (EEG) to measure cognitive load. *Educational Psychology Review, 22*, 425–438.

Atkinson, R. C., & Shiffrin, R. M. (1968). Human memory: A proposed system and its control processes. In K. W. Spence & J. T. Spence (Eds.), *The psychology of learning and motivation* (pp. 89–195). New York: Academic Press.

Ayaz, H., Shewokis, P., Bunce, S., Izzetoglu, K., Willems, B., & Onaral, B. (2012). Optical brain monitoring for operator training and mental workload assessment. *NeuroImage, 59*, 36–47.

Ayres, P. (2006). Using subjective measures to detect variations of intrinsic cognitive load within problems. *Learning and Instruction, 16*, 389–400.

Baars, B. (1986). *The cognitive revolution in psychology*. New York: The Guilford Press.

Baars, B., & Franklin, S. (2003). How conscious experience and working memory interact. *Trends in Cognitive Science, 7*, 166–172.

Baddeley, A. D. (2000). The episodic buffer: A new component of working memory? *Trends in Cognitive Sciences, 4*, 417–423.

Baddeley, A. D., & Hitch, G. (1974). Working memory. In G. H. Bower (Ed.), *The psychology of learning and motivation: Advances in research and theory* (pp. 47–89). New York: Academic Press.

Bartsch, F., Hamuni, G., Miskovic, V., Lang, P. J., & Keil, A. (2015). Oscillatory brain activity in the alpha range is modulated by the content of word-prompted mental imagery. *Psychophysiology, 52*(6), 727–735.

Basar, E. (2004). *Memory and brain dynamics: Oscillations integrating attention, perception, learning and memory*. Boca Raton, FL: CRC Press LLC.

Boucheix, J.-M., & Lowe, R. K. (2010). An eye tracking comparison of external pointing cues and internal continuous cues in learning from complex animations. *Learning and Instruction, 20*, 123–135.

Brünken, R., Plass, J., & Leutner, D. (2003). Direct measurement of cognitive load in multimedia learning. *Educational Psychologist, 38*(1), 53–61.

Canham, M., & Hegarty, M. (2010). Effects of knowledge and display design on comprehension of complex graphics. *Learning and Instruction, 20*, 155–166.

Chase, W. G., & Ericsson, K. A. (1982). Skill and working memory. In G. H. Bower (Ed.), *The psychology of learning and motivation* (pp. 1–58). New York: Academic Press.

Chomsky, N. (1959). Review of Skinner's *Verbal Behavior*. *Language, 35*, 26–58.

Chukoskie, L., Westerfield, M., & Townsend, J. (2017). A novel approach to training attention and gaze in ASD: A feasibility and efficacy pilot study. *Developmental Neurobiology, 78*, 546. https://doi.org/10.1002/dneu.22563

Conati, c., Jaques, N., & Muir, M. (2013). Understanding attention to adaptive hints in educational games: An eye-tracking study. *International Journal of Artificial Intelligence in Education, 23*, 136–161.

Cooke, N. J., Gorman, J. C., & Kiekel, P. A. (2008). Communication as team-level cognitive processing. In M. Letsky, N. Warner, & S. Fiore (Eds.), *Macrocognition in teams: Theories and methodologies* (pp. 51–64). Hants: Ashgate Publishing Ltd.

Cui, X., Bray, S., Bryant, D. M., Glover, G. H., & Reiss, A. L. (2011). A quantitative comparison of NIRS and fMRI across multiple cognitive tasks. *NeuroImage, 54*, 2808–2821.

De Koning, B. B., Tabbers, H. K., Rikers, R. M. J. P., & Paas, F. (2010). Attention guidance in learning from a complex animation: Seeing is understanding? *Learning and Instruction, 20,* 111–122.

Dehaene, S., Spelke, E., Stanescu, R., Pinel, P., & Tsivkin, S. (1999). Sources of mathematical thinking: Behavioral and brain-imaging evidence. *Science, 284,* 970–974.

Dikker, S., Wan, L., Davidesco, I., Kaggen, L., Oostrik, M., McClintock, J., et al. (2017). Brain-to-brain synchrony tracks real-world dynamic group interactions in the classroom. *Current Biology, 27,* 1375–1380.

Duchowski, A. T. (2007). *Eye tracking methodology: Theory and practice.* Berlin: Springer.

Entin, E. E., & Serfaty, D. (1999). Adaptive team coordination. *Human Factors, 41,* 312–325.

Feldon, D. F. (2004). Dispelling a few myths about learning. *UrbanEd, 1*(4), 37–39.

Ferrari, M., & Quaresima, V. (2012). A brief review on the history of human functional near-infrared spectroscopy (fNIRS) development and fields of application. *NeuroImage, 63*(2), 921–935.

Fisch, B. (1999). *Fisch and Spehlmann's EEG primer: Basic principles of digital and analog EEG.* Amsterdam: Elsevier.

Gazzaniga, M. S. (Ed.). (2009). *The cognitive neurosciences* (4th ed.). Cambridge, MA: MIT Press.

Gerjets, P., Walter, C., Rosenstiel, W., Bogdan, M., & Zander, T. O. (2014). Cognitive state monitoring and the design of adaptive instruction in digital environments: Lessons learned from cognitive workload assessment using a passive brain-computer interface approach. *Frontiers in Neuroscience, 8,* 385.

Gerlic, I., & Jausovec, N. (1999). Multimedia: Differences in cognitive processes observed with EEG. *Educational Technology Research and Development, 47*(3), 5–14.

Gevins, A., & Smith, M. E. (2003). Neurophysiological measures of cognitive workload during human-computer interactions. *Theoretical Issues in Ergonomic Science, 4,* 113–131.

Girouard, A., Solovey, E., Hirshfield, L., Peck, E., Chauncey, K., Sassaroli, A., et al. (2010). In D. S. Tan & A. Nijholt (Eds.), *From brain signals to adaptive interfaces: Using fNIRS in HCI in brain-computer interfaces* (pp. 221–237). New York: Springer.

Gobert, J., Sao Pedro, M., Baker, R. S., Toto, E., & Montalvo, O. (2012). Leveraging educational data mining for real time performance assessment of scientific inquiry skills within microworlds. *Journal of Educational Data Mining, 4,* 153–185.

Goswami, U. (2004). Neuroscience and education. *British Journal of Educational Psychology, 74,* 1–14.

Grabner, R. H., & De Smedt, B. (2011). Neurophysiological evidence for the validity of verbal strategy reports in mental arithmetic. *Biological Psychology, 87,* 128–136.

Guan, Z., Lee, S., Cuddihy, E., & Ramey, J. (2006). The validity of the stimulated retrospective think-aloud method as measured by eye tracking. In *Proceedings of the SIGCHI conference on Human Factors in computing systems* (pp. 1253–1262).

Guillory, S., Kaldy, Z., Shukla, M., & Pomplun, M. (2014). Pupil response predicts memory strength in a visual short-term memory task. *Journal of Vision, 14*(10), 235–235.

Hebb, D. O. (1949). *The organization of behavior: A neuropsychological theory.* New York: Wiley.

Hirshfield, L. M., Solovey, E. T., Girouard, A., Kebinger, J., Jacob, R. J. K., Sassaroli, A., et al. (2009). Brain measurement for usability testing and adaptive interfaces: An example of uncovering syntactic workload with functional near infrared spectroscopy. *Proceedings of the 27th International Conference on Human Factors in Computing Systems* (pp. 2185–2194). Boston

Hoshi, Y. (2003). Functional near-infrared optical imaging: Utility and limitations in human brain mapping. *Psychophysiology, 40,* 511–520.

Izzetoglu, K., Bunce, S., Onaral, B., Pourrezaei, K., & Chance, B. (2004). Functional optical brain imaging using near-infrared during cognitive tasks. *International Jounral of Human Computer Interaction, 17*(2), 211–231.

Jarodzka, H., Scheiter, K., Gerjets, P., & van Gog, T. (2010). In the eyes of the beholder: How experts and novices interpret dynamic stimuli. *Learning and Instruction, 20,* 146–154.

Jasper, H. A. (1958). The ten–twenty system of the International Federation. *Electroencephalography and Clinical Neurophysiology, 10,* 371–375.

Jensen, O., Gelfand, J., Kounios, J., & Lisman, J. E. (2002). Oscillations in the alpha band (9-12 Hz) increase with memory load during retention in a short-term memory task. *Cerebral Cortex, 12*(8), 877–882.

Jensen, O., & Tesche, C. D. (2002). Frontal theta activity in humans increases with memory load in a working memory task. *European Journal of Neuroscience, 15*, 1395–1399.

Jobard, G., Crivello, F., & Tzourio-Mazoyer, N. (2003). Evaluation of the dual route theory or reading: A meta-analysis of 35 neuroimaging studies. *NeuroImage, 20*, 693–712.

Jung, K.-J., Prasad, P., Qin, Y., & Anderson, J. R. (2005). Extraction of overt verbal response from acoustic noise from the scanner in fMRI by use of segmented active noise cancellation. *Magnetic Resonance Imaging, 53*, 739–744.

Just, M. A., & Carpenter, P. A. (1980). A theory of reading: From eye fixations to comprehension. *Psychological Review, 87*(4), 329–354.

Karpicke, J. D., & Blunt, J. R. (2011). Retrieval practice produces more learning than elaborative studying with concept mapping. *Science, 331*, 772–775.

Klimesch, W. (1999). EEG alpha and theta oscillations reflect cognitive and memory performance: A review and analysis. *Brain Research Reviews, 29*, 169–195.

Klimesch, W. (2012). Alpha-band oscillations, attention, and controlled access to stored information. *Trends in Cognitive Science, 16*, 606–617.

Klimesch, W., Doppelmayr, M., Hanslmayr, S., Christa, N., & Wolfgang, K. (2006). Upper alpha ERD and absolute power: Their meaning for memory performance. *Progress in Brain Research, 159*, 151–165.

Klimesch, W., Sauseng, P., & Hanslmayr, S. (2007). EEG alpha oscillations: The inhibition-timing hypothesis. *Brain Research Reviews, 53*(1), 63–88.

Klimesch, W., Schack, B., & Sauseng, P. (2005). The functional significance of theta and upper alpha oscillations for working memory: A review. *Experimental Psychology, 52*, 99–108.

Konvalinka, I., Bauer, M., Stahlhut, C., Hansen, L. K., Roepstorff, A., & Frith, C. D. (2014). Frontal alpha oscillations distinguish leaders from followers: Multivariate decoding of mutually interacting brains. *NeuroImage, 94*, 79–88.

Koole, S. L. (2009). The psychology of emotion regulation: An integrative review. *Cognition and Emotion, 23*(1), 4–41.

Martín-Loeches, M., Casado, P., Hernández-Tamames, J. A., & Álvarez-Linera, J. (2008). Brain activation in discourse comprehension: A 3t fMRI study. *NeuroImage, 41*, 614–622.

Mayer, R. E. (2010). Unique contributions of eye-tracking research to the study of learning with graphics. *Learning and Instruction, 20*, 167–171.

Mayer, R. E. (Ed.). (2014). *The Cambridge handbook of multimedia learning*. New York: Cambridge University Press.

National Reading Panel. (2000). *Teaching children to read: An evidence-based assessment of the scientific research literature on reading and its implications for reading instruction (NIH Publication No. 00-4769)*. Washington, DC: U.S. Government Printing Office.

Neubauer, A. C., Fink, A., Grabner, R. H., Christa, N., & Wolfgang, K. (2006). Sensitivity of alpha band ERD to individual differences in cognition. *Progress in Brain Research, 159*, 167–178.

Owen, A. M., Coleman, M. R., Menon, D. K., Berry, E. L., Johnsrude, I. S., Rodd, J. M., et al. (2005). Using a hierarchical approach to investigate residual auditory cognition in persistent vegetative state. *Progress in Brain Research, 150*, 457–471.

Paas, F. (1992). Training strategies for attaining transfer of problem-solving skill in statistics: A cognitive load approach. *Journal of Educational Psychology, 84*, 429–434.

Paas, F., & van Merriënboer, J. J. G. (1994). Variability of worked examples and transfer of geometrical problem solving skills: A cognitive-load approach. *Journal of Educational Psychology, 86*, 122–133.

Parasuraman, R., & Caggiano, D. (2005). Neural and genetic assays of mental workload. In D. McBride & D. Schmorrow (Eds.), *Quantifying human information processing* (pp. 123–155). Lanham, MD: Rowman and Littlefield.

Pernice, K., & Nielsen, J. (2009). *How to conduct eyetracking studies*. Fremont, CA: Nielsen Norman Group.

Pfurtscheller, G., & Lopes da Silva, F. H. (2005). Event-related desynchronization (ERD) and event-related synchronization (ERS). In E. Niedermeyer & F. H. Lopes da Silva (Eds.), *Electroencephalography: Basic principles, clinical applications and related fields* (5th ed., pp. 1003–1016). Philadelphia: Lippincott, Williams & Wilkins.

Plass, J. L., Kalyuga, S., & Leutner, D. (2010). Individual differences and cognitive load theory. In J. L. Plass, R. Moreno, & R. Brünken (Eds.), *Cognitive load theory.*, ch. 4. New York: Cambridge Press.

Pomplun, M., Reingold, E. M., & Shen, J. (2001). Investigating the visual span in comparative search: The effects of task difficulty and divided attention. *Cognition, 81*(2), 57–67.

Rayner, K. (1998). Eye movements in reading and information processing: 20 years of research. *Psychological Bulletin, 124*(3), 372–422.

Reuter-Lorenz, P. A., Jonides, J., Smith, E. E., Hartley, A., Miller, A., Marshuetz, C., et al. (2000). Age differences in the frontal lateralization of verbal and spatial working memory revealed by PET. *Journal of Cognitive Neuroscience, 72*(1), 174–187.

Russell, M. (2005). Using eye-tracking data to understand first impressions of a website. *Usability News, 7*(1), 1–14.

Scharinger, C., Kammerer, Y., & Gerjets, P. (2015). Pupil dilation and EEG alpha frequency band power reveal load on executive functions for link-selection processes during text reading. *PLoS One, 10*(6), e0130608.

Schmidt-Weigand, F., Kohert, A., & Glowalla, U. (2010). A closer look at split visual attention in system- and self-paced instruction in multimedia learning. *Learning and Instruction, 20*, 100–110.

Schneps, M. H., Thomson, J. M., Sonnert, G., Pomplun, M., Chen, C., & Heffner-Wong, A. (2013). Shorter lines facilitate reading in those who struggle. *PLoS One, 8*(8), e71161. https://doi.org/10.1371/journal.pone.0071161

Schreppel, T., Egetemeir, J., Schecklmann, M., Plichta, M. M., Pauli, P., Ellgring, H., et al. (2008). Activation of the prefrontal cortex in working memory and interference resolution processes assessed with near-infrared spectroscopy. *Neuropsychobiology, 57*, 188–193.

Shiffrin, R. M., & Schneider, W. (1977). Controlled and automatic human information processing: II. Perceptual learning, automatic attending, and a general theory. *Psychological Review, 84*, 1–66.

Snow, C. E., Burns, M. S., & Griffin, P. (1998). *Preventing reading difficulties in young children.* Washington, DC: National Academy Press.

Stevens, R. H., Galloway, T. L., Wang, P., & Berka, C. (2012). Cognitive neurophysiologic synchronies: What can they contribute to the study of teamwork? *Human Factors, 54*(4), 489–502.

Stieff, M. (2011). When is a molecule three-dimensional? A task-specific role for imagistic reasoning in advanced chemistry. *Science Education, 95*, 310–336.

Strait, M., & Scheutz, M. (2014). What we can and cannot (yet) do with functional near infrared spectroscopy. *Frontiers in Neuroscience, 8*, 117.

Tschentscher, N., Hauk, O., Fischer, M. H., & Pulvermüller, F. (2012). You can count on the motor cortex: fMRI reveals embodied number processing. *NeuroImage, 59*, 3139–3148.

Van Gog, T., Paas, F., & Van Merriënboer, J. J. G. (2008). Effects of studying sequences of process-oriented and product-oriented worked examples on troubleshooting transfer efficiency. *Learning and Instruction, 18*, 211–222.

Wang, J., & Antonenko, P. (2017). Instructor presence in instructional video: Effects on visual attention, recall, and perceived learning. *Computers in Human Behavior, 71*, 79–89.

Wang, J., Dawson, K., Saunders, K., Ritzhaupt, A., Antonenko, P., Lombardino, L., et al. (2018). Investigating the effects of modality and multimedia on the learning performance of college students with dyslexia. *Journal of Special Education Technology, 33*, 182. https://doi.org/10.1177/0162643418754530

Warner, N., Letsky, M., & Cowen, M. (2005). Cognitive model of team collaboration: Macro- cognitive focus. *Proceedings of the 49th Human Factors and Ergonomics Society Annual Meeting*, Orlando, FL.

Wiley, J., Sanchez, C. A., & Jaeger, A. J. (2014). The individual differences in working memory capacity principle in multimedia learning. In R. Mayer (Ed.), *The Cambridge handbook of multimedia learning* (2nd ed.). New York: Cambridge University Press.

Xie, B., & Salvendy, G. (2000). Review and reappraisal of modeling and predicting mental workload in single- and multi-task environments. *Work and Stress, 14*, 74–99.

Zago, L., Pesenti, M., Mellet, E., Crivello, F., Mazoyer, B., & Tzourio-Mazoyer, N. (2001). Neural correlates of simple and complex mental calculation. *NeuroImage, 13*, 314–327.

Pavlo D. Antonenko   is an Associate Professor of Educational Technology and Director of the NeurAL Lab at the University of Florida, USA. He received his Ph.D. in (a) Curriculum and Instructional Technology, and (b) Human–Computer Interaction from Iowa State University in 2007. In addition to using the traditional measures to study cognition and learning such as learning tests and self-reports, Dr. Antonenko is interested in multimodal analytics and psychophysiological assessment of cognitive processing to inform the design and adaptivity of technology-enhanced learning environments. Specifically he has used eye tracking, EEG, and fNIRS to explore cognition and learning with technology. Antonenko has served as a leader for AERA and NARST, designed and led professional development initiatives for K-12 and college educators, published in numerous journals, and received close to $10 million in NSF and NASA funding for his research.

Part II
Educational Technologies for Assessment and Training

Chapter 4
Close Relationships and Virtual Reality

Sabrina A. Huang and Jeremy Bailenson

Abstract The intersection between close relationships research and virtual reality holds great promise for the advancement of both fields. In social science research laboratories and mainstream society, virtual reality is becoming an increasingly popular and viable tool and method for not only studying close relationships such as romantic relationships and friendships, but also for engaging in relational processes (e.g., social interactions, relationship formation, and relationship maintenance). Initial research at the forefront of this intersection has focused on attachment theory in adult romantic relationships, exploring (a) how attachment processes occur and (b) how they may be studied using digital, immersive spaces created via virtual reality. The current chapter first provides a general overview of both attachment theory and virtual reality before delving deeper into the intersection of adult attachment theory, neuroscience, and virtual reality. The chapter then concludes with potential future directions for research at the intersection of close relationships and virtual reality.

Introduction

From infancy to adulthood, relationships color individuals' lives. As Berscheid (1999) eloquently writes, "We are born into relationships, we live our lives in relationships with others, and when we die, the effects of our relationships survive in the lives of the living, reverberating throughout the tissue of their relationships" (p. 261). Relationships are sources of intimacy, social support, sadness when conflicts occur, and happiness when the relationship goes well. During adulthood, romantic relationships are of particular salience. The initiation, maintenance, and (for some)

S. A. Huang (✉) · J. Bailenson
Department of Communication, Stanford University, Stanford, CA, USA
e-mail: saahuang@stanford.edu; bailenson@stanford.edu;
https://comm.stanford.edu/faculty-bailenson/

© Association for Educational Communications and Technology 2019   49
T. D. Parsons et al. (eds.), *Mind, Brain and Technology*, Educational
Communications and Technology: Issues and Innovations,
https://doi.org/10.1007/978-3-030-02631-8_4

dissolutions of romantic relationships constitute notable events in the tapestry of life, and play a considerable role in shaping one's self-concept, well-being, and behavior. For these reasons, understanding the processes that underlie romantic relationships is essential for furthering our understanding of the human life experience.

This chapter will begin by giving a brief overview of attachment theory, a central framework in studying close relationships, as applied to adult romantic relationships. Next, we will discuss the increasing utilization of virtual reality for close relationships in both research laboratories and mainstream culture. Finally, we will consider the potential impacts and implications that virtual reality will have on research in relationship science, and for close relationships in society at large.

Close Relationships and Attachment Theory

How are romantic relationships initiated? Once formed, how are relationships maintained, and why do certain relationships deteriorate and dissolve, while others thrive? Why are romantic relationships important, and what are the consequences of belonging in a relationship? These questions lie at the core of the study of close relationships. For the purposes of this chapter, we will limit our overview of the literature to a brief discussion of adult attachment theory, one of the major guiding frameworks in the study of close relationships, in this section.

Attachment theory describes the process of developing affection towards close others, and the ways in which a person's system of attachment behaviors influences how they behave in and perceive their social world. The origins of attachment theory lie within the realm of developmental psychology. Bowlby (1969) was interested in understanding how infants become attached, or affectionately bonded, to their primary caregiver (usually the mother figure), and distressed when separated from the caregiver or deprived of the caregiver's attention. He believed that from birth, infants are predisposed to become attached to their primary caregiver, and actively engage in attachment behaviors such as smiling, rooting, crying, and sucking that promote physical proximity and social interaction with the caregiver (Ainsworth & Bell, 1970; Bretherton, 1992). In turn, the primary caregiver's behaviors towards the infant (e.g., reciprocating proximity-seeking behaviors, being present, responsive, and sensitive to the infant's needs) can shape the infant's expectations of and attachment towards the primary caregiver (Bell & Ainsworth, 1972). For example, an infant feels more confident in exploring her surroundings when she knows that her caregiver will be available to comfort her if she needs it (Bowlby, 1988; Sroufe & Waters, 1977).

Through the combination of the infant's own activity in proximity-seeking attachment behaviors, the primary caregiver's behaviors towards the infant, and previous attachment-related experiences, the infant develops an internal working model of the self and environment that "provides a casual-temporal prototype of the ways in which attachment-related events typically unfold" (Cassidy, Jones, & Shaver, 2013, p. 3). This internal working model of attachment can then be used by the infant as a guide for navigating future attachment-related interactions. Continuing with the previous example, if an infant's past experiences of falling down involved seeking and successfully receiving comfort from her caregiver, she knows that the next time she falls down in the future, she can look towards her caregiver for reassurance and expect to receive it.

Further research in this area by Ainsworth and Bell (1970) identified three main patterns of attachment behavior: secure, avoidant, and ambivalent/resistant. They noted that children with a secure attachment style feel safe and confident in exploring their world, knowing that their caregiver will be available, responsive, and helpful if they experience any frightening or threatening situations. Avoidant children, on the contrary, expect little to no help (or even rebuttal) from their caregivers, and avoid proximity and interaction with their caregivers after frightening situations. Ambivalent/resistant children are unsure of their caregiver's availability or responsiveness, and as a result tend to cling to their caregivers. These three styles of attachment are internalized, and become part of the child's internal working model of attachment (Bartholomew & Horowitz, 1991).

Although the origins of the theory focused on infants and children, attachment theory is thought to be relevant across the life span (Ainsworth, 1982; Bowlby, 1980). In particular, Hazan and Shaver (1987) postulated that romantic love could be an attachment process between adults, similar to the attachment processes between an infant and her parent. They believed attachment theory could be used to explain how romantic affectional bonds between adults are formed. The authors conducted two studies, and found that not only was the prevalence of the different attachment styles similar in adults as in infants, but also that adults with different attachment styles experienced romantic love in different ways. Adults with a secure attachment style had happy, friendly, and trusting love experiences, avoidant adults experienced fear of closeness with their relationship partners, and ambivalent/resistant adults indicated a desire for reciprocation from their partner and many highs and lows in their relationships (Hazan & Shaver, 1987; Simpson, 1990). Moreover, adults with different attachment styles had different internal working models about "the course of romantic love, the availability and trustworthiness of love partners, and their own love-worthiness" (Hazan & Shaver, 1987, p. 521). In addition, the authors found that an adult's attachment style is related to his relationship as a child with his parents, due partially to a continuity of the adult's internal working model of relationships in general from childhood (see also Collins & Read, 1990; Feeney & Noller, 1990). In other words, a person who had a secure relationship with his parents as a child is more likely to experience secure romantic relationships as an adult.

Since the publication of Hazan and Shaver (1987), the adult romantic attachment theory literature has expanded and grown rapidly, becoming a major framework for the study of close romantic relationships (Fraley & Shaver, 2000). Researchers have examined various aspects of how attachment in adult romantic relationships affects both the self and the relationship, including beliefs about relationships (Feeney & Noller, 1990; Stackert & Bursik, 2003; Wang & Mallinckrodt, 2006), relationship satisfaction (Banse, 2004; Brennan & Shaver, 1995; Butzer & Campbell, 2008; Collins & Read, 1990; Pistole, 1989), relationship stability (Duemmler & Kobak,

2001; Simpson, 1990), and partner characteristics (Brennan & Shaver, 1995; Collins & Read, 1990). Other studies have also examined areas such as stability and change in attachment style across time (Lopez & Gormley, 2002; Scharfe & Bartholomew, 1994), conflict resolution (Pistole, 1989; Shi, 2003), and effects of romantic partner presence (Feeney & Kirkpatrick, 1996; Kane, McCall, Collins, & Blascovich, 2012).

Adult Attachment Theory and Neuroscience

More recently, researchers have begun to investigate the neurobiological underpinnings of adult attachment theory—how the attachment system affects and is affected by the brain. Coan (2010) notes that the neural systems which are involved in attachment processes such as pair bonding are also linked to "responses to rewards and punishments, emotion regulation, motivation, and personality" (p. 211; see also Vrtička & Vuilleumier, 2012). He proposes that encounters with potential mates (assuming they go well) activate the production of neurotransmitters such as dopamine and oxytocin, which induce pleasurable feelings. The release of these neurotransmitters then conditions and encourages the neural systems to seek further exposure to the potential mate or partner (Coan, 2008). Some research suggests that this combination of associating pleasurable feelings with the potential partner and seeking out the partner (to experience pleasurable feelings) can lead to a form of addiction, where separation from the partner can create feelings of distress (withdrawal) and attempts to reestablish connection with the partner (and therefore re-experience pleasurable feelings; Coan, 2010; Insel, 2003). Through the above process, the attachment behavioral system is developed.

Further research has attempted to understand how attachment styles are instantiated or encoded in the brain, though the number of studies conducted in this area remains scarce (Coan, 2010; Vrtička & Vuilleumier, 2012). Much more is known about the effects of attachment style on neural processing, especially when taken in conjunction with the existing vast literature of empirical behavioral studies on attachment styles. To give an example, from this substantive literature it is well known that adults with different attachment styles react to negative, threatening situations in different ways associated with their attachment style (e.g., individuals who have an anxious attachment style tend to continuously monitor for signs of their romantic partner's availability and attention when separated from their partner), and that, depending on their attachment style, adults may rely on their attachment figure (i.e., the romantic partner) to assist with affect regulation (Coan, 2010; Hazan & Shaver, 1987). Notably, these findings have been observed at the neurological level as well. In individuals with an anxious attachment style, the brain systems that activate neural networks associated with aversion, withdrawal, and defensive responses appear to be especially sensitive to negative social cues, thereby increasing the frequency of its activation (Vrticka et al., 2008). On the other hand, avoidant individuals experience a deactivation of the brain areas (anterior insula and dorsal ACC) related to social aversion. Individuals with a secure attachment style experience less activation of the threat-related neural networks when in the presence of their romantic partner, suggesting a greater vigilance against negative or threatening stimuli (Coan, Schaefer, & Davidson, 2006; Vrtička & Vuilleumier, 2012). Other studies examining areas such as mental state representation, memory, selective attention, and emotion regulation have drawn similar parallels between behavioral outcomes and the activation of relevant brain areas in their findings with regard to attachment styles and the attachment behavioral system (Vrtička & Vuilleumier, 2012).

Virtual Reality

Throughout history, the concept of virtual reality has evolved in conjunction with improvements and innovations in technology. Broadly defined, present-day virtual reality can be thought of as "synthetic sensory information that leads to perceptions of environments and their contents as if they were not synthetic" (Blascovich et al., 2002, p. 105). In other words, users of virtual reality employ technology such as visual displays and headphones (or speakers) to replace the sensory inputs (e.g., sight, sound) that they receive from the actual, grounded reality with digital, computer-generated sensory input from a virtual environment. For example, a person could be sitting in their living room at home, yet be seeing a rainforest instead of the open backyard sliding door (through a visual display such as a computer or television screen), and hearing sounds (through headphones or speakers) of animals living in and moving throughout the forest, instead of the radio program playing music softly in the background. Although their actual reality is their living room, for the moment, the person is engrossed in the virtual reality of the rainforest.

Through the use of head-mounted visual displays, or headsets, immersive virtual environments (IVEs) become possible. In IVEs, users feel as though they are psychological present in the virtual world—that the virtual world surrounds them and becomes the world in which they, as of that moment, inhabit. With the addition of equipment that tracks information such as current head orientation (and therefore line of sight), position in physical space, and body movements (e.g., hands, arms, legs), users are able to interact with the virtual environment, which then increases their perception of psychological presence and immersion (Cummings & Bailenson, 2016). The person in the living room could stand up and look down, observing the rich, moist soil of the rainforest ground, then look up, and see the dense green canopy with trickles of light filtering through. While walking forward in the physical world, her visual display would update based on her new physical location and head orientation, and move her forward in the virtual rainforest environment as well. Bending down, she could reach forward to virtually "touch" and flip over a leaf to examine its underside, as her handheld controller registers her hand's positions and tells the virtual reality program to move her digital hand simultaneously in order to reflect her intended actions.

The potential of virtual reality—from traveling to faraway places, creating imaginative 3D art pieces, and interacting with other people in digital worlds, to name a few—has always fascinated society and captured its imagination. Only recently, however, has VR become viable and available for mainstream access. As of the time of this writing, many of the major technology companies such as HTC, Oculus, Google, Samsung, Sony, and Microsoft now offer commercially available virtual reality headsets that the average consumer can purchase to use in their own home. Both the HTC Vive and the Oculus Rift, two of the leading options of VR headsets currently available in the market, have recently considerably decreased in price, becoming even more affordable and accessible for the general public (Kuchera, 2017a, 2017b). This increased affordability has been reflected in the sales, with over a million headsets being sold in a single business quarter in 2017, and more sales predicted for 2018 (Taylor, 2017).

Using Virtual Reality to Study Close Relationships

Recently, researchers have begun to devise new and creative ways of studying close relationships and adult romantic attachment theory. Of particular interest is the increasing utilization of virtual reality (VR) technology as a method for studying interpersonal relationship behaviors and processes. Virtual reality allows researchers to place participants into a simulated virtual environment, created by the researchers for the purpose of the experiment. When paired with a head-mounted visual display, the VR experience becomes especially immersive, and the participant feels as though they are surrounded by and almost physically present in the virtual environment. With the addition of other sensory features such as spatialized audio (via headphones or speakers) and haptic stimulation (via feedback devices such as controllers), the experience of immersion can be further augmented (Steuer, 1992). Thus, the virtual environment replaces and becomes the user's new "real" world in which they are present (Loomis, Blascovich, & Beall, 1999).

One major advantage of using VR for close relationships research is an increase in ecological validity without the tradeoff of experimental control (Loomis et al., 1999). Similar to studies conducted in laboratories, experimenters can program studies in virtual reality to precisely deliver stimuli or create specific situations of interest while minimizing the effects of external variables. However, unlike the contrived, artificial scenarios employed by laboratory studies (e.g., asking participants to read a written passage in order to induce a certain affective state, asking participants to imagine a situation before reporting how they would act in the situation), studies conducted in virtual reality can be programmed to emulate the actual real-world scenario of interest, thus increasing both ecological validity and experimental realism (Loomis et al., 1999; Rizzo, Schultheis, Kerns, & Mateer, 2004). For example, instead of asking participants to report how they believe they would act based on a written or verbal description of a specific situation, researchers can place the participants into a virtual simulation of the situation, and measure the participant's actual, real-life actions directly.

Another advantage of using virtual reality for close relationships research is the ability to create and use virtual interaction partners instead of human confederates.

As with the virtual environment, experimenters have "full experimental control over the actions and reactions" of a virtual interaction partner (Schönbrodt & Asendorpf, 2012, p. 431). Compared to human confederates, virtual confederates provide a number of benefits. Since they are programmed, virtual confederates require no training, thus reducing costs such as time and money. They are also subject to less random error compared to human confederates: Virtual confederates will always be blind to condition (unless programmed otherwise), and act exactly the same for each repetition of the experiment (unlike human confederates, virtual confederates can't forget their scripts!) (Blascovich et al., 2002). The use of virtual confederates (and VR experiments in general) also allows for near-perfect replications, both inside and across labs. Researchers need to only share the program containing the experiment through a hard drive, the cloud, or email for another researcher to gain access to the entire experiment. This direct "handing-over" of the study helps eliminates some common problems and/or difficulties of trying to replicate another laboratory's work, such as differences between the original laboratory environment and the replication laboratory's environment, accurately recreating the experimental situation and materials, training new confederates, and so on (Blascovich et al., 2002).

Due to its technological nature, virtual reality also lends itself well to certain types of data collection. Because the participant's location and movements are continuously tracked in order to render the virtual environment, data regarding distance from other virtual people or objects, direction of eye gaze, and body movement (e.g., head, hands, arms, legs; assuming trackers are being held or attached) can be automatically collected by the computer during the experiment. Such data becomes especially useful when conducting research in areas that include interpersonal distance (Bailenson, Blascovich, Beall, & Loomis, 2003; Gillath, McCall, Shaver, & Blascovich, 2008; Yee, Bailenson, Urbanek, Chang, & Merget, 2007), eye contact (Bailenson & Yee, 2006; Garau et al., 2003; Gillath et al., 2008; Yee et al., 2007), and mimicry (Bailenson & Yee, 2005; Hasler, Hirschberger, Shani-Sherman, & Friedman, 2014). For scientists interested in collecting physiological or neurological data, additional methods of data collection (e.g., skin conductance, heart rate, EEG) can be easily paired with VR. Indeed, such research may even benefit from the use of immersive virtual environments, due to VR's ability to incorporate dynamic, interactive stimuli into psychophysiological and neuropsychological assessments. Thus, adopting VR could help researchers in areas such as the social, affective, and clinical neurosciences better understand real-world functioning, compared to the traditional method of paper-and-pencil assessments (Parsons, 2015).

So far, a small handful of studies have been conducted on areas in close relationships research (such as adult romantic attachment theory) using virtual reality and virtual environments. Kane et al. (2012) examined the effects of a romantic partner's presence and the partner's nonverbal support behavior on participants during a threatening, cliff-walking task in VR. The authors believed that, similar to infants with regard to their mother, adult participants would be sensitive to their romantic partner's availability and responsiveness when experiencing a threatening or frightening situation. Participants whose partners were present, available, and responsive would feel more confident in completing the threatening task, and would experience "lower stress, a greater sense of emotional security, and reduced behavioral vigilance" (Kane et al., 2012, p. 38). On the other hand, participants whose partners were not present during the threatening task, not available, and/or not responsive would experience greater attachment needs, higher vigilance for the partner's attention, and be less able to cope with the task. For the study, the authors had participants come into the lab with their romantic partner. Participants were led to a separate room from their partner and assigned to one of three conditions: partner-absent, partner-present and unresponsive, and partner-present and responsive. After putting on a head-mounted display, participants were placed inside a virtual world, at the end of a path on the edge of a canyon, and asked to complete a cliff-walking task. Depending on the condition they were assigned to, they would either be alone in the virtual world, or their partner would be present on a visible but separate part of the canyon. In the two partner-present conditions, participants were told that their partner would be controlling the "partner" avatar from a different room in the laboratory. In reality, however, the partner avatar was actually being controlled by preprogrammed computer algorithms. In the responsive-present condition, the "partner" avatar was programmed to "wave, clap, nod their heads, and actively orient their bodies toward the participant during the task" (Kane et al., 2012, p. 39). In the unresponsive-present condition, the "partner" avatar was programmed to face away from the participant's avatar, looking over the canyon instead. Before and after the cliff-walking task, participants completed a series of questionnaires that included the study's dependent measures.

Overall, the authors found that partner responsiveness played a greater role in how participants experienced the threatening task, compared to the mere presence (and lack of presence) of the partner. As in parent–child interactions, participants reported feeling less stressed, safer, and more secure in exploring the virtual canyon world when they felt that their romantic partner was present, attentive, and responsive—a secure base which they could look to for comfort and encouragement. On the other hand, participants whose partners were present but inattentive reported experiencing levels of stress similar to those who completed the task alone, and became more preoccupied and vigilant in monitoring their partner for cues of responsiveness during the task. Additionally, partner inattentiveness during the threatening VR task affected participant's behaviors towards their partner in a subsequent task as well, where they kept a greater distance from their partner compared to participants in the other conditions. These findings suggest that attachment related-goals and behaviors are activated in adulthood similarly to childhood, and that the attachment system operates in adult intimate relationships.

In two related studies, Schönbrodt and Asendorpf (2011, 2012) examined interaction and attachment dynamics though the use of virtual environments and preprogrammed virtual agents. For both studies, the authors created and used a virtual environment, which they named "Simoland," that contained inhabitants called "Simos." Of the many Simos living in Simoland, one was a character representing the participant, and another was a character representing the participant's character's partner, or "virtual spouse." Besides the participant's own character, all other Simos (including the virtual spouse) were controlled by preprogrammed algorithms. Participants were able to move their character around Simoland, and could interact with other Simos by opening up a menu bar and choosing an action from a list of possible options.

Depending on factors such as mood, previous interactions, and familiarity with the participant's character, the Simo that the participant interacted with would then react to the participant's interactions accordingly. For example, if the participant complimented their virtual spouse, the virtual spouse would react delightedly. If the participant annoyed their spouse and then asked for a kiss, however, the spouse character would react angrily and refuse to kiss (Schönbrodt & Asendorpf, 2011).

In their first study, Schönbrodt and Asendorpf (2011) investigated whether intimacy motivations, autonomy motivations, and relationship satisfaction with a real-life partner influenced participants' behaviors towards a digital partner (the virtual spouse) in Simoland. They hypothesized that participants would behave differently towards their virtual spouse (but not other Simos), depending on their level of intimacy motive (i.e., the need for closeness to a romantic partner), their level of autonomy motive (i.e., the preference of individuality and independence from a romantic partner), and their relationship satisfaction with their real-life partner. Participants with a higher intimacy motive were expected to display more positive and less negative behaviors towards their spouse, and to be more persistent in engaging in intimate, positive behaviors, compared to participants with a lower intimacy motive. Higher relationship satisfaction with a real-life partner was also expected to lead to more positive and less negative behaviors towards the virtual spouse; moreover, the authors hypothesized that participants' real-life relationship satisfaction would set the initial level (i.e., intercept) of positivity in the interactions with the virtual spouse. Due to the unrestricted nature of the study's implementation of Simoland, and the lack of control or instructions from other Simos and the virtual spouse, the authors predicted that autonomy motives would not affect participants' actions towards the spouse or other Simos. The results of the study supported all of the authors' hypotheses, suggesting that "real-life" expectations, schemes (e.g., intimacy and autonomy motives), previous experiences, and behaviors from a current relationship can transfer over into the digital sphere, towards a virtual spouse. These findings highlight the efficacy of utilizing virtual reality paradigms for studying or observing actual, dynamic behavior in close relationships research, compared to "hypothetical choices or self-reported intentions" (Schönbrodt & Asendorpf, 2011, p. 15).

Bolstered by the findings from their first study, Schönbrodt and Asendorpf (2012) conducted a second study that extended the Simoland paradigm to address whether real-life internal working models of attachment would also transfer over into the digital world and affect behaviors towards a virtual spouse. The authors modified Simoland to include scenarios that emulated Ainsworth et al. (1978) famous "strange situation" procedure (edited from the original procedure used for infant attachment research to reflect situations relevant to adults). They hypothesized that a participant's attachment style (e.g., secure, anxious, avoidant) would predict how the participant controlled their character to act towards the virtual spouse in three different "strange" scenarios that contained an attachment-related threat: a separation scene, a conflict scene, and an illness scene. For example, participants who scored high on the anxiety dimension of attachment were predicted to "engage in hyperactivating strategies" and increase their vigilance for cues of availability from their partner during times of stress (e.g., being separated from the partner), whereas participants who scored high on the avoidance dimension were anticipated to engage in "deactivating strategies" and limit the activation of their attachment system and related attachment-seeking behaviors in response to the attachment-threatening situation (Schönbrodt & Asendorpf, 2012, p. 436). The results of the study provide evidence for their hypotheses, indicating that internal working models of attachment do indeed transfer over into the digital realm, towards virtual partners. Importantly, the authors were able to not only replicate classic, existing findings in the attachment literature originally conducted in real-life settings by using a virtual environment, but also contributed to adult attachment theory by providing supporting evidence for the emotional versus behavioral regulation model proposed by Fraley and Shaver (2000).

Close Relationships in Virtual Reality

Beyond adopting virtual reality as a means or tool to study theoretical interests (e.g., adult attachment theory) in the close relationships literature, virtual reality can also be seen as a platform for the formation and maintenance of relationships. With the influx of new VR home users, the increasing popularity of VR, and the availability of multiplayer social virtual worlds such as Facebook Spaces (by Facebook), Sansar (by the creators of Second Life), and AltspaceVR, it becomes easy to imagine a world in which people meet, interact, and form relationships with others in a virtual world—all from the comfort of their living rooms. The consequences of these relationships in VR contain further abundant research possibilities and potentially wide-reaching implications. Imagine this: Sam comes home from work and turns on his computer. Donning his VR headset, he enters a virtual town square, where he sees the avatars of other users like him. He hears the faint conversation of two friends at the small café by the corner, and notices another person browsing the quaint bookstore off to the side. Walking forward, Sam enters an open collaborative art area, where anyone can draw in the 3D space, and meets Rachael, who invites him to draw with her. While drawing together, they discover that they share similar interests and continue to meet in the virtual world, eventually forming a romantic relationship. Although this is an imaginary scenario conjured up for the purposes of providing an example, social (e.g., networked) virtual reality is slowly becoming a mainstream reality. Through the aforementioned publicly available social VR worlds, users can already interact with other users in a digital, 3D space, with the potential for forming and maintaining relationships. Understanding the consequences of these relationships, then, becomes ever more important.

Unfortunately, not much research has been conducted in this area so far. Research in social VR has mainly focused on the learning sciences (usually in a classroom context, see McCall, Bunyan, Bailenson, Blascovich, & Beall, 2009; Bailenson, Yee, Blascovich, Beall, Lundblad, & Jin, 2008; Bailenson, Yee, Blascovich, & Guadagno, 2008; Monahan, McArdle, & Bertolotto, 2008) and on specific aspects of social interaction via virtual reality, such as the ability to "transform" the physical appearance and behaviors of one's avatars (e.g., changing one's avatar's height to be taller than the interaction partner's avatar; Bailenson, Yee, Blascovich, & Guadagno, 2008; Bailenson, Beall, Loomis, Blascovich, & Turk, 2005). While the latter area of research may be useful in understanding particular aspects of relational processes in VR, such as impression formation and interaction dynamics, many of the study paradigms involved only one interaction session. Only a few researchers have conducted longitudinal studies examining the effects of social interactions in VR across time (see Bailenson & Yee, 2006). Thus, the long-term consequences of such interactions (which, assuming things go well, would lead to the formation and maintenance of a relationship) remain mostly unknown.

Despite the lack of research in a virtual reality setting, research conducted in online, web-based settings can help shed light on what the consequences of forming and/or maintaining relationships in VR may be. Many studies have examined purely online romantic relationships, where communication in the relationship occurs predominantly through computer-mediated means (e.g., instant messaging, massive multiplayer online games, online forums, chat rooms), in comparison to face-to-face relationships, where partners mainly interact in person. Three major perspectives have been offered to explain how intimacy, a major factor in relationship development and satisfaction (Anderson & Emmers-Sommer, 2006), develops in online interactions. Parks and Floyd (1996) argue that, due to the lack of cues such as facial expressions, body language, and verbal nuances, computer-mediated interactions are fundamentally impersonal, and as a result, impair the development of intimacy. Lea and Spears (1995) suggest that online interactions are interpersonal, but take longer to develop similar levels of intimacy compared to face-to-face interactions. In comparison, Walther (1996) proposes that the lack of cues, in combination with the asynchronous nature of computer-mediated communication, actually allow people to experience greater (hyperpersonal) levels of intimacy online than they would face-to-face, due to having more cognitive resources (from not having to monitor cues such as facial expressions) and time to compose messages. Walther's hyperpersonal model has been supported by research in online text-based contexts, where users believe they are better able to express their "true self" and meet others that share similar interests, leading to increased self-disclosure, trust, and intimacy, and the development of close, intimate relationships (McKenna, Green, & Gleason, 2002). Given that avatars in virtual reality can be programmed to display cues such as facial expressions and body language, and that users in virtual reality can communicate through voice-chat systems with the addition of a microphone and headphones or a speaker, it is interesting to consider which perspective may best describe intimacy development in virtual reality.

Although not fully immersive, Second Life, a freely available online 3D virtual world where users have the ability to interact with other users, provides a potentially enlightening look into the perceptions and inner workings of online relationships. In Second Life, users can control their digital avatar to engage in social activities—such as attending parties, chatting, sexual activity, and even marriage—creating opportunities to meet new people and develop intimate bonds. Gilbert, Murphy, and Clementina Ávalos (2011a) surveyed participants who were currently involved in an intimate, romantic relationship on Second Life, and found that participants perceived their relationship to be just as real as romantic relationships that take place in the physical world (i.e., face-to-face), suggesting that to those who are involved in one, online relationships go beyond gameplay and are not simply just an aspect of the online world or role-playing online. Other research in an online newsgroup setting has also described feelings of online relationships as real, deep, and meaningful (McKenna et al., 2002). Furthermore, Quackenbush, Allen, and Fowler (2015) investigated attachment bonds in romantic relationships on Second Life, and discovered that participants formed equally strong attachments in online, virtual relationships as they did in real-life relationships.

Perhaps more interestingly, participants idealized their romantic relationships on Second Life more compared to romantic relationships that occur face-to-face in real life (Gilbert et al., 2011a). Anderson and Emmers-Sommer (2006) discovered a similar finding in text-based, computer-mediated contexts, positing that the hyper-personal nature of communication with online partners creates "idealized/heightened perceptions of similarity, commitment, intimacy, trust, attributional confidence, and communication satisfaction" (p. 167), especially when participants communicated frequently and for long periods of time with their online romantic partner. Consequently, this increase in idealization and therefore positive perceptions of online romantic relationships may be one factor explaining participants' reports of higher relationship satisfaction levels in their online relationships compared to face-to-face relationships (Gilbert, Murphy, & Clementina Ávalos, 2011b).

Online relationships are not without risks however. The provision of anonymity that allows people to express their "true" self (McKenna et al., 2002) can also be used to express a "fake" or deceptive self, where a person may lie about their gender, appearance, interests, and other factors that are taken into consideration when forming relationships online (Drouin, Miller, Wehle, & Hernandez, 2016). The term "catfishing" was created specifically to describe such deceptive behavior in online romance settings, and the need for caution with regard to being "catfished" is a major concern for participants of online romances (Wildermuth & Vogl-Bauer, 2007). In a virtual reality environment, a person could create a fake avatar which they deceive others into believing is a realistic representation of them in real life. The ability to form romances online has also increased people's abilities to engage in extramarital affairs, which can then negatively impact one's relationship with their real-life partner (Gilbert et al., 2011a; Wildermuth & Vogl-Bauer, 2007).

Implications and Future Directions

Being in a romantic relationship is associated with multiple psychological benefits. One especially noteworthy benefit is that of increased health and well-being. For example, researchers have consistently established a link between relationships and mortality, finding that people who are more socially connected tend to live longer, even after controlling for factors such as socioeconomic status, health behaviors (e.g., smoking, alcohol consumption, and physical activity), and mental health (e.g., depression), among others (Sarason, Sarason, & Gurung, 2001). People who are in relationships are able to seek and receive social support from their partners to cope with negative stressors (e.g., upcoming exam or job interview) and life events (e.g., death of a loved one), helping them deal effectively with such events when they occur (Cohen & McKay, 1984). Furthermore, close relationships can function as a self-bolstering resource, not only buffering people in relationships from potentially negative or threatening information (e.g., subpar results on an intelligence test) but also increasing their openness to challenges and feedback (Kumashiro & Sedikides, 2005). The ability to capitalize on positive events such as graduations, births, and job offers together with relationship partners can also lead to important benefits for health and well-being. Sharing positive news and commemorating positive events with a partner is linked to improved relationship quality and increased positive affect, and can even increase the significance and memorability of the event (Gable, Reis, Impett, & Asher, 2004; Gosnell & Gable, 2013).

For the above reasons and others, advancing our understanding of the formation, maintenance, and consequences of close romantic relationships is essential. Further work is needed to explore the utility of virtual reality as a method for studying adult attachment processes and for theory-building. For example, the ability to manipulate the presence, distance, and actions of a partner's avatar could help shed light on the impact of nonverbal behavior on the activation of attachment-related behavior and goals. Longitudinal studies would be particularly beneficial for examining the long-term consequences of interacting socially in a virtual setting, particularly in comparison to face-to-face interactions and purely text-based communication. Given the added affordances of virtual reality (e.g., avatars, body language, perceived "physical" distance), how does intimacy develop in immersive virtual environments? The use of virtual reality would also aid researcher efforts in understanding the neurological underpinnings of adult attachment styles, especially given the growing body of literature at the intersection of cyberpsychology and the social neurosciences (Parsons, 2017). Future research should also examine the potential positive and negative effects of virtual reality as a platform for developing both online and offline relationships, especially as virtual reality becomes increasingly viable and accessible in mainstream society.

Conclusion

Social scientists have recently begun to explore the fruitful intersection of close relationships research and virtual reality. With its ability to be used both as a tool for studying close relationship processes, and as a means of forming and maintaining relationships, the use of virtual reality holds great potential for future research. The studies conducted so far at the intersection of adult attachment theory, virtual reality, and neuroscience provide both promising results and far-reaching implications for deepening our understanding of how relational processes work, especially in an increasingly digital society.

References

Ainsworth, M. D. S. (1982). *Attachment: Retrospect and prospect*. New York: Basic Books.

Ainsworth, M. D. S., & Bell, S. M. (1970). Attachment, exploration, and separation: Illustrated by the behavior of one-year-olds in a strange situation. *Child Development, 41*(1), 49–67. https://doi.org/10.2307/1127388

Ainsworth, M., Blehar, M. C., Waters, E., & Wall, S. (1978). *Patterns of attachment: A psychological study of the strange situation*. Hillsdale, NJ: Erlbaum.

Ainsworth, M. D. S., Blehar, M. C., Waters, E., & Wall, S. N. (2015). *Patterns of attachment: A psychological study of the strange situation*. New York: Psychology Press.

Anderson, T. L., & Emmers-Sommer, T. M. (2006). Predictors of relationship satisfaction in online romantic relationships. *Communication Studies, 57*(2), 153–172. https://doi.org/10.1080/10510970600666834

Bailenson, J. N., Beall, A. C., Loomis, J., Blascovich, J., & Turk, M. (2005). Transformed social interaction, augmented gaze, and social influence in immersive virtual environments. *Human Communication Research, 31*(4), 511–537. https://doi.org/10.1093/hcr/31.4.511

Bailenson, J. N., Blascovich, J., Beall, A. C., & Loomis, J. M. (2003). Interpersonal distances in virtual environments. *Personality and Social Psychology Bulletin, 29*(7), 819–833. https://doi.org/10.1177/0146167203253270

Bailenson, J. N., & Yee, N. (2005). Digital chameleons. *Society, 16*(10), 814–819. https://doi.org/10.1111/j.1467-9280.2005.01619.x

Bailenson, J. N., & Yee, N. (2006). A longitudinal study of task performance, head movements, subjective report, simulator sickness, and transformed social interaction in collaborative virtual environments. *Presence: Teleoperators and Virtual Environments, 15*(3), 309–329. https://doi.org/10.1162/pres.15.3.309

Bailenson, J. N., Yee, N., Blascovich, J., Beall, A. C., Lundblad, N., & Jin, M. (2008). The use of immersive virtual reality in the learning sciences: Digital transformations of teachers, students, and social context. *Journal of the Learning Sciences, 17*, 102. https://doi.org/10.1080/10508400701793141

Bailenson, J. N., Yee, N., Blascovich, J., & Guadagno, R. E. (2008). Transformed social interaction in mediated interpersonal communication. *Mediated Interpersonal Communication*, 77–99. https://doi.org/10.4324/9780203926864

Banse, R. (2004). Adult attachment and marital satisfaction: Evidence for dyadic configuration effects. *Journal of Social and Personal Relationships, 21*(2), 273–282. https://doi.org/10.1177/0265407504041388

Bartholomew, K., & Horowitz, L. M. (1991). Attachment styles among young adults. *Journal of Personality and Social Psychology, 61*(2), 226–244. https://doi.org/10.1037/0022-3514.61.2.226

Bell, S. M., & Ainsworth, M. D. S. (1972). Infant crying and maternal responsiveness. *Child Development, 43*(4), 1171–1190. https://doi.org/10.2307/1127388

Berscheid, E. (1999). The greening of relationship science. *American Psychologist, 54*(4), 260.

Blascovich, J., Loomis, J., Beall, A. C., Swinth, K. R., Hoyt, C. L., & Bailenson, J. N. (2002). Immersive virtual environment technology as a methodological tool for social psychology. *Psychological Inquiry, 13*(2), 103–124.

Bowlby, J. (1969). *Attachment and loss: Attachment* (Vol. 1). New York: Basic Books.

Bowlby, J. (1980). *Attachment and loss: Loss, sadness and depression* (Vol. 3). New York: Basic Books.

Bowlby, J. (1988). Attachment, communication, and the therapeutic process. In J. Bowlby (Ed.), *A secure base: Parent-child attachment and healthy human development* (pp. 137–157). New York: Basic Books.

Brennan, K. A., & Shaver, P. R. (1995). Dimensions of adult attachment, affect regulation, and romantic relationship functioning. *Personality and Social Psychology Bulletin, 21*(3), 267–283.

Bretherton, I. (1992). The origins of attachment theory: John Bowlby and Mary Ainsworth. *Developmental Psychology, 28*(5), 759–775. https://doi.org/10.1037/0012-1649.28.5.759

Butzer, B., & Campbell, L. (2008). Adult attachment, sexual satisfaction, and relationship satisfaction: A study of married couples. *Personal Relationships, 15*(1), 141–154. https://doi.org/10.1111/j.1475-6811.2007.00189.x

Cassidy, J., Jones, J. D., & Shaver, P. R. (2013). Contributions of attachment theory and research: A framework for future research, translation, and policy. *Development and Psychopathology, 25*(4 Pt 2), 1415–1434.

Coan, J. A. (2010). Adult attachment and the brain. *Journal of Social and Personal Relationships, 27*(2), 210–217. https://doi.org/10.1177/0265407509360900

Coan, J. A. (2008). Toward a neuroscience of attachment. *Handbook of attachment: Theory, research, and clinical applications, 2*, 241–265.

Coan, J. A., Schaefer, H. S., & Davidson, R. J. (2006). Lending a hand: Social regulation of the neural response to threat. *Psychological Science, 17*(12), 1032–1039.

Cohen, S., & McKay, G. (1984). Social support, stress, and the buffering hypothesis: A theoretical analysis. In A. Baum, S. E. Taylor, & J. E. Singer (Eds.), *Handbook of psychology and health*. Hillsdale, NJ: Erlbaum.

Collins, N. L., & Read, S. J. (1990). Adult attachment, working models, and relationship quality in dating couples. *Journal of Personality and Social Psychology, 58*(4), 644–663. https://doi.org/10.1037/0022-3514.58.4.644

Cummings, J. J., & Bailenson, J. N. (2016). How immersive is enough? A meta-analysis of the effect of immersive technology on user presence. *Media Psychology, 19*(2), 272–309. https://doi.org/10.1080/15213269.2015.1015740

Drouin, M., Miller, D., Wehle, S. M., & Hernandez, E. (2016). Why do people lie online? "Because everyone lies on the internet". *Computers in Human Behavior, 64*, 134–142.

Duemmler, S. L., & Kobak, R. (2001). The development of commitment and attachment in dating relationships: Attachment security as relationship construct. *Journal of Adolescence, 24*(3), 401–415.

Feeney, B. C., & Kirkpatrick, L. A. (1996). Effects of adult attachment and presence of romantic partners on physiological responses to stress. *Journal of Personality and Social Psychology, 70*(2), 255–270. https://doi.org/10.1037/0022-3514.70.2.255

Feeney, J. A., & Noller, P. (1990). Attachment style as a predictor of adult romantic relationships. *Journal of Personality and Social Psychology, 58*(2), 281–291. https://doi.org/10.1037/0022-3514.58.2.281

Fraley, R. C., & Shaver, P. R. (2000). Adult romantic attachment: Theoretical developments, emerging controversies, and unanswered questions. *Review of General Psychology, 4*(2), 132–154. https://doi.org/10.1037/1089-2680.4.2.132

Gable, S. L., Reis, H. T., Impett, E. A., & Asher, E. R. (2004). What do you do when things go right? The intrapersonal and interpersonal benefits of sharing positive events. *Journal of Personality and Social Psychology, 87*(2), 228–245. https://doi.org/10.1037/0022-3514.87.2.228

Garau, M., Slater, M., Vinayagamoorthy, V., Brogni, A., Steed, A., & Sasse, M. A. (2003). The impact of avatar realism and eye gaze control on perceived quality of communication in a shared immersive virtual environment. In *Proceedings of the Conference on Human Factors in Computing Systems—CHI '03, 529*. https://doi.org/10.1145/642700.642703

Gilbert, R. L., Murphy, N. A., & Clementina Ávalos, M. (2011a). Realism, idealization, and potential negative impact of 3D virtual relationships. *Computers in Human Behavior, 27*(5), 2039–2046. https://doi.org/10.1016/j.chb.2011.05.011

Gilbert, R. L., Murphy, N. A., & Clementina Ávalos, M. (2011b). Communication patterns and satisfaction levels in three-dimensional versus real-life intimate relationships. *Cyberpsychology, Behavior, and Social Networking, 14*(10), 585–589. https://doi.org/10.1089/cyber.2010.0468

Gillath, O., Mccall, C., Shaver, P. R., & Blascovich, J. (2008). What can virtual reality teach us about prosocial tendencies in real and virtual environments? *Media Psychology, 11*(2), 259–282. https://doi.org/10.1080/15213260801906489

Gosnell, C. L., & Gable, S. L. (2013). Attachment and capitalizing on positive events. *Attachment and Human Development, 15*(3), 281–302. https://doi.org/10.1080/14616734.2013.782655

Hasler, B. S., Hirschberger, G., Shani-Sherman, T., & Friedman, D. A. (2014). Virtual peacemakers: Mimicry increases empathy in simulated contact with virtual outgroup members.

   Cyberpsychology, Behavior, and Social Networking, 17(12), 766–771. https://doi.org/10.1089/
      cyber.2014.0213
Hazan, C., & Shaver, P. (1987). Romantic love conceptualized as an attachment process.
      Journal of Personality and Social Psychology, 52(3), 511–524. https://doi.org/10.1037/0022-
      3514.52.3.511
Insel, T. R. (2003). Is social attachment an addictive disorder? *Physiology and Behavior, 79*(3),
      351–357. https://doi.org/10.1016/S0031-9384(03)00148-3
Kane, H. S., McCall, C., Collins, N. L., & Blascovich, J. (2012). Mere presence is not enough:
      Responsive support in a virtual world. *Journal of Experimental Social Psychology, 48*(1),
      37–44. https://doi.org/10.1016/j.jesp.2011.07.001
Kuchera, B. (2017a, July 14). *Oculus rift and touch controller bundle given yet another price
      drop.* Retrieved December 7, 2017, from https://www.polygon.com/virtual-reality/2017/7/14/
      15970974/oculus-rift-touch-bundle-facebook-price-drop.
Kuchera, B. (2017b, August 21). *HTC Vive VR headset gets $200 price cut.* Retrieved December 4,
      2018, from https://www.polygon.com/2017/8/21/16177270/htc-vive-price-cut-599.
Kumashiro, M., & Sedikides, C. (2005). Taking on board liability-focused information.
      Psychological Science, 16(9), 732–739. https://doi.org/10.1111/j.1467-9280.2005.01603.x
Lea, M., & Spears, R. (1995). Love at first byte? Building personal relationships over computer
      networks. In J. T. Wood & S. Duck (Eds.), *Under-studied relationships: Off the beaten track.
      Understanding relationship processes series* (Vol. 6, pp. 197–233). Thousand Oaks, CA: Sage.
Loomis, J. M., Blascovich, J. J., & Beall, A. C. (1999). Immersive virtual environment technology as
      a basic research tool in psychology. *Behavior Research Methods, Instruments, & Computers: A
      Journal of the Psychonomic Society, Inc, 31*(4), 557–564. https://doi.org/10.3758/BF03200735
Lopez, F. G., & Gormley, B. (2002). Stability and change in adult attachment style over the first-
      year college transition: Relations to self-confidence, coping, and distress patterns. *Journal of
      Counseling Psychology, 49*(3), 355–364. https://doi.org/10.1037/0022-0167.49.3.355
McCall, C., Bunyan, D. P., Bailenson, J. N., Blascovich, J., & Beall, A. C. (2009). Leveraging
      collaborative virtual environment technology for inter-population research on persuasion in a
      classroom setting. *Presence, 18*(5), 361–369.
McKenna, K. Y. A., Green, A. S., & Gleason, M. E. J. (2002). Relationship formation on the Internet:
      What's the big attraction? *Journal of Social Issues, 58*(1), 9–31. https://doi.org/10.1111/
      1540-4560.00246
Monahan, T., McArdle, G., & Bertolotto, M. (2008). Virtual reality for collaborative e-learning.
      Computers and Education, 50(4), 1339–1353. https://doi.org/10.1016/j.compedu.2006.12.008
Parks, M. R., & Floyd, K. (1996). Making friends in cyberspace. *Journal of Communication,
      46*(1), 80–97. https://doi.org/10.1111/j.1460-2466.1996.tb01462.x
Parsons, T. D. (2015). Virtual reality for enhanced ecological validity and experimental control
      in the clinical, affective and social neurosciences. *Frontiers in Human Neuroscience, 9,* 1–19.
      https://doi.org/10.3389/fnhum.2015.00660
Parsons, T. D. (2017). *Cyberpsychology and the brain: The interaction of neuroscience and affec-
      tive computing.* Cambridge: Cambridge University Press.
Pistole, M. C. (1989). Attachment in adult romantic relationships: Style of conflict resolution and
      relationship satisfaction. *Journal of Social and Personal Relationships, 6*(4), 505–510.
Quackenbush, D., Allen, J. G., & Fowler, J. C. (2015). Comparison of attachments in real-world
      and virtual-world relationships. *Psychiatry (New York), 78*(4), 317–327. https://doi.org/10.108
      0/00332747.2015.1092854
Rizzo, A. A., Schultheis, M., Kerns, K. A., & Mateer, C. (2004). Analysis of assets for virtual real-
      ity applications in neuropsychology. *Neuropsychological Rehabilitation, 14*(1–2), 207–239.
Sarason, B., Sarason, I., & Gurung, R. (2001). Close personal relationships and health outcomes:
      A key to the role of social support. In B. R. Sarason & S. Duck (Eds.), *Personal relationships:
      Implications for clinical and community psychology* (pp. 15–41). New York: Wiley.
Scharfe, E., & Bartholomew, K. I. M. (1994). Reliability and stability of adult attachment patterns.
      Personal Relationships, 1(1), 23–43. https://doi.org/10.1111/j.1475-6811.1994.tb00053.x

Schönbrodt, F. D., & Asendorpf, J. B. (2011). Virtual social environments as a tool for psychological assessment: Dynamics of interaction with a virtual spouse. *Psychological Assessment, 23*(1), 7–17. https://doi.org/10.1037/a0021049

Schönbrodt, F. D., & Asendorpf, J. B. (2012). Attachment dynamics in a virtual world. *Journal of Personality, 80*(2), 429–463. https://doi.org/10.1111/j.1467-6494.2011.00736.x

Shi, L. (2003). The association between adult attachment styles and conflict resolution in romantic relationships. *American Journal of Family Therapy, 31*(3), 143–157. https://doi.org/10.1080/01926180301120

Simpson, J. A. (1990). Influence of attachment styles on romantic relationships. *Journal of Personality and Social Psychology, 59*(5), 971–980. https://doi.org/10.1037/0022-3514.59.5.971

Sroufe, L. A., & Waters, E. (1977). Attachment as an organizational construct. *Child Development, 48*, 1184–1199.

Stackert, R. A., & Bursik, K. (2003). Why am I unsatisfied? Adult attachment style, gendered irrational relationship beliefs, and young adult romantic relationship satisfaction. *Personality and Individual Differences, 34*(8), 1419–1429. https://doi.org/10.1016/S0191-8869(02)00124-1

Steuer, J. (1992). Defining virtual reality: Dimensions determining telepresence. *Journal of Communication, 42*(4), 73–93. https://doi.org/10.1111/j.1460-2466.1992.tb00812.x

Taylor, H. (2017, November 28). *More than one million VR headsets sold last quarter.* Retrieved December 7, 2017, from https://www.gamesindustry.biz/articles/2017-11-28-vr-headset-sales-exceed-one-million-units-last-quarter.

Vrtička, P., & Vuilleumier, P. (2012). Neuroscience of human social interactions and adult attachment style. *Frontiers in Human Neuroscience, 6*, 1–17. https://doi.org/10.3389/fnhum.2012.00212

Vrticka, P., Andersson, F., Grandjean, D., Sander, D., & Vuilleumier, P. (2008). Individual attachment style modulates human amygdala and striatum activation during social appraisal. *PLoSONE, 3*, e2868. https://doi.org/10.1371/journal.pone.0002868

Walther, J. B. (1996). Computer-mediated communication: Impersonal, interpersonal, and hyperpersonal interaction. *Communication Research, 23*(1), 3–43.

Wang, C. C. D. C., & Mallinckrodt, B. S. (2006). Differences between Taiwanese and U.S. cultural beliefs about ideal adult attachment. *Journal of Counseling Psychology, 53*(2), 192–204. https://doi.org/10.1037/0022-0167.53.2.192

Wildermuth, S. M., & Vogl-Bauer, S. (2007). We met on the net: Exploring the perceptions of online romantic relationship participants. *Southern Communication Journal, 72*(3), 211–227. https://doi.org/10.1080/10417940701484167

Yee, N., Bailenson, J. N., Urbanek, M., Chang, F., & Merget, D. (2007). The unbearable likeness of being digital: The persistence of nonverbal social norms in online virtual environments. *Cyberpsychology & Behavior, 10*(1), 115–121. https://doi.org/10.1089/cpb.2006.9984

Sabrina A. Huang is a Ph.D. candidate at the Department of Communication at Stanford University. She is interested in studying how people form and maintain friendships and romantic relationships through the use of technology.

Jeremy Bailenson is founding director of Stanford University's Virtual Human Interaction Lab, Thomas More Storke Professor in the Department of Communication, Professor (by courtesy) of Education, Professor (by courtesy) Program in Symbolic Systems, a Senior Fellow at the Woods Institute for the Environment, and a Faculty Leader at Stanford's Center for Longevity. He earned a B.A. cum laude from the University of Michigan in 1994 and a Ph.D. in cognitive psychology from Northwestern University in 1999. He spent 4 years at the University of California, Santa Barbara as a Post-Doctoral Fellow and then an Assistant Research Professor Bailenson studies the psychology of Virtual and Augmented Reality, in particular how virtual experiences lead to changes in perceptions of self and others. His lab builds and studies systems that allow people to meet in virtual space and explores the changes in the nature of social interaction. His most recent research focuses on how virtual experiences can transform education, environmental conservation, empathy, and health. He is the recipient of the Dean's Award for Distinguished Teaching at Stanford.

Chapter 5
Uses of Physiological Monitoring in Intelligent Learning Environments: A Review of Research, Evidence, and Technologies

H. Chad Lane and Sidney K. D'Mello

Abstract Two of the most important benefits of using computer-based learning environments are that (1) they allow for interactive learning experiences and (2) it becomes possible to assess learning at a fine level of granularity based on learner actions, choices, and performance. Using these assessments, modern systems can deliver tailored pedagogical interventions, such as through feedback or adjustment of problem difficulty, in order to enhance learning. To magnify their power to promote learning, researchers have also sought to capture additional information, such as physiological data, to make even finer-grained and nuanced pedagogical decisions. A wide range of technologies have been explored, such as depth-sensing cameras (e.g., Kinect), electrodermal activity (EDA) sensors, electroencephalography (EEG), posture/seat detectors, eye- and head-tracking cameras, and mouse-pressure sensors, among many others. This chapter provides an overview and examples of how these techniques have been used by educational technology researchers. We focus on how these additional inputs can improve technology-based pedagogical decision-making to support *cognitive* (i.e., knowledge and information processing), *affective* (i.e., emotions, including motivational factors), and *metacognitive* (i.e., attention and self-regulatory behaviors) aspects of learning. Though not a comprehensive review, we take a selective look at classic and recent developments in this area. The chapter concludes with a brief discussion of emerging topics and key open questions related to the use of physiological tracking in the context of education and learning with technology.

H. C. Lane (✉)
Department of Educational Psychology, College of Education, University of Illinois, Urbana-Champaign, Champaign, IL, USA
e-mail: hclane@illinois.edu; http://hchadlane.net

S. K. D'Mello
Institute of Cognitive Science, University of Colorado, Boulder, Boulder, CO, USA
e-mail: sidney.dmello@colorado.edu; https://sites.google.com/site/sidneydmello/

© Association for Educational Communications and Technology 2019
T. D. Parsons et al. (eds.), *Mind, Brain and Technology*, Educational Communications and Technology: Issues and Innovations,
https://doi.org/10.1007/978-3-030-02631-8_5

Introduction

Sidney Pressey, an early twentieth-century psychologist and pioneer of educational technology, was a vocal proponent of modernizing education. He described it as one of the few areas of society that rarely witnessed any kind of innovation and was in need of its own "industrial revolution" (Pressey, 1932). Inspired by another famous educational psychologist, Edward Thorndike, who was possibly the first to publish the concept of an adaptive learning technology, Pressey built the first drill-and-practice teaching machine (Pressey, 1926). It was capable of capturing student answers to multiple choice questions, recording and assessing student answers, and (eventually) adjusting questions based on student performance. In subsequent years, new versions of the machine emerged with additional functionality improve its teaching power. In one extension, Pressey implemented Thorndike's "laws" such as requiring a question to be answered twice before being removed from the question set. Just as he sought to improve the original teaching machine, the search for techniques to improve computer-based teaching and learning boldly marches forward today.

Today's computer-based learning environments provide expanded opportunities for *authentic*, *social*, and *highly interactive* learning experiences for nearly every imaginable topic. Digital devices allow learners to navigate through digital learning materials, interact with realistic simulations, solve personalized problems, interact with their peers and teachers, all while receiving feedback and guidance. The enormous cross product of devices (computers, tablets, phones, virtual reality hardware, etc.), algorithms (for modeling pedagogy, learner modeling, prediction, personalization, social interactivity, etc.), and sensing technologies (cameras, eye trackers, pressure sensors, skin conductance, etc.) has produced a vast and complex body of research on human learning. On top of technological advances, content of the systems is also maturing, often branching into narrative-based and social experiences with the power to evoke emotional changes in learners.

The interdisciplinary roots of this work are broad, leveraging a wide range of technological advances, findings from cognitive, behavioral, and social psychology, research on schools and education, anthropological studies of classrooms, and more. In this chapter, we look at a specific subset of this vast literature by investigating the uses of physiological monitoring tools for pedagogical decision-making, primarily in the context of intelligent tutoring systems. In other words, we ask: *how have advances in user sensing enabled educational technologies to make better decisions about learning?*

What counts as a physiological sensor or physiological data may or may not always be clear. For example, clickstreams—patterns exhibited by learners with a mouse, keyboard, or touchpad—are a common target for analysis by intelligent learning environments (ILE), and can be informative, such as in measuring time delays between responses or time spent reversing previous actions. Although clickstream data does indeed result from physical interaction with a machine, it exists as more of a by-product of human–computer interaction rather than for the sole purpose of physiological monitoring. Thus, we do not consider a standard mouse as providing physiological data, but we would consider a pressure sensitive mouse (that senses the amount of pressure applied during a mouse click event) as a physiological device. Throughout the chapter, we focus on popular physiological monitoring tools used in educational research, and specifically those used in the articles reviewed. Comprehensive reviews of the field can be found elsewhere (Calvo & D'Mello, 2011; D'Mello, Dieterle, & Duckworth, 2017; Healey, 2015; Mukhopadhyay, 2015; Zeng, Pantic, Roisman, & Huang, 2009).

The decision-making space that intelligent learning environments, like tutoring systems, must navigate is enormous (e.g., When to give feedback? What kind of support to provide? How to select problems to solve?). We discuss this space in the next section, then work through three aspects of learning which physiological monitoring in the context of interactive learning technologies has sought to extend and improve:

- *Cognitive* support refers to strategies used to make decisions with respect to a learner's knowledge acquisition and information processing. For example, functional magnetic resonance imaging techniques (fMRI, fNIRS) can be used to estimate cognitive load of a learner and adjust problem difficulty (Yuksel et al., 2016).
- *Affective* support involves helping learners manage academic emotions, and development of methods that seek to map physiological sensor data into relevant emotional models. Common targets for such research include detecting emotions relevant to learning, such as frustration, confusion, and boredom and adjusting instruction accordingly (D'Mello & Graesser, 2014; Harley, Lajoie, Frasson, & Hall, 2017). We include motivation in this category, which though conceptually distinct, is more closely related to affect than the other two categories.
- Finally, *metacognitive* support focuses on self-regulatory skills, such as attention and strategy selection. For example, sensed electrodermal activity has been measured in coordination with solicited *judgements of learning* (JOLs) to better measure a learner's emotions in reaction to such a (metacognitive) request (Harley, Bouchet, Hussain, Azevedo, & Calvo, 2015).

We conclude the chapter with a brief discussion of emerging research in physiological computing and potential new directions for uses of physiological monitoring in educational contexts.

Pedagogical Decision-Making in Intelligent Learning Environments

Like experts in many domains, it is widely understood that teachers and tutors navigate a massive space of pedagogical choices. An ILE is software that seeks to promote effective and efficient learning by monitoring a learner during some learning activity, actively inferring the state of that learner, and finally (optionally) providing support and guidance. Historically, ILEs tend to emulate the tactics of expert human educators, although they are not necessarily bound by human limitations (e.g., physiological monitoring can go well beyond what a human can infer from observable cues). For the purposes of this chapter, we are concerned with ILEs that monitor the acquisition of knowledge and skills, usually during problem-solving, while the student is practicing and learning from feedback and explanations.

Generic Model for an Intelligent Learning Environment

In one form or another, ILEs typically consist of specific modules that enable them to support learning. These include a learning environment ("front end"), a model of expertise (target knowledge), a learner model (estimate of learner), and an instructional model. This is depicted in Fig. 5.1.

Briefly, as a learner engages in learning activities in the learning environment (often, a digital one), each action is tracked and mapped against a representation of what the ILE believes the learner *should* be doing. Learner actions are recorded and incorporated into a learner model via *update rules*, which is a persistent estimate of that learner's knowledge and/or affective/motivational state. These rules attempt to capture the meaning of learner actions in terms of what they reveal about the learner's evolving understanding of the task domain. For example, if a math learner successfully converts two fractions to have the same denominator, the system's belief in that learner's skill to find common denominators will increase.

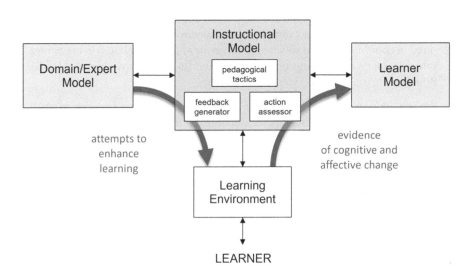

Fig. 5.1 A generic model of an intelligent learning environment. As the learner takes actions, the system infers cognitive and affective changes, which in turn are used to make that are intended to enhance learning in some way

The instructional model is responsible for any actions taken in an ILE that are intended to influence the learner state, such as helping the learner learn to find common denominators. Two key decisions include *whether* (and *when*) to intervene, as well as *how* to go about it. Guidance can be *unsolicited* (the system decides when to help), *solicited* (the learner requests help when needed), or achieved in more subtle ways via modifications to the learning environment or narrative (Lane & Johnson, 2009). Ideally, the learner model provides input to inform these instructional choices and identify the most needed interventions. It is intuitive to think about the decision space as consisting of two primary loops (VanLehn, 2006):

1. *Outer loop,* for selection and identification of learning activities or tasks, and an,
2. *Inner loop* that operates at a finer level of granularity by providing step-by-step support through a specific problem.

At the lowest level, the instructional model makes these decisions based on the problem-solving context (e.g., Is the student stuck on a step? Did the student struggle with the last task?). This involves monitoring the learning environment as well consulting the learner model, if one is maintained (not a requirement). For example, intelligent tutoring systems (ITSs) have to decide what kind of feedback to present, such as a hint, leading question, or give-away (Shute, 2008). At a higher-level, decisions on the outer loop support navigation through problem sets and curricula. A great deal of scholarship has focused on the roles of artificial intelligence (AI) techniques in building the models that enable these decisions (Graesser, Conley, & Olney, 2012; Wenger, 1987; Woolf, 2009). Our focus addresses a component of this broad effort by looking at very specific roles that physiological monitoring can play in improving estimates of the learner's state, and deciding what support may be best.

Efficacy of Intelligent Learning Environments

Decades of evidence has demonstrated that systems employing techniques from artificial intelligence (AI), when used in ways consistent with how people learn, outperform traditional "computer-aided" instructional systems (Anderson, Corbett, Koedinger, & Pelletier, 1995; Kulik & Fletcher, 2016; Kulik & Kulik, 1991; Ma, Adesope, Nesbit, & Liu, 2014; Mark & Greer, 1995). ITS researchers have historically pursued the holy grail of *the two-sigma effect* (Bloom, 1984), which suggested the best human tutors produce effect sizes of about 2.0 (roughly two grade levels). Recent evidence and lack of replication of the two sigma effect has brought this result into question leading to the possibility of "an interaction plateau" at an effect size of about 1.0 (VanLehn, 2011), which is still a positive result as it suggests ITSs are now as good as human tutors (in tightly controlled circumstances). For reference, non-AI based learning systems tend to achieve an effect size of about 0.3 (Kulik & Kulik, 1991). It also begs the question, *can ITSs surpass the effectiveness of human tutors?*

In reviewing this history, one must be aware of the kinds of knowledge being acquired—in the case of ITS research, it is most often *cognitive skills*, such as solving algebra equations, producing geometry proofs, or writing computer programs. As research on ITSs has evolved and morphed into new kinds of learning environments—that are often not tutoring systems, such as educational games, or inquiry environments—researchers have also begun to consider outcome measures other than simple cognitive gains. These have included metacognitive skills, emotional self-regulatory skills, interest, and other "non-cognitive" outcomes. Many of the systems reviewed here do focus on knowledge or skills, however, given their continued importance and desire to understand the value-added by incorporating physiological measurements.

In the remainder of the chapter, we review a variety of approaches for using physiological monitoring tools to enhance the decision-making of intelligent learning environments. The question of whether physiological monitoring enables ILEs to surpass the 1.0 sigma plateau remains unanswered as of now, but given the potential for sensors to go well beyond what humans can practically monitor, there are good reasons to try. We focus here on the question of whether physiological data can enhance the decision-making ability of ILEs to improve learning and learning-related outcomes (the arrow labeled "attempts to improve learning" in Fig. 5.1), and describe the pedagogical techniques such systems have tried to employ.

Support for Cognitive Aspects Learning

The first category we address is how physiological monitoring has been used to support cognitive aspects of learning, which generally refers to activities that involve reasoning, (human) pattern recognition, problem-solving, question-asking, information synthesis, and so on (Anderson & Krathwohl, 2001). Cognitive outcomes are by far the most emphasized outcomes in education research and often the sole target of exams and standardized testing, and so, ILEs have historically followed suit. Indeed, for most of the first two decades of research on ITSs, cognitive learning was the exclusive target of a wide range of systems, covering many domains, such as geography, algebra, computer programming, history, and more (Anderson et al., 1995; Wenger, 1987).

Given the relative success of these systems (Kulik & Fletcher, 2016; Ma et al., 2014; VanLehn, 2011), significant headway has been made on the question of how to design and deploy ILEs for learning. What is not yet known, however, is whether the use of physiological monitoring to support cognitive activities brings the possibility of surpassing what has already been achieved. Is it possible that the finer level of granularity afforded by physiological monitoring tools enable ILEs to surpass existing systems, or even human tutors? Or perhaps the potential gains are so minimal the needed investments are not justified? At this time, a conclusive answer is far from within reach; however, as explored in later sections, physiological sensing has established a robust and reliable link to affective aspects of learning, and as learning sciences research matures, the critical role of emotions is becoming increasingly more apparent (Graesser, D'Mello, & Strain, 2014; Pekrun & Linnenbrink-Garcia, 2012).

Cognitive Load

One of the most important questions for educational technologists and instructional designers to address is whether systems impose too many cognitive demands on a learner. As learning occurs, especially when the goal is cognitive skill acquisition (e.g., solving equations), learners have not yet automated many of the subskills they are practicing. Thus, it is important to gently introduce complexity and challenge based on their growing mastery of the skill. The idea of *cognitive load* has a long history in cognitive psychology (Sweller, 1988) and provides a theoretical and empirical frame for the design of ILEs. As competence increases through practice, more of the skill becomes automatic, thus reducing its burden (or cognitive load) on working memory. Therefore, detecting when these growth phases are likely to occur is an important technical challenge. Cognitive load is usually considered to take three forms: (1) *intrinsic load:* complexity of the content and its relation to the learner's prior knowledge, (2) *germane load:* related to the design of the task and the necessary cognitive activities, and (3) *extraneous load:* undesirable elements, associated with poor design or learner self-regulatory skills (Sweller, 2010).

Although most tutoring systems are able to manage cognitive load based on behavioral and interface data, a few projects have explored the use of physiological monitoring tools. For example, based on a technique called *knowledge tracing,* CMU's Cognitive Tutors track student changes in knowledge over multiple sessions and select problems at the right difficulty, based purely on problem-solving actions (Anderson et al., 1995). This includes gradual introduction of complexity and use of system feedback, thus indirectly helping manage learners' cognitive load. In more recent work, functional magnetic resonance imaging (fMRI) has been used to predict when students are cognitively engaged in problem-solving tasks, but not making progress (Anderson, Betts, Ferris, & Fincham, 2010). This work was extended and combined with extant behavioral models, enabling the system to predict which step learners were attempting and whether those steps were correct (Anderson, Betts, Ferris, & Fincham, 2012). At the time of this writing, it is unclear if the additional information enables the system to surpass what were already large cognitive gains (effect sizes of over 1), however the use of fMRI to glean a more detailed assessment of learners is a significant advance.

In a different project, the Brain Automated Chorales (BaCH) system uses functional Near Infrared Spectroscopy (fNIRS) to automatically gauge when cognitive workload crosses an individually determined threshold, and adjusts the difficulty of instruction accordingly (Yuksel et al., 2016). With a focus on music skill, the system is able to infer from fNIRS signals when a learner has mastered a given musical segment, and then increases difficulty to take the learner closer to the desired level of cognitive workload. The authors relate their approach to Vygotsky's *zone of proximal development* (Vygotsky, 1978) as well as cognitive load theory (Sweller, 1988). fNIRS is a "non-invasive imaging technique that measures levels of activation in the brain due to the hemodynamic response" (Yuksel et al., 2016, p. 5374), and is widely believed to be more resilient to other potential physiological noise, such as heartbeat and motion. A within-subjects study of 16 participants who played 15 easy pieces followed by 15 hard pieces with BaCH resulted in increased accuracy and reduced errors when compared to simplified control condition. Although it is not difficult to imagine a simpler technique for adjusting difficulty based on performance data alone, the study shows that a real-time, brain-based adaptive system is now feasible and effective.

Adapting to Challenge and Difficulty

The level of perceived difficulty of material by learners is an important factor when considering how best to adjust instruction. The *AttentiveReview* system monitors learners as they watch videos on their (unmodified) smartphones, and senses perceived difficulty via implicit photoplethysmography (PPG) (Pham & Wang, 2016). PPG is a sensing technique that requires a user cover the rear facing camera on the phone with their finger, which is then used to detect blood volume changes in the microvascular bed of tissue. The system tracks which videos and what content is being discussed, while tracking fluctuations in heart rate. When a learner removes their finger from the camera, playback is paused. Based on these readings across different kinds of videos and determination of difficulty from heart rate changes, *AttentiveReview* is able to suggest which topics may be best suited for review later, and assigns these topics to individual learners. Preliminary studies of the system report significant improvements in both recall and learning gains, when compared against systems that provide no review.

A different approach can be found in the MENTOR ITS, a tutoring system that uses electroencephalogram (EEG) signals to adaptively sequence the learning content according to the learners' mental states (Chaouachi, Jraidi, & Frasson, 2015). Specifically, MENTOR attempts to predict the suitability of a *worked example* or a question to solve based on the valence of the EEG signals. Learners who are in a more "negative" state, such as frustration, are given worked examples based on the rationale that they require less generative work on the part of the learner. Learners who are assessed to be in more of a positive state are assigned questions to answer, which of course, require greater focus and introduce the possibility of providing a wrong answer. In a pilot study ($N = 14$), the authors report a 22.7% increase in learning outcomes when employing this pedagogical strategy for students in the adaptive condition, versus those receiving the same content based solely on the answers they provide. MENTOR is one of the few systems to date that directly adjusts instruction based on EEG signals in real-time.

Attention and Gaze

Eye gaze is another important area of augmenting the assessment of learning with physiological monitoring. Where a learner is looking at any given moment can be very revealing about their attention, focus, goals, and more. If they are looking away from a screen or device for an extended time, for example, an adaptive system can reasonably infer that the learner's attention has been diverted. These sorts of judgements should be useful in terms of how the system makes judgements and plans instruction. Although a number of techniques exist for eye tracking, effective methods have emerged that are both affordable and non-intrusive, such as depth-sensing cameras and consumer-off-the-shelf eye trackers (Calvo & DMello, 2010; Hutt et al., 2017; Murphy, Carroll, Champney, & Padron, 2015).

D'Mello et al. describe the need for "attention-aware" learning technologies that are able to adapt instruction based on changes in the attention of the learner, such as mind wandering and gaze (D'Mello, 2016; D'Mello, Mills, Bixler, & Bosch, 2017). Specifically, their system combines machine learning for mind wandering detection with a real-time interpolated testing and restudy intervention. An eye tracker is used to classify attentional focus vs. mind wandering during the reading of educational texts. When the system detects mind wandering, it intervenes with just-in-time questions along with encouragement to re-read sections of text that may have received too little attention. A pilot study of the system with 104 participants showed that the intervention was successful in correcting mind wandering related comprehension deficits versus a yoked control condition. The authors comment that the eye-tracker used in the study was (at the time) cost prohibitive, and that the learned classifiers may not generalize well beyond the studied population. Nonetheless, the study is evidence that detection of attention can lead to improved reading comprehension under certain conditions, and thus represents an important example of physiological monitoring providing direct support for cognitive aspects of learning.

Support for Emotional and Motivational Aspects of Learning

The links between physiology, brain activity, and emotions run deep, and have been the focus of considerable academic research (Ekman, 1992; Panksepp, 2004; Simonov, 2013). In educational psychology research, quite a bit of effort has gone into mapping physiological signals into emotional states that are believed to relevant for learning, such as boredom, frustration, happiness, and more (Arroyo et al., 2009; Brawner & Gonzalez, 2016; D'Mello & Graesser, 2010; Kort, 2009). Here, we adopt common definitions that somewhat differentiate between affect and emotions (Rosenberg, 1998). Specifically, *affect* is primarily a subjective feeling that influences cognition, and is defined as a state that arises from, influences, and is influenced by neurobiology and physiology. *Emotions*, on the other hand, are relatively brief, sometimes intense states for which we have conscious awareness (although perhaps not always the words to describe them). In this chapter, we focus our attention on strategies that have been employed in ILEs to support learning based on physiological assessment of affect and emotions.

Affect-Sensitive Instructional Strategies

It is useful to begin with a discussion of emotion regulation strategies people already employ, to varying degrees, to manage the emotions that arise during learning. Gross and Barrett (2011) identify five distinct strategies of relevance to this discussion:

- *Situation selection* and *situation modification:* these involve selection or modification of contexts or situations for learning that are believed to minimize or maximize specific affective states.
- *Attentional deployment:* avoidance of situations that elicit specific affective states (distraction) or increased attention to aspects of a situation (rumination).
- *Cognitive change:* adjustment of the perceived meaning of a situation with the intent to change its affective content.
- *Response modulation:* after an affective state is experienced, this strategy involves managing how it is perceived and remembered.

D'Mello, Blanchard, Baker, Ocumpaugh, and Brawner (2014) provide an overview of how different ILEs have worked to support and promote use these strategies. Given that these are strategies that many learners employ naturally, the question is *how can an ILE be designed to prompt or promote their effective use?*

One obvious strategy is to change the learning environment directly. Because an ILE has (nearly) complete control of what the learner sees and what options are available at any given time, it is easy to select appropriate problems (situation selection) or hide certain features that may be less useful for easier problems (situation modification). These changes can also be faded over time to promote self-regulation. This tactic relates closely to *pedagogical experience manipulation*, a technique for adjusting simulation behaviors within an acceptable window of fidelity for purposes related learning (Lane & Johnson, 2009).

D'Mello et al. (2014) describe tactics to promote the remaining three self-regulation tactics as well. For example, attentional deployment can be managed by delivering attentional reorientation messages when overt disengagement is detected (i.e., the learner looks away from the screen) (D'Mello, Olney, Williams, & Hays, 2012). Cognitive change (adjusting the meaning of content so that is more favorably appraised) can be promoted in several ways, including providing encouraging and motivational messages and with direct support for affective states (e.g., encouraging a frustrated student) (D'Mello et al., 2010). Finally, response modulation can be promoted via empathetic system messages or with pedagogical agents that engage in nonverbal mirroring (that is building rapport through alignment of nonverbal communication) (Burleson & Picard, 2007). In summary, these are all tactics designed to enhance or induce the strategies learners may use already. Physiological monitoring tools, in this context, enable the detection of when they are likely to be active, but also to scaffold them when they are not.

Induction of Emotions That Are Conducive to Learning

Our next category of ILE interventions are those that seek to induce specific emotional reactions based on judgments made via physiological sensor inputs. In other words, just as a cognitive tutor will seek to promote revisions in knowledge or reflection on learning, an affective tutor may also take actions that nudge learners into a specific affective or emotional state that is believed to be conducive to learning. Those emotions, in turn, are believed to have positive downstream consequences on learning.

In this category, Chaffar, Derbali, and Frasson (2009) describe an ILE for computer science students that uses electromyography (EMG) to infer the valence of learners' emotional states, and respond with affective feedback. The aim of the work is to induce positive emotions for what is usually difficult material for students to grasp (data structures). Feedback in the system takes one of three primary forms: *encouragement*, *recommendation*, or *congratulation*, and can include problem-focused content (often as part of a recommended action). A small study confirmed what might be expected: recommendation and encouragement had a positive impact on learners with lower to mid-level achievement, while congratulatory actions had no impact on higher achieving learners. Related work using EEG and shifting to a game context, focused on the impact of ITS feedback on motivation, and concluded that EEG was appropriate for evaluating the success of motivation-focused ITS strategies (Derbali & Frasson, 2012). In other words, physiological monitoring tools were used to confirm the success or failure of affective tutoring strategies.

Similarly intuitive findings occurred with AutoTutor (Graesser, D'Mello, et al., 2012), a dialogue-based tutoring system that includes pedagogical agents and incorporates several different physiological sensors, including heart rate, facial expressions, and electrodermal activity (Pour, Hussain, AlZoubi, D'Mello, & Calvo, 2010). Specifically, while detecting how learners reacted to different forms of feedback: delight was experienced frequently after positive feedback, while surprise dominated after negative feedback (most likely due to learners not expecting to be wrong). These findings suggest that, for the most part, our intuitive expectations about the emotional impact of different kinds of feedback hold up in terms of how physiological sensors reveal those emotions.

Multichannel Affect Detection and Response

As demonstrated by AutoTutor, it is sometimes advantageous to incorporate multiple channels into assessment of affective and emotional states, which allows for more fine-grained analysis and verification across channels (Calvo & D'Mello, 2010). For example, a more confident assessment of boredom could be made if facial expressions, posture, and gaze simultaneously suggest a lack of attention and focus. Such multichannel (or multimodal) approaches have gained widespread attention in affective computing that often expand beyond physiological inputs to include audio, textual, and behavioral data as well (Poria, Cambria, Bajpai, & Hussain, 2017).

As an example, we take a closer look at an ITS that incorporates numerous physiological signals in order to make pedagogical decisions. The system, developed by Woolf et al. (2009) and called *Wayang Outpost* tasks learners with solving math problems that are relevant to nature, and include an emotional element to the story. For example, one problem requires the use of geometry to find the shortest route for orangutans to escape a forest fire. The system incorporates four kinds of physiological data: facial expressions, posture analysis (on a seat), finger pressure (on a pressure-sensitive mouse), and skin conductance. Bayesian networks are used to infer affective states based on problem-solving behavior and sensor data, using student post-practice surveys for training. The classifiers in this project ranged between 80% and 90% accuracy, though there is some concern of overfitting since student-level cross-validation was not done.

To further emphasize emotional aspects of learning, the system includes pedagogical agents, which have been shown to enhance social presence and learning, when properly deployed (Lane, 2016). The agents in Wayang Outpost display a wide range of emotions, such as confidence, excitement, boredom, frustration, and more, and are deployed strategically in response to detected learner emotions. For example, the agent may *mirror* student emotions to build solidarity, *praise* effort, or *acknowledge* potential frustration when it is detected. The authors report that use of these tactics lead to greater persistence in the face of challenge, an important finding that could be argued to justify the use of physiological monitoring when support for motivation is the focus of an intervention.

Along with research on the general challenge of interpreting multiple channels of physiological data together, sometimes called *fusion* (Castellano, Kessous, & Caridakis, 2008; Poria et al., 2017), other ILEs have been developed that attempt to leverage such data for learning. For example, Arroyo et al. (2009) instrumented a computer-based classroom with physiological monitoring equipment to provide teachers with affective assessments of instruction. Further, a multimodal affect detector using conversational cues, gross body language, and facial features for AutoTutor, was found to outperform single-channel models (D'Mello & Graesser, 2010). The key tradeoff in all cases is whether the added complexity, both with practical issues related to use of hardware and computational demands that come with real-time processing of the data, pays off in terms of affective and cognitive gains. Even when multiple signals may provide a more accurate assessment of affective state, it may not always be important pedagogically. For example, in one study of AutoTutor, it was found that affective-sensitive tutor responses only benefited learners with low domain knowledge (D'Mello et al., 2010). It is therefore important that future studies continue to unpack the conditions under which affect-sensitivity is effective, and when it is not, rather than racing to add more sensing modalities.

Support for Metacognitive Aspects of Learning

The last dimension of learning we review is how physiological monitoring can be used to support metacognitive aspects of learning. Treating metacognition independently of cognition is potentially questionable, since in the previous section, emotional self-regulation was considered alongside emotional support. Indeed, it remains unclear if there is a meaningful demarcation between physiological aspects of metacognition and cognition. Nonetheless, we recognize that the small number of examples we are able to review reveals the difficulty of imagining such boundaries.

Metacognition, often used interchangeably with self-regulated learning (SRL), is described by Flavell (1976) as "knowledge concerning one's own cognitive processes or anything related to them, e.g., the learning-relevant properties of information or data." Metacognition includes many skills that are domain independent, such as confirming one's understanding of material as it is learned (monitoring), reviewing earlier work to better understand what worked and what did not (evaluating), and selecting harder problems because they address known weaknesses (planning). Strong metacognitive skills have been linked to a number of important 21st Century competencies (Partnership for 21st Century Skills (P21), 2012) and have remained a consistent focus of educational technology research for decades.

Affect-Sensitive Acquisition of Learning Strategies

One potential link between affect and cognitive gains is to promote the use of effective learning strategies when a student experience negative affective states. This is exactly the approach taken in *Meta-Tutor* (VanLehn, Zhang, Burleson, Girard, & Hidago-Pontet, 2017) where "non-cognitive techniques" are used in a training phase to "persuade students to continue using the learning strategy on into the transfer phase" (p. 278). Learning strategies in this context have two criteria: (1) they can be used when studying but not required by the instructional objectives, and (2) are believed to be helpful for robust learning (not simply performance). With the help of a learning companion, the system supports learners while they construct simulation models (e.g., predator/prey) with support along numerous cognitive (e.g., domain-focused hints) and metacognitive dimensions (e.g., staying on task, promoting planning, and encouraging use of help). Affective states are estimated based on facial expressions and a posture sensor.

A study of the impact of Meta-Tutor showed that the system was successful in persuading learners to use effective learning strategies during the training phase, and with the tutor's support. However, use of the strategies was not detected in a transfer task when the Meta-Tutor was not available. The study provides evidence that it is possible to influence cognitive performance in the short term through physiological assessments (plus a learning companion), but that it remains a high bar to see these changes persist. The authors speculate that the transfer task may have been too difficult (floor effects), but it is also possible that further training and support from Meta-Tutor was necessary in order to see successful transfer of the learning strategies.

Metacognitive Tools and Self-Regulation

In a second example of metacognitive support, we consider a system also called *MetaTutor* (without a hyphen) that addresses a wider range of metacognitive and emotional self-regulatory skills (Azevedo, Johnson, Chauncey, & Burkett, 2010). Based on the idea that complex learning cannot occur without effective self-regulation, MetaTutor supports learning of biological systems with concrete tools that allow learners to use SRL techniques. For example, learning goals are clearly presented in the interface along with activities that will contribute to their completion. Earlier versions of the system based its assessments purely from clickstream and behavioral data, however recent versions have begun to incorporate physiological data to better assess metacognitive activities.

In particular, a more recent version of MetaTutor incorporates eye-tracking data along with extant behavioral data to monitor and support SRL (Taub & Azevedo, 2018). The system focuses on *fixations* on specific areas relevant to self-regulated learning, such as those related to goal-setting and planning. Gaze is a critical physiological signal for metacognition in the sense that it reveals critical information both about what the learner may be considering at any given moment, as well as which actions they may be deliberating on. In a study of 194 college students, there were no significant differences based on prior knowledge on single areas of interest, however there were differences in *pairs* and *sequential patterns* of areas of interest. In other words, the data revealed that learners with higher levels of prior knowledge were engaging in cognitive and metacognitive processes (tracked by their use of MetaTutor tools), whereas those with lower prior knowledge did to a lesser degree. Very much in line with the results reported above about support for affective processes related to learning, individual differences are profoundly important when it comes to providing learning support, and physiological tracking appears to be capable of identifying key dimensions on which to adapt that support.

Conclusion

In this chapter we provide a selective review of systems that attempt to use real-time physiological data as part of pedagogical decision-making and assessment. Techniques explored include brain scans, skin-based measurements, posture detection, gaze, facial expressions, pressure sensitive mice, and more. These systems are certainly not yet ready for the mainstream and exist primarily in lab-based or temporary school-based settings. Surprisingly few can be classified as "closed-loop" systems (see Fig. 5.1). Most studies report positive, but modest findings, and are normally linked to a short-term gain in some learning relevant behavior or variable. No known studies of physiological monitoring in ILEs have yet occurred over a longer period of time, which is an important area of future research for the field. How learner emotions vary across learning contexts, social contexts, and domains could provide a wealth of information with respect to personalization and learning support, and especially support emerging technologies for lifelong learning (Kay, 2008).

Given the strong link between physiological responses and affect, affective computing receives much of the focus in the research literature. As seen in our review, one of the more promising applications of physiologically based assessments of affective states is to verify induced affective states in learners. For example, if an ITS delivers positive feedback, can physiological assessments be used to confirm that the feedback improved the learner's confidence or motivation. This mirrors how cognitively focused feedback is typically tracked, and thus continues to be a prime area for continued research, along with interactions between the two.

An intriguing example of how physiological tools can be used in a similar manner can be found in the horror video game *Nevermind*.[1] Using a standard webcam or compatible heart rate monitor, the game adjusts play based on detected levels of stress and anxiety. The description on *Steam* states: "Nevermind picks up on indications of fear—lashing out if you allow your feelings of anxiety to get the better of you." In other words, when the player grows more anxious, the game becomes more stressful, but when the player is able to calm herself or himself, the frightening elements are dialed back. Engagement such as this is only possible with the help of physiological sensing of some kind and an adaptive system.

Physiological data represents only one part of a much larger decision space for ILEs, of course. In the chapter, we discuss the *fusion* of physiological data with other information streams, such as behavioral data, and this has been shown to enable more accurate judgments of affective states. The challenge, which very much remains an open question, is how best to integrate increasingly accurate physiological assessments into a pedagogical decision process. Expert human tutors are not incredibly helpful in this respect, since their access to information is limited to standard human communication channels (sight, sound). Thus, it is possible that this is an actually an advantage for ILEs over human tutors, and one that could feasibly allow them to surpass humans in terms of learning gains (VanLehn, 2011). Creating tools for human tutors that provide such information in real time, and allowing them to use them over extended time to improve their tutoring skills, is one possible direction of future research. Whether or not these are the best goals for the research community to pursue is certainly debatable.

Progress to enhance the efficacy of computer-based learning environments has been dramatic since the early work of Pressey and early ILEs of the 60s and 70s. The systems reported here demonstrate how physiological data may provide insights into learners that were not previously possible, though questions of how best to use this data remain largely open. We are certainly still at the beginning of understanding the

---

[1] http://nevermindgame.com/

full potential of physiological monitoring to enhance learning with technology, and encourage the field to continue exploring creative applications and conduct critical underlying empirical research that will inform future, scaled-up versions of the systems reviewed in this chapter.

Acknowledgements We would like to thank the editors for their valuable feedback on this chapter, as well as the National Science Foundation, Institute of Education Sciences, and the US Department of Defense that have funded large portions of the work cited in this chapter.

References

Anderson, J. R., Betts, S., Ferris, J. L., & Fincham, J. M. (2010). Neural imaging to track mental states while using an intelligent tutoring system. *Proceedings of the National Academy of Sciences, 107*(15), 7018–7023. https://doi.org/10.1073/pnas.1000942107

Anderson, J. R., Betts, S., Ferris, J. L., & Fincham, J. M. (2012). Tracking children's mental states while solving algebra equations. *Human Brain Mapping, 33*(11), 2650–2665.

Anderson, J. R., Corbett, A., Koedinger, K., & Pelletier, R. (1995). Cognitive tutors: Lessons learned. *Journal of the Learning Sciences, 4*(2), 167–207.

Anderson, L. W., & Krathwohl, D. R. (Eds.). (2001). *A taxonomy for learning, teaching, and assessing: A revision of Bloom's taxonomy of eductional outcomes.* New York: Longman.

Arroyo, I., Cooper, D. G., Burleson, W., Woolf, B. P., Muldner, K., & Christopherson, R. (2009). Emotion sensors go to school. In *Proceedings of the 14th International Conference on Artificial Intelligence in Education* (pp. 17–24).

Azevedo, R., Johnson, A., Chauncey, A., & Burkett, C. (2010). Self-regulated learning with MetaTutor: Advancing the science of learning with metacognitive tools. In M. Khine & I. Saleh (Eds.), *New science of learning: Computers, cognition, and colloboration in eduction* (pp. 225–247). Amsterdam: Springer.

Bloom, B. S. (1984). The 2 sigma problem: The search for methods of group instruction as effective as one-to-one tutoring. *Educational Researcher, 13*(6), 4–16.

Brawner, K. W., & Gonzalez, A. J. (2016). Modelling a learner's affective state in real time to improve intelligent tutoring effectiveness. *Theoretical Issues in Ergonomics Science, 17*(2), 183–210.

Burleson, W., & Picard, R. W. (2007). Gender-specific approaches to developing emotionally intelligent learning companions. *IEEE Intelligent Systems, 22*(4), 62–69.

Calvo, R. A., & D'Mello, S. K. (2010). Affect detection: An interdisciplinary review of models, methods, and their applications. *IEEE Transactions on Affective Computing, 1*(1), 18–37.

Calvo, R. A., & D'Mello, S. K. (2011). *New perspectives on affect and learning technologies.* New York: Springer.

Castellano, G., Kessous, L., & Caridakis, G. (2008). *Emotion recognition through multiple modalities: Face, body gesture, speech affect and emotion in human-computer interaction* (pp. 92–103). Berlin: Springer.

Chaffar, S., Derbali, L., & Frasson, C. (2009). *Inducing positive emotional state in intelligent tutoring systems.* Paper presented at the AIED.

Chaouachi, M., Jraidi, I., & Frasson, C. (2015). Adapting to learners' mental states using a physiological computing approach. In *FLAIRS Conference* (pp. 257–262).

D'Mello, S. K. (2016). Giving eyesight to the blind: Towards attention-aware AIED. *International Journal of Artificial Intelligence in Education, 26*(2), 645–659.

D'Mello, S. K., Blanchard, N., Baker, R., Ocumpaugh, J., & Brawner, K. (2014). I feel your pain: A selective review of affect-sensitive instructional strategies. In R. A. Sottilare, A. C.

Graesser, X. Hu, & B. Goldberg (Eds.), *Design recommendations for intelligent tutoring systems: Adaptive instructional strategies* (Vol. 2, pp. 35–48). Orlando, FL: US Army Research Laboratory.

D'Mello, S. K., Dieterle, E., & Duckworth, A. (2017). Advanced, analytic, automated (AAA) measurement of engagement during learning. *Educational Psychologist, 52*(2), 104–123.

D'Mello, S. K., & Graesser, A. C. (2010). Multimodal semi-automated affect detection from conversational cues, gross body language, and facial features. *User Modeling and User-Adapted Interaction, 20*, 147–187.

D'Mello, S. K., & Graesser, A. C. (2014). Feeling, thinking, and computing with affect-aware learning. In R. A. Calvo, S. K. D'Mello, J. Gratch, & A. Kappas (Eds.), *Oxford library of psychology. The Oxford handbook of affective computing* (pp. 419–434). New York: Oxford University Press.

D'Mello, S. K., Lehman, B., Sullins, J., Daigle, R., Combs, R., Vogt, K., et al. (2010). A time for emoting: When affect-sensitivity is and isn't effective at promoting deep learning. In V. Aleven, J. Kay, & J. Mostow (Eds.), *Intelligent tutoring systems* (Vol. 6094, pp. 245–254). Heidelberg: Springer.

D'Mello, S. K., Mills, C., Bixler, R., & Bosch, N. (2017). Zone out no more: Mitigating mind wandering during computerized reading. In *Proceedings of the 10th International Conference on Educational Data Mining* (pp. 8–15).

D'Mello, S. K., Olney, A., Williams, C., & Hays, P. (2012). Gaze tutor: A gaze-reactive intelligent tutoring system. *International Journal of Human-Computer Studies, 70*(5), 377–398.

Derbali, L., & Frasson, C. (2012). Assessment of learners' motivation during interactions with serious games: A study of some motivational strategies in food-force. *Advances in Human-Computer Interaction, 2012*, 5.

Ekman, P. (1992). An argument for basic emotions. *Cognition & Emotion, 6*(3–4), 169–200.

Flavell, J. H. (1976). Metacognitive aspects of problem solving. In M. Resnick (Ed.), *The nature of intelligence* (pp. 231–236). Hillsdale, NJ: Erlbaum.

Graesser, A. C., Conley, M., & Olney, A. (2012). Intelligent tutoring systems. In K. R. Harris, S. Graham, & T. Urdan (Eds.), *APA educational psychology handbook, Vol 3. Applications to learning and teaching* (pp. 451–473). Washington, DC: American Psychological Association.

Graesser, A. C., D'Mello, S. K., Hu, X., Cai, Z., Olney, A., & Morgan, B. (2012). AutoTutor. In P. McCarthy & C. Boonthum-Denecke (Eds.), *Applied natural language processing: Indentification, investigation, and resolution* (pp. 169–187). Hershey, PA: IGI Global.

Graesser, A. C., D'Mello, S. K., & Strain, A. C. (2014). Emotions in advanced learning technologies. In R. Pekrun & L. Linnenbrink-Garcia (Eds.), *International handbook of emotions in education* (pp. 473–493). New York, NY: Routledge.

Gross, J. J., & Barrett, L. F. (2011). Emotion generation and emotion regulation: One or two depends on your point of view. *Emotion Review, 3*(1), 8–16.

Harley, J. M., Bouchet, F., Hussain, M. S., Azevedo, R., & Calvo, R. (2015). A multi-componential analysis of emotions during complex learning with an intelligent multi-agent system. *Computers in Human Behavior, 48*, 615–625. https://doi.org/10.1016/j.chb.2015.02.013

Harley, J. M., Lajoie, S. P., Frasson, C., & Hall, N. C. (2017). Developing emotion-aware, advanced learning technologies: A taxonomy of approaches and features. *International Journal of Artificial Intelligence in Education, 27*(2), 268–297. https://doi.org/10.1007/s40593-016-0126-8

Healey, J. (2015). Physiological sensing of emotion. In R. A. Calvo, S. K. D'Mello, J. Gratch, & A. Kappas (Eds.), *Handbook of affective computing* (pp. 204–216). New York: Oxford University Press.

Hutt, S., Mills, C., Bosch, N., Krasich, K., Brockmole, J. R., & D'Mello, S. K. (2017). Out of the Fr-Eye-ing pan: Towards gaze-based models of attention during learning with technology in the classroom. In M. Bielikova, E. Herder, F. Cena, & M. Desmarais (Eds.), *Proceedings of the 2017 Conference on User Modeling, Adaptation, and Personalization* (pp. 94–103). New York: ACM.

Kay, J. (2008). Lifelong learner modeling for lifelong personalized pervasive learning. *IEEE Transactions on Learning Technologies, 1*(4), 215–228.

Kort, B. (2009, May 10). *Cognition, affect, and learning: The role of emotions in learning.* Retrieved from http://knol.google.com/k/cognition-affect-and-learning.

Kulik, C.-L. C., & Kulik, J. A. (1991). Effectiveness of computer-based instruction: An updated analysis. *Computers in Human Behavior, 7*(1–2), 75–94. https://doi.org/10.1016/0747-5632(91)90030-5

Kulik, J. A., & Fletcher, J. (2016). Effectiveness of intelligent tutoring systems: A meta-analytic review. *Review of Educational Research, 86*(1), 42–78.

Lane, H. C. (2016). Pedagogical agents and affect: Molding positive learning interactions. In S. Y. Tettegah & M. Gartmeier (Eds.), *Emotions, technology, design, & learning* (pp. 47–61). London: Academic Press.

Lane, H. C., & Johnson, W. L. (2009). Intelligent tutoring and pedagogical experience manipulation in virtual learning environments. In D. Schmorrow, J. Cone, & D. Nicholson (Eds.), *The handbook of virtual environments for training and education, Volume 2: VE components and training technologies* (pp. 393–406). Westport, CT: Praeger Security International.

Ma, W., Adesope, O. O., Nesbit, J. C., & Liu, Q. (2014). Intelligent tutoring systems and learning outcomes: A meta-analysis. *Journal of Educational Psychology, 106*(4), 901.

Mark, M. A., & Greer, J. E. (1995). The VCR tutor: Effective Instruction for device operation. *The Journal of the Learning Sciences, 4*(2), 209–246.

Mukhopadhyay, S. C. (2015). Wearable sensors for human activity monitoring: A review. *IEEE Sensors Journal, 15*(3), 1321–1330. https://doi.org/10.1109/JSEN.2014.2370945

Murphy, J. S., Carroll, M. B., Champney, R. K., & Padron, C. K. (2015). *Investigating the role of physiological measurement in intelligent tutoring.* Paper presented at the Generalized Intelligent Framework for Tutoring (GIFT) Users Symposium (GIFTSym2).

Panksepp, J. (2004). *Affective neuroscience: The foundations of human and animal emotions.* New York: Oxford University Press..

Partnership for 21st Century Skills (P21). 2012. *Framework for 21st Century Learning.* Retrieved from http://www.p21.org/overview/skills-framework.

Pekrun, R., & Linnenbrink-Garcia, L. (2012). Academic emotions and student engagement. In S. L. Christenson, A. L. Reschly, & C. Wylie (Eds.), *Handbook of research on student engagement* (pp. 259–282). New York: Springer.

Pham, P., & Wang, J. (2016). *Adaptive review for mobile MOOC learning* via *implicit physiological signal sensing.* Paper presented at the Proceedings of the 18th ACM International Conference on Multimodal Interaction.

Poria, S., Cambria, E., Bajpai, R., & Hussain, A. (2017). A review of affective computing: From unimodal analysis to multimodal fusion. *Information Fusion, 37*, 98–125. https://doi.org/10.1016/j.inffus.2017.02.003

Pour, P. A., Hussain, M. S., AlZoubi, O., D'Mello, S. K., & Calvo, R. A. (2010). The impact of system feedback on learners' affective and physiological states. In V. Aleven, J. Kay, & J. Mostow (Eds.), *Intelligent tutoring systems* (Vol. 6094, pp. 264–273). Berlin: Springer.

Pressey, S. L. (1926). A simple apparatus which gives tests and scores—And teaches. *School and Society, 23*(586), 373–376.

Pressey, S. L. (1932). A third and fourth contribution toward the coming "industrial revolution" in education. *School and Society, 36*(934), 668–672.

Rosenberg, E. L. (1998). Levels of analysis and the organization of affect. *Review of General Psychology, 2*(3), 247–270.

Shute, V. J. (2008). Focus on formative feedback. *Review of Educational Research, 78*(1), 153–189. https://doi.org/10.3102/0034654307313795

Simonov, P. V. (2013). *The emotional brain: Physiology, neuroanatomy, psychology, and emotion.* New York: Springer.

Sweller, J. (1988). Cognitive load during problem solving: Effects on learning. *Cognitive Science, 12*, 257–285.

Sweller, J. (2010). Element interactivity and intrinsic, extraneous, and germane cognitive load. *Educational Psychology Review, 22*(2), 123–138.

Taub, M., & Azevedo, R. (2018). How does prior knowledge influence eye fixations and sequences of cognitive and metacognitive SRL processes during learning with an intelligent tutoring system? *International Journal of Artificial Intelligence in Education* (pp 1–28). https://doi.org/10.1007/s40593-018-0165-4

VanLehn, K. (2006). The Behavior of tutoring systems. *International Journal of Artificial Intelligence in Education, 16*(3), 227–265.

VanLehn, K. (2011). The relative effectiveness of human tutoring, intelligent tutoring systems, and other tutoring systems. *Educational Psychologist, 46*(4), 197–221. https://doi.org/10.1080/00461520.2011.611369

VanLehn, K., Zhang, L., Burleson, W., Girard, S., & Hidago-Pontet, Y. (2017). Can a non-cognitive learning companion increase the effectiveness of a meta-cognitive learning strategy? *IEEE Transactions on Learning Technologies, 10*(3), 277–289.

Vygotsky, L. S. (1978). Zone of proximal development: A new approach. In M. Cole, V. John-Steiner, S. Scribner, & E. Souberman (Eds.), *Minds in society: The development of higher psychological processes* (pp. 84–91). Cambridge, MA: Harvard University Press.

Wenger, E. (1987). *Artificial intelligence and tutoring systems.* San Francisco, CA: Morgan Kaufmann.

Woolf, B. P. (2009). *Building intelligent interactive tutors: Student-centered strategies for revolutionizing E-learning.* Amsterdam: Morgan Kaufmann.

Woolf, B. P., Burleson, W., Arroyo, I., Dragon, T., Cooper, D. G., & Picard, R. (2009). Affect-aware tutors: Recognising and responding to student affect. *International Journal of Learning Technology, 4*(3–4), 129–164.

Yuksel, B. F., Oleson, K. B., Harrison, L., Peck, E. M., Afergan, D., Chang, R. et al. (2016). *Learn piano with BACh: An adaptive learning interface that adjusts task difficulty based on brain state.* Paper presented at the Proceedings of the 2016 Chi Conference on Human Factors in Computing Systems.

Zeng, Z., Pantic, M., Roisman, G. I., & Huang, T. S. (2009). A survey of affect recognition methods: Audio, visual, and spontaneous expressions. *IEEE Transactions on Pattern Analysis and Machine Intelligence, 31*(1), 39–58.

H. Chad Lane is an Associate Professor of Educational Psychology and Informatics at the University of Illinois, Urbana-Champaign, USA. Prof. Lane's research focuses on the design, use, and impacts of intelligent technologies for learning and behavior change. This work involves blending techniques from the entertainment industry (that foster engagement) with those from artificial intelligence and intelligent tutoring systems (that promote learning), as well as running studies to better understand whether and how the resulting learning experiences impact learners. He has led design-based research projects involving educational games, intelligent tutoring systems, and immersive technologies. His current work focuses on the uses of game and sensing technologies for science learning and interest development in informal learning contexts. He has over 80 publications, delivered invited talks around the USA and Europe, and has hands-on experiences in informal and formal learning contexts. He earned his Ph.D. in Computer Science from the University of Pittsburgh in 2004. There, he conducted his doctoral research on intelligent learning technologies for problem understanding and solving skills.

Sidney K. D'Mello is an Associate Professor at the Institute of Cognitive Science and the Department of Computer Science at the University of Colorado Boulder (since July 1, 2017). He was previously an Assistant and then Associate Professor in the departments of Psychology and Computer Science at the University of Notre Dame. D'Mello conducts basic research on affective and cognitive states (e.g., confusion, boredom, and mind wandering) during complex learning and problem-solving, develops real-time computational models of these states, and integrates the models in learning environments that intelligently respond to learner mental states. His research uses a range of techniques such as eye tracking, speech recognition, physiological sensing, computer vision, nonlinear time series analyses, discourse modeling, and machine learning. The learning contexts include intelligent tutoring, educational games, collaborative problem-solving, classroom discourse, text, scene, and film comprehension. Data is collected in the lab, online, and in schools. D'Mello has coedited six books and has published over 220 journal papers, book chapters, and conference proceedings in these areas.

Chapter 6
Gaze-Based Attention-Aware Cyberlearning Technologies

Sidney K. D'Mello

Abstract Over a century of cognitive psychology has taught us that attention plays a central role in cognition, especially in learning. Accordingly, the central thesis of this chapter is that next-generation learning technologies should include mechanisms to model and respond to learners' attentional states. As a step in this direction, this chapter proposes a macro-theoretic framework that encompasses various forms of overt and covert states of attention (e.g., alternative vs. divided attention) and inattention (e.g., zone outs vs. tune outs). It then provides examples of three attention-aware cyberlearning technologies that utilize eye tracking as a window into learners' attentional states. The first of these is GazeTutor, which uses eye movements to detect overt inattentional lapses and attempts to redirect attention with a set of gaze-reactive dialogue moves. The second system address more covert forms of inattention by using eye movements to detect instances of mind wandering and responding with interpolated questions, self-explanations, and re-reading opportunities. The third example attempts to graduate such technologies from the lab into real-world classrooms by using consumer-off-the-shelf eye trackers as entire classes of students individually interact with a cyberlearning technology. The chapter concludes by suggesting key next-steps for the field of attentional-aware cyberlearning.

Introduction

> "My experience is what I agree to attend to. Only those items which I notice shape my mind—without selective interest, experience is an utter chaos."
> *William James, The Principles of Psychology, 1980, p. 402.*

"I can't believe how many random thoughts I have," reported a learner when asked to monitor and report on the contents of his/her "zone outs" while reading a text or

S. K. D'Mello (✉)
Institute of Cognitive Science, University of Colorado Boulder, Boulder, CO, USA
e-mail: sidney.dmello@colorado.edu; https://www.colorado.edu/ics/sidney-dmello

© Association for Educational Communications and Technology 2019
T. D. Parsons et al. (eds.), *Mind, Brain and Technology*, Educational Communications and Technology: Issues and Innovations, https://doi.org/10.1007/978-3-030-02631-8_6

viewing a film in a lab study. Indeed, people are often surprised to discover that a sizable number of their thoughts have nothing to do with the task at hand. These lapses in attention—called mind wandering (Smallwood & Schooler, 2015)—can occur even when learners make a concerted effort to concentrate on the learning task. Further, maintaining attentional focus is not sufficient in and of itself. Learners must also effectively allocate limited attentional resources in a manner that aligns with changing task demands, and with the dynamics of the learning environment. For example, learners must effectively alternate attention between a text and diagram when learning from illustrated texts (Hegarty & Just, 1993; Schnotz, 2005). When diagnosing problems with complex systems, learners must allocate information to critical components to deeply comprehend the underlying mechanisms (Graesser, Lu, Olde, Cooper-Pye, & Whitten, 2005). Processing animations requires learners to allocate attention in a manner that aligns with changes in the animation and in concert with any accompanying narration (van Gog & Scheiter, 2010). Effective problem-solving also demands an appropriate allocation of attentional resources (Knoblich, Öllinger, & Spivey, 2005; van Gog, Jarodzka, Scheiter, Gerjets, & Paas, 2009).

Thus, the ability to sustain and effectively allocate limited attentional resources is critical for effective learning. Accordingly, researchers have begun to develop attention-aware learning technologies that sense and respond to learners attentional states (D'Mello, 2016). The idea of attention-aware user interfaces was proposed almost a decade ago (Roda & Thomas, 2006). Prior to this, Gluck, Anderson, and Douglass (2000) discussed the use of eye tracking to increase the bandwidth of information available to an intelligent tutoring system (ITS). Anderson (2002) followed up on some of these ideas by demonstrating how certain beneficial instructional strategies could only be implemented via a real-time analysis of eye gaze. Since then, most of the work has been on leveraging eye gaze to dynamically adapt the learning session (Bondareva et al., 2013; Conati, Aleven, & Mitrovic, 2013; Conati & Merten, 2007; Jaques, Conati, Harley, & Azevedo, 2014; Kardan & Conati, 2012; Muir & Conati, 2012).

Eye gaze has emerged as a leading candidate for implementing attention-aware mechanisms, ostensibly motivated by decades of research in support of an *eye-mind link,* which posits a tight coupling between cognitive processing and eye movements (Deubel & Schneider, 1996; Hoffman & Subramaniam, 1995; Rayner, 1998). Conati et al. (2013) provide an overview of much of the existing work on eye movements and learning. It can be grouped into (1) offline-analyses of eye gaze to understand attentional processes (e.g., Graesser et al., 2005; Hegarty & Just, 1993; Mathews, Mitrovic, Lin, Holland, & Churcher, 2012; Muir & Conati, 2012; Ponce & Mayer, 2014); (2) attempts to incorporate learners' attentional states into learner (or student) models (e.g., Graesser et al., 2005; Hegarty & Just, 1993; Mathews et al., 2012; Muir & Conati, 2012; Ponce & Mayer, 2014); and (3) closed-loop systems that track and respond to attention in real-time (for a more or less exhaustive list, see D'Mello, Olney, Williams, & Hays, 2012; Gluck et al., 2000; Sibert, Gokturk, & Lavine, 2000; Wang, Chignell, & Ishizuka, 2006).

The present focus is on closed-loop attention-aware cyberlearning technologies that utilize eye movements to monitor and respond to some aspect of learners' attentional state. The emphasis on eye gaze is motivated by the fact that it is one of the most direct and nonintrusive ways to measure the locus of attentional focus (see above). That said, attentional states can also be estimated from facial expressions (Stewart, Bosch, Chen, Donnelly, & D'Mello, 2017; Whitehill, Serpell, Lin, Foster, & Movellan, 2014), electroencephalography (EEG) (Liu, Chiang, & Chu, 2013; Sun & Yeh, 2017), physiology (Blanchard, Bixler, Joyce, & D'Mello, 2014; Pham & Wang, 2015), acoustic-prosodic features (Drummond & Litman, 2010), and behavioral data, such as reading times (Franklin, Smallwood, & Schooler, 2011; Mills & D'Mello, 2015). However, eye gaze has most successfully been used in closed-loop attention-aware learning technologies, so it is emphasized here. The remainder of this chapter provides a theoretical overview of attention during learning followed by examples of attention-aware cyberlearning technologies that have been tested in the lab and in the wild.

Attention During Learning

Attention is crucial for effective learning. Contemporary theories of learning, including the cognitive-affective theory of learning with multimedia (CATLM) (Moreno, 2005; Moreno & Mayer, 2007), the integrated model of text and picture comprehension (ITPC) (Schnotz, 2005; Schnotz & Bannert, 2003), and cognitive load theory (CLT) (Chandler & Sweller, 1991; Paas, Renkl, & Sweller, 2003), espouse the critical role of attention. For example, CATLM posits that the three key processes that underlie deep learning include the selection of relevant information to *attend to*, the mental organization of the *attended* information into coherent units, and the appropriate use of *attentional focus* to integrate the newly organized knowledge into existing knowledge structures in long term memory.

In general, cognitive processes such as prior knowledge activation, rehearsal, inference generation, causal reasoning, and comprehension all demand attentional resources (Azevedo, 2009; Fredricks, Blumenfeld, & Paris, 2004; Graesser et al., 2007; Guthrie & Wigfield, 2000; Linnenbrink, 2007; Shernoff, Csikszentmihalyi, Shneider, & Shernoff, 2003; Strain, Azevedo, & D'Mello, 2013; Tobias, 1994). A lack of attention counters these processes and leads to radically different behaviors and outcomes (Baker, D'Mello, Rodrigo, & Graesser, 2010; Fisher, 1993; Larson & Richards, 1991; Pekrun, Goetz, Daniels, Stupnisky, & Perry, 2010; Strain & D'Mello, 2014). Students who cannot sustain attentional focus are more likely to passively attend to learning materials (Damrad-Frye & Laird, 1989; Drummond & Litman, 2010; Forbes-Riley & Litman, 2011; Kane et al., 2007; Mann & Robinson, 2009; Moss et al., 2008; Sparfeldt, Buch, Schwarz, Jachmann, & Rost, 2009), which in turn leads to superficial understanding rather than deep comprehension.

Attention can be thought of as a filter in that it has an object or location of focus. Attentional filtering governs which aspects of the environment (e.g., relevant content vs. distractions and extraneous details) are selected for further processing, and attentional focus is needed for the construction of mental models. It can be driven by top-down goal-directed control or captured by bottom-up stimulus-driven processing (Egeth & Yantis, 1997; Kinchla, 1992). However, the locus of attention is not synonymous with where attention appears to be directed, because a person can be looking at one thing but thinking about something else.

In line with this, Table 6.1. outlines a 2 × 2 (perceived direction of attention × content of thoughts) framework to organize attentional states during learning with technology. At a very basic level, one can distinguish between attention that *appears* to be directed towards the learning environment or elsewhere. *Overt inattention* occurs when the learner directs attention elsewhere, as when the learner intentionally goes off-task or is distracted by external stimuli. Inattention can also be *covert,* when attention drifts away from the learning task to content-unrelated thoughts even though the learner may appear to be concentrating. These mind wandering thoughts can be directed towards external factors (e.g., "the temperature in the room"), task-factors (e.g., "this tutor agent looks funny"), or something else entirely (e.g., "I wonder what's for dinner") (Stawarczyk, Majerus, Maj, Van der Linden, & D'Argembeau, 2011). Mind wandering can occur both *intentionally* (e.g., tuning out) and *unintentionally* (zoning out) (Seli, Risko, & Smilek, 2016).

An interesting situation arises when attention appears to be directed away from the learning environment, but the focus of thoughts is content-related; this is referred to as *covert attention.* For example, a learner could talk to a peer about a particular problem (on-task conversation), could engage in help seeking behaviors, or could close his or her eyes and deeply reflect on the content. In contrast, *overt attention* occurs when attention is both directed toward the learning environment and consists of content-related thoughts. This is also referred to as *sustained attention*, which can take on different forms. *Focused attention* occurs when attention is directed towards a particular component of the learning environment. *Alternating attention* consists of rapidly switching attention between different interface components; for example, reading a sentence from the text, then looking at the image, back to the text, and so on. Finally, *divided attention* is the highest level of attention and involves simultaneously attending to multiple components of the environment (e.g., attending to the narration of a multimedia presentation while simultaneously processing an accompanying animated image).

Table 6.1 Organizing framework to differentiate between various attentional states

Content of thoughts	Perceived direction of attention	
	Learning environment	Elsewhere
Content-related	*Overt attention* (sustained attention) Focused attention Alternating attention Divided attention	*Covert attention* On-task conversation Help seeking Concentrating with eyes closed Others….
Content-unrelated	*Covert inattention* (mind wandering) Tune outs Zone outs	*Overt inattention* Off-task Distracted

Attention-Aware Learning Technologies

Attention-aware learning technologies model one or more types of attentional state. They should not be conflated with related systems that monitor different, albeit related, states like stress, affect, cognitive load, engagement, and so on. In particular, automated detection of complex mental states—with the goal of developing interfaces that close the loop by responding to the sensed states—is an active research area in a number of areas, such as social signal processing (Mehu & Scherer, 2012; Vinciarelli, Pantic, & Bourlard, 2009), affective computing (Calvo & D'Mello, 2010; Picard, 1997), and augmented cognition (Marshall, 2005; St. John, Kobus, Morrison, & Schmorrow, 2004). Attention-aware technologies can be distinguished by their emphasis on attention.

Technologies that track and respond to attentional states have been explored in a number of domains, including the auto-industry (e.g., monitoring driver fatigue and susceptibility to external distractions—see review by Dong, Hu, Uchimura, and Murayama (2011)), educational scaffolds (e.g., to select adaptive hints in educational games (Muir & Conati, 2012)), adaptive information visualization (Carenini et al., 2014; Steichen, Wu, Toker, Conati, & Carenini, 2014), and various other applications (e.g., to prioritize the position of news items on a screen as in Navalpakkam, Kumar, Li, and Sivakumar (2012) or to study perceived object saliency during video viewing as in Yonetani, Kawashima, and Matsuyama (2012)).

In the context of learning, most of the adaptive systems have focused on modeling attentional lapses. These systems are discussed below as concrete examples of attention-aware learning technologies.

Example 1: Addressing Inattention During Multimedia Learning

GazeTutor is a multimedia interface consisting of an animated conversational agent that provides explanations on biology concepts with synthesized speech that is synchronized with annotated images (D'Mello et al., 2012). GazeTutor attempted to address states of *overt inattention* (see above).

Gaze-Sensitive Intervention

GazeTutor used a Tobii T60 eye tracker to detect inattention, which was assumed to occur when gaze was not on critical parts of the interface. Specifically, the screen was divided into zones for the tutor (zone 0), the image (zone 1), the text box (zone 2), and the blank areas (zones 3 and 4)—see Fig. 6.1a. There was also an off-screen zone for gaze patterns that were not classified as falling into any of these five zones.

GazeTutor assumed that learners were not attending when their gaze was not on the tutor or image for a period of time. When this occurred, it attempted to re-engage learners with statements that directed them to reorient their attention towards the agent or the image.

The gaze-reactive intervention was triggered when (1) the tutor was speaking; (2) the tutor was not in the middle of a gaze-reactive statement; (3) the student had continuously not looked at the agent or image for more than 5 s; and (4) it had been more than 10 s since the last gaze-reactive statement.

If these conditions were satisfied, the tutor would stop speaking in mid-sentence, pause for 1 s, and then deliver a gaze-reactive statement, such as, "Please pay attention." The tutor would then repeat the interrupted sentence from the beginning. Each gaze-sensitive response was randomly selected from a set of four predefined responses designed to reorient students' attention towards the tutor in a somewhat direct manner: "Please pay attention," "I'm over here you know," "You might want to focus on me for a change," and "Snap out of it. Let's keep going."

Validation Study

The efficacy of GazeTutor in promoting learning, motivation, and engagement was evaluated in an experiment where 48 learners were tutored on four biology topics: two with the gaze-reactive component enabled (experimental condition) and two with the gaze-reactive component disabled (control condition). Learners completed a posttest on all four topics after interacting with the system.

The results indicated that the gaze-sensitive intervention was successful in dynamically reorienting learner attention to the important areas of the interface (see Fig. 6.1b). Prior to the intervention, the probability that students were looking away from the screen steadily increased while there was a corresponding decrease in focus on the tutor and the image. A reverse pattern occurred after the intervention message, where off-screen gaze rapidly decreased, while focus on the tutor increased.

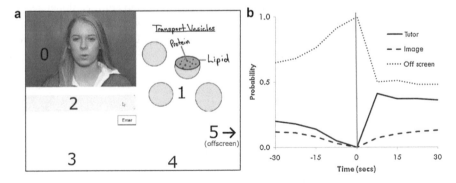

Fig. 6.1 (a) GazeTutor. Screen shot of interface on left. (b) Gaze before and after intervention on right

With respect to learning, posttest scores for deep reasoning questions were higher when learners interacted with the gaze-sensitive interface compared to its non-reactive counterpart. Individual differences in scholastic aptitude moderated the impact of gaze-reactivity on learning gains. Gaze-reactivity was associated with a small improvement in overall learning for learners with average aptitude, but learning gains were substantially higher for those with high aptitude and somewhat lower for their low-aptitude counterparts.

In summary, the results of this study suggest that gaze-sensitive statements can reorient attention, and thereby improve comprehension and learning for a subset of learners. There were no corresponding increases in self-reported motivation and engagement, suggesting there is considerable room for improvement. Future enhancements of the system include replacing the expensive eye-tracker with low-cost alternatives, improved modeling of inattention (rather than exclusively relying on off-screen gaze), a larger repertoire of context-specific gaze-reactive messages, and incorporating individual differences in selecting appropriate gaze-sensitive responses.

Example 2: Mitigating Mind Wandering During Computerized Reading

Considerable research points to the high incidence of mind wandering during learning and its negative relationship with learning outcomes (D'Mello, 2019; Smallwood, Fishman, & Schooler, 2007). Thus, next-generation learning technologies should include mechanisms to detect and address mind wandering. One such technology uses eye tracking and machine learning to detect mind wandering and dynamically responds with interpolated comprehension questions and re-reading opportunities (D'Mello, Mills, Bixler, & Bosch, 2017).

Mind Wandering Detection and Intervention

A supervised learning approach was used to detect mind wandering. Data used to train the detector was collected as 98 learners read a 57-page (or 57-computer screens) scientific text on surface tension in liquids (Boys, 1895). Learners used the arrow key to navigate forward. They self-reported when they caught themselves mind wandering throughout the reading session. Eye gaze was tracked with a Tobii TX 300 eye tracker. Global eye-gaze features (e.g., fixation durations, saccade amplitudes) were used to train a support vector machine classifier to discriminate between mind wandering (pages with a self-report—32%) and normal reading (see Faber, Bixler, & D'Mello, 2018) for an overview of the methodology) in a manner that generalizes to new learners. The model had a precision of 69% and a recall of 67%, which was deemed sufficiently accurate for dynamic intervention.

The mind wandering detector was integrated into the computerized reading inter-face in order to provide real-time, page-by-page estimates of the likelihood of mind wandering for new learners. The main intervention strategy consisted of asking comprehension questions on the page where mind wandering was detected and pro-viding opportunities to re-read. Specifically, two surface-level multiple choice ques-tions were created for each of the 57 pages. Mind wandering detection occurred when the learner attempted to navigate to the next page, upon which eye gaze from the page just read was submitted to the mind wandering detector, which provided a mind wandering likelihood. If the likelihood was sufficiently high (based on a prob-abilistic prediction), one of the questions (randomly selected) was presented to the learner. If the learner answered the question correctly, feedback was provided, and the learner could advance to the next page. If the learner answered incorrectly, he/she was encouraged to re-read the page. When ready to continue, the learner received a second (randomly selected) question, but was allowed to advance regardless of the correctness of their response (Fig. 6.2).

Validation Study

The experiment ($N = 104$) had two conditions: an intervention condition and a yoked control condition. Participants in the intervention condition received the intervention as described above (i.e., based on detected mind wandering likeli-hoods). Each participant in the yoked control condition was paired with a partici-pant in the intervention condition. The control participant received an intervention question on the same pages as their paired intervention participant regardless of the mind wandering likelihood. After reading, participants completed a 38-item multiple choice comprehension assessment. The questions were randomly selected from the 57 pages (one per page) with the exception that a higher selection priority was given to pages that were re-read as part of the dynamic intervention. Participants in the yoked control condition received the same posttest questions as their intervention condition counterparts.

The key dependent variable was posttest performance on unseen questions (i.e., questions not presented as part of the intervention). There was no significant condition difference on overall scores ($p = 0.846$) between the intervention ($M = 57.6\%$, SD = 15.7%) and control conditions ($M = 58.1\%$, SD = 12.9%). The data were more telling when the posttest was examined as a function of mind wandering during reading. As expected, there were no significant differences on pages where both the intervention and control participants had low ($p = 0.759$) or high ($p = 0.922$) mind wandering likelihoods. There was also no significant dif-ference ($p = 0.630$) for pages where the intervention condition had high, but the control condition had low, mind wandering likelihoods. However, the interven-tion condition ($M = 64.3\%$, SD = 26.3%) significantly ($p = 0.003$, $d = 0.47$ sigma) outperformed the control condition ($M = 48.9\%$, SD = 29.8%) for pages where the intervention participants had low, but the control condition had high, mind wandering likelihoods. This pattern of results suggests that the intervention had

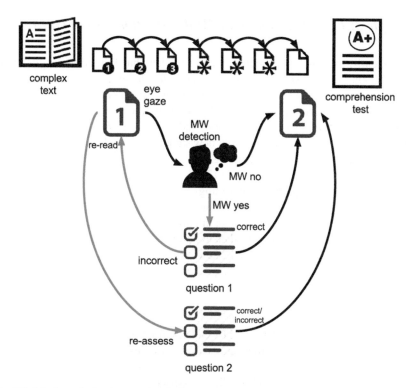

Fig. 6.2 Mind wandering intervention during computerized reading

the intended effect of reducing comprehension deficits attributable to mind wandering because it led to equitable performance when mind wandering was high and improved performance when it was low.

Next Steps

Despite the promising result, there were several limitations with the technology as elaborated in D'Mello et al. (2017). Most significantly, it encouraged keyword spotting and a general shallow-level processing style. To address this, Mills, Bixler, and D'Mello (in prep.) modified the technology by: (a) segmenting the 57 pages into 15 coherent units and only intervening at the end of a unit; (b) replacing the surface-level multiple-choice questions with deeper-level questions that required learners to generate self-explanations in natural language; and (c) providing feedback and opportunities to re-read and revise the explanations. The validation study measured both surface—and inference-level comprehension, immediately and after a 1-week delay. Preliminary results suggest a positive effect for the intervention (compared to a yoked-control) for delayed inference-level questions, though analyses are still ongoing.

Example 3: From the Lab to the Wild: Attention-Aware Guru

Until recently, the cost of research-grade eye trackers has limited the applicability of eye tracking in real-world environments at scale. However, the relatively recent introduction of consumer off-the-shelf (COTS) eye trackers (retailing for $100 to $150) has ushered forth an exciting era by affording the application of decades of lab-based research on eye gaze, attention, and learning to real-world classrooms, thereby affording new discoveries about how students learn while designing innovations to sustain attention during learning.

It is currently unknown whether COTS eye trackers can be implemented with sufficient fidelity in noisy classroom settings to enable collection of actionable gaze data. To address this challenge, Hutt et al. (2017) collected eye gaze while high-school students learned biology from an intelligent tutoring system (ITS) as part of their biology classes. They used the data to build automated detectors of mind wandering, similar to the aforementioned studies involving reading.

Guru

This research used a conversational ITS called GuruTutor (or Guru) (Olney et al., 2012), which was modeled after interactions with expert human tutors. Guru engages the student through natural language conversations, using an animated tutor agent that references a multimedia workspace (see Fig. 6.3). The tutor communicates via synthesized speech and gestures, while students communicate by typing responses, which are analyzed using natural language processing techniques. Guru maintains a student model (Sottilare, Graesser, Hu, & Holden, 2013) throughout the session, which it uses to tailor instruction to individual students. Guru has been shown to be effective at promoting learning at levels similar to human tutors in small group tutoring sessions (Olney et al., 2012).

Guru teaches introductory biology topics (e.g., osmosis; protein function) from state curriculum standards in short sessions, typically lasting 15–40 min. Each topic involves interrelated concepts and facts. Guru begins with a basic introduction to motivate the topic, which is then followed by a five-phase session that develops students' understanding of the topic. First, Guru engages the student in a *Collaborative Lecture* that covers basic information and terminology relevant to the topic. Following this, students construct their own natural language *Summaries* of the material just covered. These summaries are automatically analyzed to determine which concepts require further tutoring in the remainder of the session. For the target concepts, students complete skeleton *Concept Maps*, node-link structures that cover essential relationships between concepts. Next, students complete a *Scaffolded Natural Language Dialogue,* where Guru uses a Prompt → Feedback → Verification Question → Feedback → Elaboration cycle to cover target concepts. If a student shows difficulty mastering particular concepts, a second Concept Maps phase is initiated

Fig. 6.3 Heatmap overlay showing participants eye gaze on the Guru interface. Red indicates high concentration of fixations, purple low concentration of fixations

followed by an additional Scaffolded Dialogue phase. The session concludes with a *Cloze Task* that requires students to complete an ideal summary of the topic by filling in missing information from memory.

Previous work has shown that mind wandering can be detected using eye tracking in Guru (Hutt, Mills, White, Donnelly, & D'Mello, 2016), but this was done using data collected in a very controlled lab environment. How do detectors developed using similar methods perform on data collected in a more noisy and complex environment? If successful, this opens the possibility of an attention-aware version of Guru for real-world classrooms.

Mind Wandering Detection

Hutt et al. (2017) developed the first gaze-based mind wandering detector for in-class use. The 'in the wild' data collection involved 135 eighth and ninth graders enrolled in a Biology 1 class. Class sizes ranged from 14 to 30 students based on regular class enrollment. The classroom layout remained unchanged from the setup used for standard instruction, with the addition of laptops to run Guru and an EyeTribe gaze tracker per desk (note that the EyeTribe is no longer available but there are alternatives). Each student completed two approximately 30-min sessions with Guru. Mind wandering was measured using auditory thought probes occurring every 90–120 s during the Guru sessions.

The eye tracker records a validity for each sample based on number of eyes tracked and the quality of the tracking. Of the 85% of the sessions where eye tracking was successfully collected, the median validity rate was 95% (mean was 89%).

If a stricter validity threshold of both eyes tracked was enforced, mean validity dropped to 71% with a median of 75%. These results are promising given the difficulties presented by the relatively unconstrained classroom environment, where students were free to fidget, look around the room, and even occasionally laid their heads on the table as they interacted with Guru.

The next important question pertains to whether the eye gaze data was of sufficient fidelity for mind wandering detection. To address this question, features were computed in 30-s windows preceding each auditory probe and were used to train Bayesian networks to detect mind wandering in a manner that generalized to new students. Global gaze features focused on general gaze patterns and are independent of the content on the screen, whereas locality features encode where gaze is fixated (see Hutt et al., 2017, for details). A set of context features that encoded information from the session, such as time into the session, student performance, response times, and so on were also considered. The results indicated that global and locality models achieved similar overall performance with a slight tradeoff with respect to precision (global = 55%; locality = 51%) and recall (global = 65%; locality = 70%).

Students completed a posttest assessment after the tutoring session. The *predicted* mind wandering rate for the global (Spearman's *rho* = −0.112, $p = 0.269$) and locality (rho = −0.177, $p = 0.076$) models were correlated with posttest scores similar to self-reported mind wandering rates (rho = −0.189 $p = 0.058$), thereby providing evidence for the predictive validity of the detector.

The results thus far indicate that it is feasible to (a) track eye-gaze using COTS gaze-trackers despite the complexities of real-world classroom environments and (b) the collected data was of sufficient fidelity to consider real-time mind wandering detection. The team is now working on embedding the detector into Guru so as to provide real-time assessments of mind wandering, which will be used to trigger interventions.

Mind Wandering Intervention

What strategies should an attention-aware Guru utilize when it detects that a student is mind wandering? Some possibilities are proposed below, though a more student-centered design approach is needed to identify a set of candidates for implementation.

It is important to devise different strategies for isolated episodes of mind wandering vs. instances when it is concentrated over short periods of time. At an immediate level, one initial effect of mind wandering is that the student simply fails to attend to a unit of information (e.g., a tutor question) or a salient event in the learning environment (e.g., the multimedia panel displays a critical part of a diagram that is missed). If the unattended information, question, or event is needed to construct a mental model so that subsequent knowledge can be assimilated, a student who mind wanders will be left behind. For example, when discussing a complex biology topic that has multiple phases like mitosis, failure to comprehend the first phase (interphase) reduces the likelihood that subsequent phases (prophase, metaphase, anaphase) can be comprehended. Therefore, it is important that intermediate comprehension deficiencies attributed to mind wandering are corrected before progressing further into the session.

Accordingly, a direct approach might be to simply reassert the unattended information ("e.g., Isabella, let me repeat that…") or highlight the information by directing attention to specific areas of the display (e.g., "Martin, you might want to look at the highlighted image showing the chromosomes duplicating"). The use of the student's first name (i.e., Martin in this example) is intended to help in capturing attention as selective attention is biased towards personal information, especially one's own name (i.e., the well-known cocktail-party effect (Cherry, 1953).

Taking a somewhat different approach, Guru can launch a sub-dialogue where it asks a content-specific question (e.g., "Anthony, what happens to the chromosomes when they duplicate?") or asks the student to complete a mini-activity (e.g., "Kiara, we now have a simulation of the first phase in mitosis. Can you…."). This form of interleaved questions and embedded activities has been shown to reduce mind wandering (Szpunar, Khan, & Schacter, 2013). Guru can also ask the student to self-explain a concept, as this has been known to reduce mind wandering (Moss, Schunn, Schneider, & McNamara, 2013).

The aforementioned strategies are expected to refocus attention when momentary episodes of mind wandering are detected. However, additional measures might be needed if mind wandering persists despite these interventions, as it might signal prolonged boredom or disengagement. One option is to simply suspend the current activity and launch a new activity. For example, if a large concentration of mind wandering is detected during *Concept Mapping*, then Guru might suggest moving on to a different activity, such as inviting the student to engage in a *Scaffolded Discussion*. Guru might even suggest changing topics or offering students to choose what they would like to do next, which is a likely effective strategy given the positive role of choice in inspiring engagement (Patall, Cooper, & Robinson, 2008). If all else fails, Guru might even suggest that the student take a break. These strategies are intended to disrupt the status quo, thereby giving the student an opportunity to start the new activity fresh.

Conclusion

Attention is a necessary condition of learning. We have known this for over a century. Yet current learning technologies are blissfully unaware of the learners' level and locus of attention, an oversight that can lead to tedious, unproductive, boring, and occasionally "hair pulling" experiences. Attentional-aware cyberlearning technologies aim to address this challenge by incorporating multimodal sensing and computational modeling to automatically detect learners' attentional states and intelligently adapt the interaction in a manner that coordinates external (what the learner does) with internal (what the learner attends to) behaviors.

This chapter illustrated some of the progress made in this area. Despite some successes, it is clear that much more needs to be done. In particular, future systems should (1) forgo a micro-theoretic view of attention that narrowly focuses on isolated components in lieu of a more integrated approach that does justice to an inherently multicomponential construct (e.g., covert vs. overt inattention, alternating vs. divided attention), (2) go beyond micro-optimizing to a narrow set of tasks and interfaces to making generalizability and transferability a design constraint not an afterthought; and (3) apply the basic principles of attention-aware cyberlearning to a broader set of real-world tasks that requires concentration and vigilance, such as air traffic control, flight simulation, medical diagnosis, advertising, and so on. Implementing these steps is one important way to ensure that attentional-aware cyberlearning will come of age.

Acknowledgements This research was supported by the National Science Foundation (NSF) (DRL 1235958 and IIS 1523091). Any opinions, findings, and conclusions, or recommendations expressed in this paper are those of the authors and do not necessarily reflect the views of NSF.

References

Anderson, J. R. (2002). Spanning seven orders of magnitude: A challenge for cognitive modeling. *Cognitive Science, 26*(1), 85–112.

Azevedo, R. (2009). Theoretical, methodological, and analytical challenges in the research on metacognition and self-regulation: A commentary. *Metacognition & Learning, 4*, 87–95.

Baker, R., D'Mello, S. K., Rodrigo, M., & Graesser, A. (2010). Better to be frustrated than bored: The incidence, persistence, and impact of learners' cognitive–affective states during interactions with three different computer-based learning environments. *International Journal of Human-Computer Studies, 68*(4), 223–241.

Blanchard, N., Bixler, R., Joyce, T., & D'Mello, S. K. (2014). Automated physiological-based detection of mind wandering during learning. In S. Trausan-Matu, K. Boyer, M. Crosby, & K. Panourgia (Eds.), *Proceedings of the 12th International Conference on Intelligent Tutoring Systems (ITS 2014)* (pp. 55–60). Switzerland: Springer.

Bondareva, D., Conati, C., Feyzi-Behnagh, R., Harley, J. M., Azevedo, R., & Bouchet, F. (2013). Inferring learning from gaze data during interaction with an environment to support self-regulated learning. In K. Yacef, C. Lane, J. Mostow, & P. Pavlik (Eds.), *Proceedings of the 16th International Conference on Artificial Intelligence in Education (AIED 2013)* (pp. 229–238). Berlin: Springer.

Boys, C. V. (1895). *Soap bubbles, their colours and the forces which mold them.* London: Society for Promoting Christian Knowledge.

Calvo, R. A., & D'Mello, S. K. (2010). Affect detection: An interdisciplinary review of models, methods, and their applications. *IEEE Transactions on Affective Computing, 1*(1), 18–37. https://doi.org/10.1109/T-AFFC.2010.1

Carenini, G., Conati, C., Hoque, E., Steichen, B., Toker, D., & Enns, J. (2014). Highlighting interventions and user differences: Informing adaptive information visualization support. In *Proceedings of the 32nd Annual ACM Conference on Human Factors in Computing Systems* (pp. 1835–1844). New York: ACM.

Chandler, P., & Sweller, J. (1991). Cognitive load theory and the format of instruction. *Cognition and Instruction, 8*(4), 293–332.

Cherry, E. C. (1953). Some experiments on the recognition of speech, with one and with two ears. *The Journal of the Acoustical Society of America, 25*(5), 975–979.

Conati, C., Aleven, V., & Mitrovic, A. (2013). Eye-tracking for student modelling in intelligent tutoring systems. In R. Sottilare, A. Graesser, X. Hu, & H. Holden (Eds.), *Design Recommendations for intelligent tutoring systems—Volume 1: Learner modeling* (pp. 227–236). Orlando, FL: Army Research Laboratory.

Conati, C., & Merten, C. (2007). Eye-tracking for user modeling in exploratory learning environments: An empirical evaluation. *Knowledge-Based Systems, 20*(6), 557–574. https://doi.org/10.1016/j.knosys.2007.04.010

D'Mello, S., Olney, A., Williams, C., & Hays, P. (2012). Gaze tutor: A gaze-reactive intelligent tutoring system. *International Journal of Human-Computer Studies, 70*(5), 377–398.

D'Mello, S. K. (2016). Giving eyesight to the blind: Towards attention-aware AIED. *International Journal of Artificial Intelligence in Education, 26*(2), 645–659.

D'Mello, S. K. (2019). What do we think about when we learn? In K. Millis, J. Magliano, D. Long & K. Wiemer (Eds.), *Understanding Deep Learning, Educational Technologies and Deep Learning, and Assessing Deep Learning.* New York, NY: Routledge/Taylor and Francis.

D'Mello, S. K., Mills, C., Bixler, R., & Bosch, N. (2017). Zone out no more: Mitigating mind wandering during computerized reading. In X. Hu, T. Barnes, A. Hershkovitz & L. Paquette (Eds.), *Proceedings of the 10th International Conference on Educational Data Mining* (pp. 8–15). International Educational Data Mining Society.

Damrad-Frye, R., & Laird, J. D. (1989). The experience of boredom: The role of the self-perception of attention. *Journal of Personality and Social Psychology, 57*(2), 315.

Deubel, H., & Schneider, W. X. (1996). Saccade target selection and object recognition: Evidence for a common attentional mechanism. *Vision Research, 36*(12), 1827–1837.

Dong, Y., Hu, Z., Uchimura, K., & Murayama, N. (2011). Driver inattention monitoring system for intelligent vehicles: A review. *IEEE Transactions on Intelligent Transportation Systems, 12*(2), 596–614.

Drummond, J., & Litman, D. (2010). In the zone: Towards detecting student zoning out using supervised machine learning. In V. Aleven, J. Kay & J. Mostow (Eds.), Intelligent tutoring systems (Vol. 6095, pp. 306–308). Berlin: Springer.

Egeth, H. E., & Yantis, S. (1997). Visual attention: Control, representation, and time course. *Annual Review of Psychology, 48*(1), 269–297.

Faber, M., Bixler, R., & D'Mello, S. K. (2018). An automated behavioral measure of mind wandering during computerized reading. *Behavior Research Methods, 50*(1), 134–150.

Fisher, C. D. (1993). Boredom at Work—A neglected concept. *Human Relations, 46*(3), 395–417.

Forbes-Riley, K., & Litman, D. (2011). When does disengagement correlate with learning in spoken dialog computer tutoring? In S. Bull & G. Biswas (Eds.), *Proceedings of the 15th International Conference on Artificial Intelligence in Education* (pp. 81–89). Berlin: Springer.

Franklin, M. S., Smallwood, J., & Schooler, J. W. (2011). Catching the mind in flight: Using behavioral indices to detect mindless reading in real time. *Psychonomic Bulletin & Review, 18*(5), 992–997.

Fredricks, J. A., Blumenfeld, P. C., & Paris, A. H. (2004). School engagement: Potential of the concept, state of the evidence. *Review of Educational Research, 74*(1), 59–109.

Gluck, K. A., Anderson, J. R., & Douglass, S. A. (2000). Broader bandwidth in student modeling: What if ITS were "Eye" TS? In C. Gauthier, C. Frasson, & K. VanLehn (Eds.), *Proceedings of the 5th International Conference on Intelligent Tutoring Systems* (pp. 504–513). Berlin: Springer.

Graesser, A., Louwerse, M., McNamara, D., Olney, A., Cai, Z., & Mitchell, H. (2007). Inference generation and cohesion in the construction of situation models: Some connections with computational linguistics. In F. Schmalhofer & C. Perfetti (Eds.), *Higher level language processes in the brain: Inferences and comprehension processes.* Mahwah, NJ: Erlbaum.

Graesser, A., Lu, S., Olde, B., Cooper-Pye, E., & Whitten, S. (2005). Question asking and eye tracking during cognitive disequilibrium: Comprehending illustrated texts on devices when the devices break down. *Memory and Cognition, 33*, 1235–1247. https://doi.org/10.3758/BF03193225

Guthrie, J. T., & Wigfield, A. (2000). Engagement and motivation in reading. In M. L. Kamil, P. D. Pearson, & R. Barr (Eds.), *Handbook of reading research* (Vol. 3, pp. 403–422). Mahwah, NJ: Lawrence Erlbaum.

Hegarty, M., & Just, M. (1993). Constructing mental models of machines from text and diagrams. *Journal of Memory and Language, 32*(6), 717–742.

Hoffman, J. E., & Subramaniam, B. (1995). The role of visual attention in saccadic eye movements. *Attention, Perception, & Psychophysics, 57*(6), 787–795.

Hutt, S., Mills, C., Bosch, N., Krasich, K., Brockmole, J. R., & D'Mello, S. K. (2017). Out of the Fr-Eye-ing Pan: Towards gaze-based models of attention during learning with technology in the classroom. In M. Bielikova, E. Herder, F. Cena, & M. Desmarais (Eds.), *Proceedings of the 2017 Conference on User Modeling, Adaptation, and Personalization* (pp. 94–103). New York: ACM.

Hutt, S., Mills, C., White, S., Donnelly, P. J., & D'Mello, S. K. (2016). The eyes have it: Gaze-based detection of mind wandering during learning with an intelligent tutoring system. In *Proceedings of the 9th International Conference on Educational Data Mining (EDM 2016)* (pp. 86–93). International Educational Data Mining Society.

Jaques, N., Conati, C., Harley, J. M., & Azevedo, R. (2014). *Predicting affect from gaze data during interaction with an intelligent tutoring system.* Paper presented at the Intelligent Tutoring Systems.

Kane, M. J., Brown, L. H., McVay, J. C., Silvia, P. J., Myin-Germeys, I., & Kwapil, T. R. (2007). For whom the mind wanders, and when an experience-sampling study of working memory and executive control in daily life. *Psychological Science, 18*(7), 614–621.

Kardan, S., & Conati, C. (2012). Exploring gaze data for determining user learning with an interactive simulation. In S. Carberry, S. Weibelzahl, A. Micarelli, & G. Semeraro (Eds.), *Proceedings of the 20th International Conference on User Modeling, Adaptation, and Personalization (UMAP 2012)* (pp. 126–138). Berlin: Springer.

Kinchla, R. A. (1992). Attention. *Annual Review of Psychology, 43*, 711–743.

Knoblich, G., Öllinger, M., & Spivey, M. J. (2005). Tracking the eyes to obtain insight into insight problem solving. In G. Underwood (Ed.), *Cognitive processes in eye guidance* (pp. 355–375). Oxford: Oxford University Press.

Larson, R. W., & Richards, M. H. (1991). Boredom in the middle school years—Blaming schools versus blaming students. *American Journal of Education, 99*(4), 418–443.

Linnenbrink, E. (2007). The role of affect in student learning: A mulit-dimensional approach to considering the interaction of affect, motivation and engagement. In P. Schutz & R. Pekrun (Eds.), *Emotions in education* (pp. 107–124). San Diego, CA: Academic Press.

Liu, N.-H., Chiang, C.-Y., & Chu, H.-C. (2013). Recognizing the degree of human attention using EEG signals from mobile sensors. *Sensors, 13*(8), 10273–10286.

Mann, S., & Robinson, A. (2009). Boredom in the lecture theatre: An investigation into the contributors, moderators and outcomes of boredom amongst university students. *British Educational Research Journal, 35*(2), 243–258.

Marshall, S. P. (2005). Assessing cognitive engagement and cognitive state from eye metrics. In D. D. Schmorrow (Ed.), *Foundations of augmented cognition* (pp. 312–320). Mahwah, NJ: Lawrence Erlbaum Associates.

Mathews, M., Mitrovic, A., Lin, B., Holland, J., & Churcher, N. (2012). Do your eyes give it away? Using eye tracking data to understand students' attitudes towards open student model representations. In S. A. Cerri, W. J. Clancey, G. Papadourakis, & K.-K. Panourgia (Eds.), *Proceedings of the 11th International Conference on Intelligent Tutoring Systems* (pp. 422–427). Berlin: Springer.

Mehu, M., & Scherer, K. (2012). A psycho-ethological approach to social signal processing. *Cognitive Processing, 13*(2), 397–414.

Mills, C., Gregg, J., Bixler, R., & D'Mello, S. K. (in prep.). Dynamic "deep" attentional reengagement during reading via automated mind wandering detection.

Mills, C., & D'Mello, S. K. (2015). Toward a real-time (day) dreamcatcher: Detecting mind wandering episodes during online reading. In C. Romero, M. Pechenizkiy, J. Boticario, & O. Santos (Eds.), *Proceedings of the 8th International Conference on Educational Data Mining (EDM 2015)*. International Educational Data Mining Society.

Moreno, R. (2005). Instructional technology: Promise and pitfalls. In L. PytlikZillig, M. Bodvarsson, & R. Bruning (Eds.), *Technology-based education: Bringing researchers and practitioners together* (pp. 1–19). Greenwich, CT: Information Age Publishing.

Moreno, R., & Mayer, R. (2007). Interactive multimodal learning environments. *Educational Psychology Review, 19*(3), 309–326. https://doi.org/10.1007/s10648-007-9047-2

Moss, J., Schunn, C. D., Schneider, W., & McNamara, D. S. (2013). The nature of mind wandering during reading varies with the cognitive control demands of the reading strategy. *Brain Research, 1539*, 48–60.

Moss, J., Schunn, C. D., VanLehn, K., Schneider, W., McNamara, D. S., & Jarbo, K. (2008). They were trained, but they did not all learn: Individual differences in uptake of learning strategy training. In B. C. Love, K. McRae, & V. M. Sloutsky (Eds.), *Proceedings of the 30th Annual Meeting of the Cognitive Science Society* (pp. 1389–1395). Austin, TX: Cognitive Science Society.

Muir, M., & Conati, C. (2012). An analysis of attention to student–adaptive hints in an educational game. In S. A. Cerri, W. J. Clancey, G. Papadourakis, & K. Panourgia (Eds.), *Proceedings of the International Conference on Intelligent Tutoring Systems* (pp. 112–122). Berlin: Springer.

Navalpakkam, V., Kumar, R., Li, L., & Sivakumar, D. (2012). *Attention and selection in online choice tasks*. Paper presented at the Proceedings of the International Conference on User Modeling, Adaptation, and Personalization.

Olney, A., D'Mello, A., Person, N., Cade, W., Hays, P., Williams, C., et al. (2012). Guru: A computer tutor that models expert human tutors. In S. Cerri, W. Clancey, G. Papadourakis, & K. Panourgia (Eds.), *Proceedings of the 11th International Conference on Intelligent Tutoring Systems* (pp. 256–261). Berlin: Springer.

Paas, F., Renkl, A., & Sweller, J. (2003). Cognitive load theory and instructional design: Recent developments. *Educational Psychologist, 38*(1), 1–4.

Patall, E., Cooper, H., & Robinson, J. (2008). The effects of choice on intrinsic motivation and related outcomes: A meta-analysis of research findings. *Psychological Bulletin, 134*(2), 270–300.

Pekrun, R., Goetz, T., Daniels, L., Stupnisky, R. H., & Perry, R. (2010). Boredom in achievement settings: Exploring control–value antecedents and performance outcomes of a neglected emotion. *Journal of Educational Psychology, 102*(3), 531–549. https://doi.org/10.1037/a0019243

Pham, P., & Wang, J. (2015). AttentiveLearner: Improving mobile MOOC learning via implicit heart rate tracking. In *International Conference on Artificial Intelligence in Education* (pp. 367–376). Berlin: Springer.

Picard, R. (1997). *Affective computing*. Cambridge, MA: MIT Press.

Ponce, H. R., & Mayer, R. E. (2014). Qualitatively different cognitive processing during online reading primed by different study activities. *Computers in Human Behavior, 30*(1), 121–130.

Rayner, K. (1998). Eye movements in reading and information processing: 20 years of research. *Psychological Bulletin, 124*(3), 372–422.

Roda, C., & Thomas, J. (2006). Attention aware systems: Theories, applications, and research agenda. *Computers in Human Behavior, 22*(4), 557–587. https://doi.org/10.1016/j.chb.2005.12.005

Schnotz, W. (2005). An integrated model of text and picture comprehension. In R. Mayer (Ed.), *The Cambridge handbook of multimedia learning* (pp. 49–69). New York: Cambridge University Press.

Schnotz, W., & Bannert, M. (2003). Construction and interference in learning from multiple representation. *Learning and Instruction, 13*(2), 141–156.

Seli, P., Risko, E. F., & Smilek, D. (2016). On the necessity of distinguishing between unintentional and intentional mind wandering. *Psychological Science, 27*(5), 685–691.

Shernoff, D. J., Csikszentmihalyi, M., Shneider, B., & Shernoff, E. S. (2003). Student engagement in high school classrooms from the perspective of flow theory. *School Psychology Quarterly, 18*(2), 158.

Sibert, J. L., Gokturk, M., & Lavine, R. A. (2000). The reading assistant: Eye gaze triggered auditory prompting for reading remediation. In *Proceedings of the 13th annual ACM Symposium on User Interface Software and Technology* (pp. 101–107). New York, NY: ACM.

Smallwood, J., Fishman, D. J., & Schooler, J. W. (2007). Counting the cost of an absent mind: Mind wandering as an underrecognized influence on educational performance. *Psychonomic Bulletin & Review, 14*(2), 230–236.

Smallwood, J., & Schooler, J. W. (2015). The science of mind wandering: Empirically navigating the stream of consciousness. *Annual Review of Psychology, 66*, 487–518.

Sottilare, R., Graesser, A., Hu, X., & Holden, H. K. (Eds.). (2013). *Design recommendations for intelligent tutoring systems: Volume 1: Learner modeling*. Orlando, FL: U.S. Army Research Laboratory.

Sparfeldt, J. R., Buch, S. R., Schwarz, F., Jachmann, J., & Rost, D. H. (2009). "Maths is boring"—Boredom in mathematics in elementary school children. *Psychologie in Erziehung und Unterricht, 56*(1), 16–26.

St. John, M., Kobus, D. A., Morrison, J. G., & Schmorrow, D. (2004). Overview of the DARPA augmented cognition technical integration experiment. *International Journal of Human Computer Interaction, 17*(2), 131–149.

Stawarczyk, D., Majerus, S., Maj, M., Van der Linden, M., & D'Argembeau, A. (2011). Mind-wandering: Phenomenology and function as assessed with a novel experience sampling method. *Acta Psychologica, 136*(3), 370–381.

Steichen, B., Wu, M. M., Toker, D., Conati, C., & Carenini, G. (2014). Te, Te, Hi, Hi: Eye gaze sequence analysis for informing user-adaptive information visualizations. In V. Dimitrova, T. Kuflik, D. Chin, F. Ricci, P. Dolog, & G.-J. Houben (Eds.), *Proceedings of the 22nd International Conference on User Modeling, Adaptation, and Personalization* (pp. 183–194). Basel: Springer.

Stewart, A., Bosch, N., Chen, H., Donnelly, P., & D'Mello, S. (2017). Face forward: Detecting mind wandering from video during narrative film comprehension. In E. André, R. Baker, X. Hu, M. Rodrigo, & B. du Boulay (Eds.), *Proceedings of the 18th International Conference on Artificial Intelligence in Education (AIED 2017)* (pp. 359–370). Berlin: Springer.

Strain, A., Azevedo, R., & D'Mello, S. K. (2013). Using a false biofeedback methodology to explore relationships between learners' affect, metacognition, and performance. *Contemporary Educational Psychology, 38*(1), 22–39.

Strain, A., & D'Mello, S. (2014). Affect regulation during learning: The enhancing effect of cognitive reappraisal. *Applied Cognitive Psychology, 29*(1), 1–19. https://doi.org/10.1002/acp.3049

Sun, J. C.-Y., & Yeh, K. P.-C. (2017). The effects of attention monitoring with EEG biofeedback on university students' attention and self-efficacy: The case of anti-phishing instructional materials. *Computers & Education, 106*, 73–82.

Szpunar, K. K., Khan, N. Y., & Schacter, D. L. (2013). Interpolated memory tests reduce mind wandering and improve learning of online lectures. *Proceedings of the National Academy of Sciences, 110*(16), 6313–6317.

Tobias, S. (1994). Interest, prior knowledge, and learning. *Review of Educational Research, 64*, 37–54.

van Gog, T., Jarodzka, H., Scheiter, K., Gerjets, P., & Paas, F. (2009). Attention guidance during example study via the model's eye movements. *Computers in Human Behavior, 25*(3), 785–791. https://doi.org/10.1016/j.chb.2009.02.007

van Gog, T., & Scheiter, K. (2010). Eye tracking as a tool to study and enhance multimedia learning. *Learning and Instruction, 20*(2), 95–99.

Vinciarelli, A., Pantic, M., & Bourlard, H. (2009). Social signal processing: Survey of an emerging domain. *Image and Vision Computing, 27*(12), 1743–1759.

Wang, H., Chignell, M., & Ishizuka, M. (2006). Empathic tutoring software agents using real-time eye tracking. In *Proceedings of the 2006 Symposium on Eye Tracking Research & Applications* (pp. 73–78). New York: ACM.

Whitehill, J., Serpell, Z., Lin, Y.-C., Foster, A., & Movellan, J. (2014). The faces of engagement: Automatic recognition of student engagement from facial expressions. *IEEE Transactions on Affective Computing, 5*(1), 86–98.

Yonetani, R., Kawashima, H., & Matsuyama, T. (2012). *Multi-mode saliency dynamics model for analyzing gaze and attention.* Paper presented at the Proceedings of the Symposium on Eye Tracking Research and Applications.

Sidney K. D'Mello (Ph.D. in Computer Science) is an Associate Professor in the Institute of Cognitive Science and Department of Computer Science at the University of Colorado Boulder. He is interested in the dynamic interplay between cognition and emotion while people engage in complex real-world tasks. He applies insights gleaned from this basic research program to develop intelligent technologies that help people achieve their fullest potential by coordinating what they think and feel with what they know and do. D'Mello has coedited six books and published over 220 journal papers, book chapters, and conference proceedings (13 of these have received awards). His work has been funded by over 25 grants and he serves/has served as associate editor for three journals, on the editorial boards for four others, and has played leadership roles in several professional organizations.

Chapter 7
Using Motion Capture Technologies to Provide Advanced Feedback and Scaffolds for Learning

Andreja Istenic Starcic, William Mark Lipsmeyer, and Lin Lin

Abstract In this chapter, we take the stand that cognition and learning are embodied in psychomotor activities and socio-cultural contexts, and they are mediated by technologies on the enactive, iconic, and symbolic representational levels. We discuss motion or body movements as an integral part of cognition and learning. The particular focus is on the role of motion capture technologies in integrating body, sensorimotor engagement, and feedback in learning. Motion capture technologies may help assist learning in several ways: (1) fascilitating seamless human–computer interaction; (2) connecting the enactive learning to observation and to model-based learning; (3) linking body motion to psychological reactions and states. Traditionally, computer-based learning has supported visual and symbolic representations. Advanced motion capture technologies connect physical and virtual environments, support enactive representations, connect different types of representations, and provide smart and sophisticated feedback to improve learning.

Introduction

The idiom "practice makes perfect" may be better stated as "practice with proper feedback makes perfect," because practice without feedback may actually lead to a wrong concept or bad habit that is difficult to unlearn (Schwartz, Tsang, & Blair, 2016). This chapter focuses on the more recent advancements being made in smart technologies, learning sciences, and learning theories that are dramatically

A. I. Starcic
Faculty of Education, University of Primorska, Koper, Slovenia

University of Ljubljana, Ljubljana, Slovenia

W. M. Lipsmeyer
Zoic Studios, LA, Culver City, CA, USA

L. Lin (✉)
University of North Texas, Denton, TX, USA
e-mail: lin.lin@unt.edu

© Association for Educational Communications and Technology 2019
T. D. Parsons et al. (eds.), *Mind, Brain and Technology*, Educational
Communications and Technology: Issues and Innovations,
https://doi.org/10.1007/978-3-030-02631-8_7

changing the learning landscape. These changes are helping us better incorporate model-based learning, adding enactive learning to the visual and conceptual representations of a learner's cognitive dissonance. We discuss how motion capture can help augment the zone of proximal development (Vygotsky, 1978), and how models of learners' scaffolding can be enhanced through virtual technologies integrating motor actions.

When a learner suddenly becomes aware that he or she is lacking in some area of ability or is having a gap in learning, either through a newly acquired knowledge or through a mentoring process, the cognitive dissonance becomes a prime motivational mover (Festinger, 1962). Cognitive dissonance can emerge within the learner in numerous ways. For the purpose of this chapter, we are interested in the new capabilities of fast-developing technologies that may help a learner eliminate the cognitive dissonance and create consistency more quickly.

The JOHARI window (Luft & Ingham, 1955) provides a map of a learner's self-knowledge as situated in a self-awareness framework and a feedback model (Fig. 7.1). It describes the difference between how one views himself or herself, and how others view him or her with regard to their behavior, knowledge, skills, attitudes, deep-seated issues, and personal history. Within the four quadrants, quadrant 1 is the part that we and others see or know about us. Quadrant 2 contains aspects that others see but we are unaware or do not know. Quadrant 3 is the private space we know but hide from others. Quadrant 4 is the unconscious part of us that neither others nor we see or know. This is a useful framework to discuss the beginning emergence of cognitive dissonance.

Technology-supported feedback could contribute in the area of blind self and in unknown self. Technology-supported feedback could provide teachers with information on the learning process and the learning outcomes. This information could be used as feedback to students directly or indirectly through teaching mediation. In

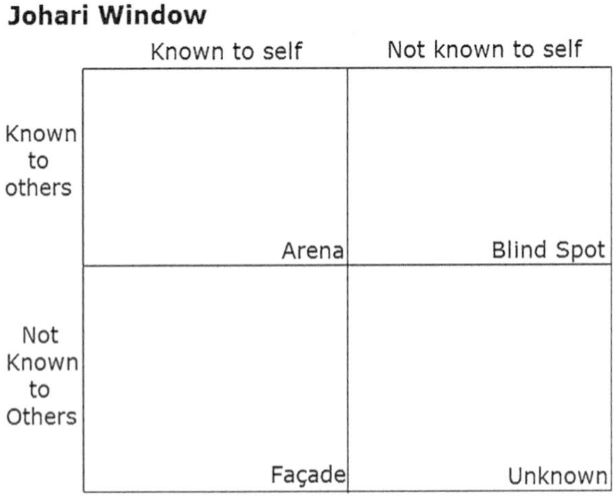

Johari Window

	Known to self	Not known to self
Known to others	Arena	Blind Spot
Not Known to Others	Façade	Unknown

Fig. 7.1 JOHARI window (public domain)

the classroom situation where one teacher is responsible for feedback to many students, the technology-supported feedback could add in efficiency and quality. Below, we will discuss the motion capture feedback connecting physical and virtual environments and connecting different types of representations.

Embodied Cognition and Learning

In this section, we will discuss four important components, that is, the observation, occlusions, detachment, and resonance that form as foundations for multiple representations, reflective feedback, and embodied learning.

Observation is possibly the oldest form of learning. Bandura's social cognitive learning theory (1977) emphasized observation and modelling taking a variety of forms in real-life or imaginative/fictional contexts. He distinguished between life, verbal, and symbolic models. Observation oftentimes must precede planning. As part of the scientific method, categorizing or unpacking observations can be key to human understanding. Intertwined with observation is the issue of one's particular point of view. A person's awareness and observation tend to be anchored to one observation point or angle. From that relative viewpoint, the observer has but one unique perspective on the world. As told in the parable of the blind men and an elephant, humans have a tendency to project their partial experiences as the whole truth, ignore other people's partial experiences. One can look at this as both an advantage and a disadvantage. While the angle may be unique in that no other person has that observation from that one point in time, a single viewer of an activity has unique blind spots or occlusions as well.

An *occlusion* occurs when a single viewer cannot see something due to the perspective being blocked or shadowed by another actor or object blocking their line of sight, thereby creating an obstruction in space and time. Occlusions occur naturally and are a result of a singular point of view. Occlusions present a problem to be solved when activities or observations in time are being recreated for learning purposes (Cheng & Davis, 2000). The resolutions of these awareness issues generally come by selecting a different point of view that does not have the occlusion, an opportunity to see and recreate from a collective omniscient perspective, as the resultant lack of knowledge is then mitigated by unmasking the blind spots which have been collectively processed from within the observed volume. When these blind spots are mitigated over intervals of time, a full reconstruction of all activity in the 3D volume can be made with no blind spots present. This is the omniscient view.

A basic premise of learning is that a teacher does not knowingly put out false information to a student (Bodner, 1986). Accurate awareness is key to understanding; suggesting otherwise for the purpose of brevity often puts the learners at a disadvantage, since more time is then required to "un-learn" or deconstruct something that was taught inappropriately or characterized untruthfully (von Glasersfeld, 1995). Partial representation of the facts often has the same negative impact as a learner's lack of the complete picture can negatively affect his or her full under-standing of the activities and relationships being presented. These philosophical precepts seem basic enough so that mentors and teachers spend the requisite time in making sure that representations and observations are made accurately.

Alexander (1964) talks at length about design nodes and the connectivity between linked nodes in a design. One of the things he highlights is that functionality in a design is oftentimes constricted by the hard links made (Alexander, 1964). These hard links are characterized by connections in the physical world of construction like cables, girders, and other material objects that limit flexibility but add structure and rigidity. While others may think of this as a loss of a degree of freedom, Alexander points to both the advantages and disadvantages of hard connections that humans make in their designs. Alexander clearly believes that when hard connec-tions are made, many designers have not fully considered the loss of functionality as a result of a connection to a particular node. Today, as we further investigate network theory, we are more aware of the loss of freedom or functionality because of a hard connection to a specific design node. A simple life example would be that a person holding an object in his or her hands would have to put down the object to free up the hands to pick up something else. Using this example, we can better understand what we mean by detachment and the importance of being detached or invoking detachment in order to gain a different perspective, free of occlusions.

Detachment is a higher form of observation (Trungpa & Fremantle, 2000). Trungpa and Fremantle (2000) placed great value on the experience of being "in the flow" of, and devoting one's total awareness of being in the focused moment of "being one" with one's activity such as dancing, playing the piano, or jogging. Meanwhile, they also placed great emphasis on one's ability to be able to detach, refocus one's center of awareness outside of the activity, pulling the self outside of the flow, to acquire the perspective of being a detached observer. While the detach-ment might cause one to lose the feeling and intuition of the flow, one is now afforded a new perspective of being the detached observer of one's own actions, a trusted position of observation. This new perspective is no longer burdened by emo-tional investment in the proximate happenings of the evolving actor. Through our detachment we are no longer part of the flow, but are afforded a new position of detached, logical, and informed observation, viewing our own activity from the desired position of impartial judgment.

Since the case has been made for detachment, it would only be fair to make a similar case for **resonance**. Kozulin (1999) talks at length about the importance of resonance in human psychology and learning. Kozulin characterizes resonance between and among humans as almost a supernatural or otherworldly, preferring to describe the feelings that ensue because of one human expressing something that resonates deeply with another as a newly forged but lasting bond that cannot be eas-ily broken. Since many things resonate with others purely on the emotional level or feelings, it is sometimes difficult to accurately measure or account for the impact of this resonance on a learner. For learning that can occur on a logical, factual, kines-thetic, and emotional level, the learner can be deeply touched. If this kind of learning

can transpire on all of these levels simultaneously it can make a substantially positive impact on the learner.

Observation, occlusion, detachment, and resonance help us understand different
levels of feedback, which we will discuss in more detail below.

Feedback for Learning

There exist different kinds of feedback. Feedback is information that flows back to
learners about their hidden or unknown selves, or about the quality of their ideas
and behaviors (Schwartz et al., 2016). For instance, reinforcement feedback uses
rewards to encourage a learner to repeat, or uses punishments to force a learner to
change their behaviors. Good informative feedback helps a learner to locate a dis-
crepancy between the current outcome and the desired goal, so the learner can
make improvements. Both positive feedback and negative feedback can be informative for learning (Schwartz et al., 2016). Kluger and DeNisi (1996) conducted a
meta-analysis of 131 studies that compared learning with and without feedback.
Their analysis demonstrated that on average, feedback interventions raised student
scores compared to interventions that did not include opportunities for feedback.
Hattie and Timperley (2007) reported the results of a meta-analysis of meta-analy-
ses, which indicated that on average, including feedback had a large positive effect
on student learning.

Representations are essential in learning and have been considered from a developmental perspective, where the transition from enactive to abstract has been seen
as progressing towards the development of abstract thinking. The cognitive developmental theory by Piaget (1952) indicates stages of child development although
the theory has informed instructional design beyond preschool and elementary
education. The stages include the sensory stage, perceptional, concrete operational,
and the formal operational stage. Vygotsky (1978) considered learning and development in interaction with the socio-cultural environment and mediated by tools.
Bruner's model of learning (1966) was based on modelling and transiting between
representations. The representations according to Bruner (1966) are on the level of
actions (enactive), images (iconic), and symbolic or logical propositions (symbolic). Bandura explores the enactive mastery (performance), vicarious learning
(observation and modelling), verbal enhancement and psychological and affective
states and responses in learning through interaction in a social environment. The
observation and modelling take a variety of forms in real-life or in imaginative/
fictional contexts. He distinguished between life, verbal, and symbolic models.
These processes are underlined by symbolization, self-reflection, self-regulation,
and anticipation (Bandura, 1977).

The role of the sensorimotor system and bodily experience has been connected
to the enactive level. The notion of cognitive activity as compared with perception
and psychomotor activity lies within the focus of embodied cognition. In socio-

cultural theories, cognition is situated in a socio-cultural context and is mediated by tools and/or symbolic systems such as language (Vygotsky, 1978). The embodied technology engages the body through human–computer interaction and supports cognition and learning with body activities. Embodied cognition focuses on perception and bodily activity as an integral part of learning, taking into account cognitive activities in the context of the physical world and social interactions (Anderson, 2003; Barsalou, 2008).

In the learning processes, the diagnostic, formative, and summative feedback are essential for scaffolding and guiding learners. Diagnostic feedback focuses on prerequisite knowledge and the learners' readiness for learning, while formative and summative feedback are concerned about learning outcomes and learners' engagements. The engagement paradigm refers to emotional, behavioral, cognitive, and agentic engagements (D'Mello, Dieterle, & Duckworth, 2017). Black and Wiliam (2009) define formative feedback as a formative interaction situation in which an external stimulus such as a feedback interacts with a learner's activity and influences his or her cognition. In skills learning, the intrinsic feedback comes from the sensory perceptual information and is a natural part of performance while the extrinsic feedback is discussed as an augmented feedback, an add-on to the intrinsic feedback (Walchli, Ruffieux, Bourquin, Keller, & Taube, 2016). According to Rosati, Oscari, Spagnol, Avanzini, and Masiero (2012), augmented feedback could be visual, auditory, haptic, or multimodal, and it is classified according to the task execution, during the task, concurrent, real-time feedback or after task, the terminal feedback.

Embodied cognition focuses on the link between the neurological, bodily, and psychological states, providing bio-feedback learning support. D'Mello et al. (2017) discuss the eye-mind link, brain-mind link, and the mind-body link. Learning technology integrates computer simulations with physical or embodied interactions (Wallon & Lindgren, 2017), providing the enactive feedback in a range of frequency and contexts. Connecting the three perspectives—person-in-context, context-oriented perspective, and person-in-context perspective (Sinatra, Heddy, & Lombardi, 2015), advanced motion capture technology could provide scaffolds and feedback related to changes of learning individually (person-oriented perspective) and in groups in diverse real-life or virtual environments (the context-oriented perspective). The person-in-context perspective is facing new opportunities in mixed learning environments that require more complex learning analytics. The motion capture technologies utilize seamless human–computer interactions, provides feedback connecting the enactive learning to observation and model-based learning, and links body motion to psychological reactions and states (Johnson-Glenberg, Birchfield, Tolentino, & Koziupa, 2014).

Using Motion Capture Technologies to Scaffold Expertise and Reflective Feedback

Digital practices, for example, digital games, have the potential to introduce whole-body experiences (Bianchi-Berthouze, Kim, & Patel, 2007). Important streams of motion capture technology have been used to offer more natural types of interactions. An example is the Wii console, which uses a type of embedded motion capture device (Bianchi-Berthouze et al., 2007). This motion capture technology could be used for transitioning body movements from a physical into a virtual space in the process of creating a mixed reality (Istenic Starcic, Lipsmeyer, & Lin, 2018).

With the development of learning technologies and motion tracking sensors, the psychomotor learning domain and embodiment of learning in physical activity are considered. The affordance of the motion capture technology supports the inclusion of sensual knowledge and body motion in the cognitive processes of learning. In the current landscape of increasingly digitalized schooling and social practices in general, the affordance of motion capture technology adds to learning in two ways: seamless human–computer interaction and model-based learning. It includes body movement in different types of representations in learning and connects real-life physical environments to virtual space.

In traditional motion capture on a movie set, a massive framework called a trestle is created which might house over 100 cameras, capture motions accurately, and are collectively integrated over time. A lot of time, effort, and money are invested in getting rid of all of the occlusions to recreate the activity that transpired inside of the 3D volume. What goes unspoken though is that all of this effort is expended for the purpose of getting a true representation of what actually transpired on set with all of the actors interacting, working, and relating in unison with one another.

Motion capture technologies have been implemented to link body movements to various psychological reactions and states. For instance, they have been used to support the communication of emotional information, whole-body movement, biological movement, and the analysis of affective states or responses based on posture features, body gestures, and expressive body movements (Castellano, Villalba, & Camurri, 2007; Crane & Gross, 2007; Kim, Maloney, Bruder, Bailenson, & Welch, 2017; Kleinsmith & Bianchi-Berthouze, 2007).

Moving and working from within a controlled 3D volume offers unique capabilities for both learners and teachers. Among the many advantages offered by working kinesthetically in a motion capture volume is the ability to approach an omniscient view. Motion tracking sensors in a physical space, on a computer console, or attached to a person (smart suit), allow the possibility to look at observed activities with no occlusions. In other words, the collective observers can look at something with no blind spots. The technology allows the capture of the activity from many more viewpoints simultaneously; so that any blind spots or occlusions can be overcome and the skeletal structure of the activity can be known from any point of view. In re-creating the activity from within the 3D volume being examined, this capability has a dramatic impact on the veracity of the representations being captured or being observed and played back for purposes of repeatability.

Imagine, for example, in a learning space such as the Second Life, the actor/learner is able to enter the volume or simulation wearing a 3D motion capture suit. Now, instead of using only a computer and keyboard interface, the learner enters the simulation with the potential for full body emersion and a holistic learning experience. He or she now has the potential to learn and experience the activity thinking from the perspective of the whole body, moving about in the new environment as an integral part of the environment rather than relying on a somewhat abstract haptic experience of merely touching a keyboard and looking at a screen (Cordes & Miller, 2000; Lindgren & Moshell, 2011).

Humans appropriate knowledge in many different ways. The human brain has a profound ability to characterize and generalize observable findings from an experience creating abstractions. Such abstractions can be extracted and elevated to a meta-level for further generalization and analysis. However, on an individual learner's level, it is critical to examine the positive and negative impacts of the user interface deeply since these interfaces either enhance the learning experience or create a filter or roadblock for the motivated learner. From the view of the learner, oftentimes the interface being used works against the viability of learning the intended learning objective. In some cases, the clumsiness of the interface actually inhibits the possibility of the learner learning the intended learning point. Motion capture has the potential of removing some important barriers to learning (Waibel, Vo, Duchnowski, & Manke, 1996). While the method of appropriation may not be well understood, a learner often appropriates or obtains knowledge through mimicry and practice, usually adopted or evolved as these actions are fit for some specific purposes. A sea otter might use a rock to crack open an oyster shell to get at the food source inside; a chimpanzee might use a stick to root out some tasty insect from a hole in the ground. These acquired developments and the fashioning of tools from one's environment point to the ability of acquiring knowledge at the most basic kinesthetic level.

Any discussion of motion capture for learning should include a discussion about the bifurcation or split in requirements that are currently being demonstrated in the area of design. As the state of the art of design requirements seems to be splitting to design requirements for human learning and design requirements for machine learning, it is quite apparent that through Artificial Intelligence (AI) it will not be long before human designers are designing learning environments for both humans and machines (Asada, MacDorman, Ishiguro, & Kuniyoshi, 2001). This brings up an important dichotomy. Sometime soon within the next 10 years, it will be important in requirements engineering to make the distinction as to whether we are writing design requirements for humans or machines to implement (Russell & Norvig, 2016). The design of learning environments is no exception in this regard. One can envision that the design requirements for a human learning system would be quite different from the design requirements of a machine learning system. Yet, it will become very important to make the distinctions of learning systems for humans or learning systems for machines. As machines take over the role of creating design requirements for Artificial Intelligence and other machines, humans need to pay attention to the nuances and needs of their own evolved state vis-à-vis machine learning. It is interesting to think about the types of shortcuts that might be feasible once machines start designing requirements to advance their own intelligence. Motion capture helps preserve the requirements that allow for the full body experience of a human being acting seamlessly and independently in a three-dimensional space (Waibel et al., 1996).

The saying "all models are wrong, but some are useful" is largely attributed to the British statistician George Edward Pelham Box (Box, 1976). The wisdom largely proceeds from the fact that every model, due to its nature as a representation, does not, in fact, perfectly represent the real nature of the object it tries to represent. By nature, models are generally simplifications and oftentimes exaggerations of the activity or object being modelled. When we extract, analyze, generalize, and extrapolate sometimes we make assumptions that are inaccurate and over-simplified. Yet, as Box states, some models can be useful.

As shown in Fig. 7.2 below, some very basic physical attributes are examined in detail during the process of motion capture. In the most basic of states, an object's position is plotted or tracked over time. Each connected position is integrated relationally over the same equidistant interval of time to calculate the precise new position in a given sequence. To be more accurate, one does not make a prediction of where the object will be in the future, one merely records what happened in the past or is currently happening, and then lets the fluid motion representation stand on its own merit. In effect, the detailed representation literally takes on a "life" of its own. This record of movement represents a change in state over time. Scientists, technologists, engineers, mathematicians, musicians, athletes, and other artists spend a lot of time looking at, noticing, and recording moving objects over time so that they

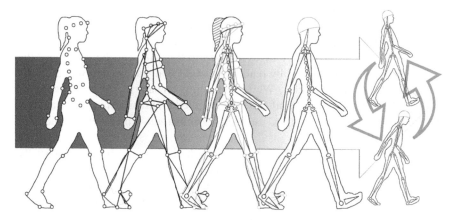

Fig. 7.2 Example of one possible motion capture feedback loop. *Note: in the sequence of: Physical Markers—Labelling—Solved Skeleton—End Result—Realistic Variations of the End Result(s)*

can better understand the nature of the thing that they are studying. We might say that the study of movement is largely a cross-cutting effort that involves all aspects of human endeavor.

In motion capture, the value of the undertaking comes from the fact that the points in a three-dimensional volume are tracked to be rotated and examined, over time. The value of this effort cannot be attained without two very important things: rotation and position. Points are being examined through rotation in a 3D space to look for occlusions and blind spots. A highly trained technical expert visually examines plotted points in space, rotates the volume, tracks and corrects the point's position, and corrects the relational or missing point position in order to recreate the smooth flow of the object through space and time. The "relationships" of relative points are then accurately tracked through space and time. This allows the object's motion to be represented accurately, captured, played back, shared, and characterized. The importance of these collected states in terms of representing the nature of something cannot be over-emphasized, as collectively they largely represent the essence of the value of the sense of sight. To be able to sense the nature of the thing over time, and to be able to do this in a detached or separated state from the object being examined, represents a new technology. We have yet to understand its full ramifications for teaching and learning.

In statistics, a *Varimax Rotation* largely derives its value through the accurate plotting of the relationship of a group of valued numbers over a set interval (Kaiser, 1958). The actual coordinate system is unchanged; rather it is the orthogonal basis being rotated to align with a set of coordinates. Responding to a representative field of plotted values, mathematicians have discovered that often times the value of the relationships exist independent of the axis of rotation of the field, and that all the observer needs to do is simply rotate the relative plot, keeping the relationships of the various points the same, while finding a rotation that resonates with the observer for purposes of observation of multiple viewers. That is, mathematicians are not about to let the static and initially discovered axis of rotation improperly characterize a set of relationships when all they need to do is to rotate the relational mass to the correct axis to better represent what they are trying to model. While there may be exceptions to this rule, for the most part, the model becomes useful merely by realizing that all that was needed was a proper rotation in order to be useful. While some might characterize this change as flawed, others see it only as another degree of freedom in mathematics created by the ability to unlink from a restrictive constraint and view something independently.

Ontologically, humans have evolved largely based on our abilities to visually process the observation of movement of objects and things. We make decisions all the time based on contrast, movement, and the resultant characterization of movement that is fit for our own particular adaptive and evolutionary processes. Sometimes, we call these evolutionary processes learning.

Defined Feedback Loops for Motion Capture

Here, we define five separate feedback loops necessary for learning using motion capture. First, there needs to be "the director's intention feedback loop" (i.e., the Strategic Intention Loop) (Troy, Erignac, & Murray, 2006). When a director decides to make a movie or film using motion capture the director lays out an intended path even before the pre-visualization technicians plan the visual layouts. In learning, the equivalent step is for the instructional (system) designer to lay out the learning objectives necessary for the intended learning. A movie director is guided by the script or story line, while the instructional designer will decide the sequence of the learning objectives to be met and the desired motions that will be captured for visual discovery. The expected cognitive dissonance opportunities would be mapped and planned.

Second, the actual planning of how the motion capture of the learning motion is planned (i.e., Capture Planning) and directed with its cameras, suits, and 3D volume set. This feedback loop involves a number of technicians who actually plan and capture the motion using cameras or other relevant technologies. These technicians advise the director and ensure the truthfulness of the scene, episode, or learning point. They ensure that the "look" and "feel" that the director intends is faithfully represented so the proper events are captured accurately and are available for playback in a fashion that will ultimately benefit the learner.

Third, the technicians who planned the event execute the capture process and use their multiple perspectives to illuminate and discard the natural occlusions [i.e., Veracity Loop] that might present during the capture process. They strive to approximate the omniscient view. These technicians strive for a highly accurate view or representation, but work together to ensure that multiple perspectives are incorporated and that the event in progress is an accurate representation of reality.

Fourth, before the viewer or learner is presented with the representation of the learning episode or recreation the technicians review the motion capture with the Director of Learning to make certain the style, intention, and feel of the motion capture was achieved as intended [i.e., Intended Effect Loop]. During the production of a film or movie, these reviews occur often and are referred to as "dailies" as they tend to occur each day to ensure the look of the motion being captured achieves the intuitive "feel" that the director intended is actually taking shape as planned. Oftentimes the technicians will need to adjust the timing, layout or edit the episode or vignette in order to achieve the desired effect. Once the director and the technicians are in agreement and the desired effect has been achieved it is then ready for the learner to view.

Fifth, the learner is finally shown the motion capture representation and becomes familiar with the first level of awareness which is his or her entry level state or awareness of self-state (i.e., Cognitive Dissonance Loop). This motion capture then becomes the entry level for the cognitive dissonance which is expected to occur. On multiple incidences of motion capture, the progressive states of the learner are captured and analyzed for improvement.

As this process matures over time and through multiple iterations, each player (director, technician, ISD designer, teacher, learner) becomes more familiar with the limits of his or her authority the degrees of freedom afforded inside of the process. The learner will become more aware of difference between his or her entry level state and his desired state and incrementally makes improvements in his actions to refine his understanding of the causes of the differences. At the same time, the finished products of the motion capture videos act both as evidence and as learning artifacts that can be shared with realistic measurement of the improvements being made over time.

Conclusions and the Future Directions

Many educational programs have well-conceptualized instructions, but they fail to provide provisions of effective feedback (Schwartz et al., 2016). Feedback that is specific, timely, understandable, and nonthreatening can help students learn the desired task and reach the desired outcome. Good feedback is aligned with the learner's prior knowledge and experiences as well as the projected models and goals. The digitalization of life has been aligned with body-mind dualism and the passivation and decontextualization of the body in human–computer interaction. With motion capture technologies, the embodiment of the cognition in psychomotor activity is taking place. To draw our conclusion from the developmental perspective, which informs learning in all stages, a child's development depends on the child's psychophysical and emotion social activities. With the computer's proliferation into our day-to-day life and especially human leisure activity, locomotion and sensorimotor experiences are being downgraded. The enactive activities and the feedback of such authentic engagements, which are essential in a child's learning and development, have been missing in the environment.

Through embodied cognition, we recognize the importance of the physical body in defining cognition and learning. Learning technologies have been predominantly based visually on symbolic representations. Using motion capture technology based on the notion of embodied cognition, body motion and sensual perceptions could be equally considered.

References

Alexander, C. (1964). *Notes on the synthesis of form*. Cambridge, MA: Harvard University Press.
Anderson, M. L. (2003). Embodied cognition: A field guide. *Artificial inteligence, 149*, 91–130.
Asada, M., MacDorman, K., Ishiguro, H., & Kuniyoshi, Y. (2001). Cognitive developmental robotics as a new paradigm for the design of humanoid robots. *Robotics and Autonomous Systems, 37*(2–3), 185–193.
Bandura, A. (1977). *Social learning theory*. Englewood Cliffs, NJ: Prentice Hall.
Barsalou, L. W. (2008). Grounded cognition. *Annual Review of Psychology, 59*, 617–645.

Bianchi-Berthouze, N., Kim, W. W., & Patel, D. (2007). Does body movement engage you more in digital game play? And why? In A. Paiva, R. Prada, & R. W. Picard (Eds.), *ACII 2007, LNCS* (Vol. 4738, pp. 102–113). New York: ACM.

Black, P., & Wiliam, D. (2009). Developing the theory of formal assessment. *Educational Assessment, Evaluation and Accountability, 21*(1), 5.

Box, G. E. P. (1976). Science and Statistics. *Journal of the American Statistical Association, 71*, 791–799. https://doi.org/10.1080/01621459.1976.10480949

Bruner, J. S. (1966). *Toward a theory of instruction.* Cambridge, MA: Harvard University Press.

Bodner, G. (1986). Constructivism: A theory of knowledge. *Journal of Chemical Education, 63*, 873–878. https://doi.org/10.1021/ed063p873.

Castellano, G., Villalba, S. D., & Camurri, A. (2007). Recognising human emotions from body movement and gesture dynamics. In A. Paiva, R. Prada, & R. W. Picard (Eds.), *ACII 2007, LNCS* (Vol. 4738, pp. 71–82). Heidelberg: Springer.

Cheng, X., & Davis, J. (2000). *Camera placement considering occlusion for robust motion capture* (Stanford Computer Science Technical Report, CS-TR-2000-07). Stanford University.

Cordes, C., & Miller, E. (Eds.). (2000). *Fool's gold: A critical look at computers in childhood.* College Park, MD: Alliance for Childhood.

Crane, E., & Gross, M. (2007). Motion capture and emotion: Affect detection in whole body movement. In A. Paiva, R. Prada, & R. W. Picard (Eds.), *ACII 2007, LNCS* (Vol. 4738, pp. 95–101). Heidelberg: Springer.

D'Mello, S., Dieterle, E., & Duckworth, A. (2017). Advanced, analytic, automated (AAA) measurement of engagement during learning. *Educational Psychologist, 52*(2), 104–123. https://doi.org/10.1080/00461520.2017.1281747

Festinger, L. (1962). Cognitive dissonance. *Scientific American, 207*(4), 93–106.

Hattie, J., & Timperley, H. (2007). The power of feedback. *Review of Educational Research, 77*(1), 81–112. https://doi.org/10.3102/003465430298487

Istenic Starcic, A., Lipsmeyer, W. M., & Lin, L. (2018). Motion capture technology supporting cognitive, psychomotor, and affective-social learning. In Wu, Huang, Istenic Starcic, Shadijev, Lin (Eds.), *2018 International Conference of Innovative Technologies in Learning, LNCS* (pp. 311–322).

Johnson-Glenberg, M. C., Birchfield, D. A., Tolentino, L., & Koziupa, T. (2014). Collaborative embodied learning in mixed reality motion-capture environments: Two science studies. *Journal of Educational Psychology, 106*(1), 86–104. https://doi.org/10.1037/a0034008

Kaiser, H. (1958). The varimax criterion for analytic rotation in factor analysis. *Psychometrika, 23*(3), 187–200. https://doi.org/10.1007/BF02289233

Kim, K., Maloney, D., Bruder, G., Bailenson, J. N., & Welch, G. F. (2017). The effects of virtual human's spatial and behavioral coherence with physical objects on social presence in AR. *Computer Animation and Virtual Worlds, 28*, e1771.

Kleinsmith, A., & Bianchi-Berthouze, N. (2007). Recognizing affective dimensions from body posture. In A. Paiva, R. Prada, & R. W. Picard (Eds.), *ACII 2007, LNCS* (Vol. 4738, pp. 48–58). Heidelberg: Springer.

Kluger, A. N., & DeNisi, A. (1996). The effects of feedback interventions on performance: Historical review, a meta-analysis and a preliminary feedback intervention theory. *Psychological Bulletin, 119*, 254–284.

Kozulin, A. (1999). *Vygotsky's psychology.* Cambridge: Harvard University Press.

Lindgren, R., & Moshell, J. (2011). Supporting children's learning with body-based metaphors in a mixed reality environment. In *Proceedings of the 10th International Conference on Interaction Design and Children* (pp. 177–180). New York: ACM.

Luft, J. & Ingham, H. (1955). The Johari window, a graphic model of interpersonal awareness. In *Proceedings of the Western Training Laboratory in Group Development.* Los Angeles: University of California, Los Angeles.

Piaget, J. (1952). *The origins of intelligence in children.* New York: International Universities Press.

Rosati, G., Oscari, F., Spagnol, S., Avanzini, F., & Masiero, S. (2012). Effect of task-related continuous auditory feedback during learning of tracking motion exercises. *Journal of Neuroengineering and Rehabilitation, 9*(79), 2–13. https://doi.org/10.1186/1743-0003-9-79

Russell, S., & Norvig, P. (2016). *Artificial intelligence: A modern approach.* Malaysia: Pearson Education Limited. Tin hoc Collection. Global Edition.

Schwartz, D. L., Tsang, J. T., & Blair, K. P. (2016). *The ABCs of how we learn: 26 scientifically proven approaches, how they work, and when to use them.* New York: W. W. Norton & Company.

Sinatra, G. M., Heddy, B. C., & Lombardi, D. (2015). The challenges of defining and measuring student engagement in science. *Educational Psychologist, 50*(1), 1–13.

Troy, J., Erignac, C., & Murray, P. (2006). Closed-loop feedback control using motion capture systems. US Grant – US7643893B2. *Boeing Aircraft Corporation.* Retried August 18, from https://patents.google.com/patent/US7643893B2/en

Trungpa, C., & Fremantle, F. (2000). *Tibetan book of the dead: The great liberation through hearing in the Bardo.* Boston: Shambhala Publications.

von Glasersfeld, E. (1995). *Radical constructivism: A way of knowing and learning, Studies in Mathematics Education, Series: 6.* Bristol, PA: Falmer Press.

Vygotsky, L. (1978). *Mind in society: The development of higher mental process.* Cambridge, MA: Harvard University Press.

Waibel, A., Vo, M. T., Duchnowski, P., & Manke, S. (1996). Multimodal interfaces. *Artificial Intelligence Review, 10*(3–4), 299–319.

Walchli, M., Ruffieux, J., Bourquin, Y., Keller, M., & Taube, W. (2016). Maximizing performance: Augmented feedback, focus of attention, and/or reward? *Medicine and Science in Sports and Exercise, 48*(4), 714–719. https://doi.org/10.1249/MSS.0000000000000818

Wallon, R. C., & Lindgren, R. (2017). Considerations for the design of gesture-augmented learning environments. In M. J. Spector, B. B. Lockee, & M. D. Childress (Eds.), *Learning, design, and technology: An international compendium of theory, research, practice and policy* (pp. 1–21). Cham: Springer. https://doi.org/10.1007/978-3-319-17727-475-1

Andreja Istenic Starcic is full professor in didactics and educational technology. Her teaching and research interests include educational technology, media and communication, teacher education, higher education, research evaluation, and, particularly, interdisciplinary research. She has been editor of British Journal of Educational Technology for Europe and Scandinavia. She is one of funding convenors of EERA—European Educational Research Association network Didactics. She is a member of European Network for Research Evaluation in the Social Sciences and the Humanities (ENRESSH) and is leading research on data publishing. She was visiting professor at Macquarie University, Sydney, Kazan Federal University and University of North Texas. Andreja was awarded by Slovenian research agency for the exceptional research achievement in social science in Slovenia for the year 2012. She received an award of University of Primorska for scientific excellence in social sciences and humanities for the year 2014. She has been mentor to Ph.D. students in educational technology, nursing education, education in sustainable development, speech and language therapy, and inclusive education. Andreja was nominated for a mentor of the year 2016. She was leading many international research projects in all educational levels and lifelong learning and professional development. As a chair and a program committee member of international conferences, she supports young researchers. She is committed to interdisciplinary research and research evaluation in social science and humanities.

William Mark Lipsmeyer For almost 19 years in the visual effects industry, Mark has worked on television series, commercials, and blockbuster feature films such as Polar Express, Monster House, Beowulf, A Christmas Carol, and Mars Needs Moms. Early in his career as a motion capture artist, he worked for director Robert Zemeckis at Sony Pictures Imageworks and ImageMovers Digital to push motion capture technology forward using vicon systems and house of moves many different hardware and software. Mark is an award-winning visual effects technical director, a VES (Visual Effects Society) member, and a long time character effects artist working for many leading studios including Lucasfilm | Industrial Light & Magic, Sony Pictures Imageworks, Rhythm & Hues, Digital Domain, Blur, and Zoic Studios.

Lin Lin is a Professor of Learning Technologies at the University of North Texas (UNT). Lin's research looks into interactions between mind, brain, and technology in smart learning environments. Specially, she has conducted research on (1) media multitasking; (2) learning in online/blended/virtual reality environments; and (3) Computer-supported Collaborative Learning (CSCL). Lin is the Editor-in-Chief for the development section of *Educational Technology Research and Development*, one of the most respected journals in the field. She is also Associate Editor for the *International Journal of Smart Technology and Learning* (IJSmartTL) as well as serving on the several other journal editorial boards. Lin has played leadership roles in several professional organizations (e.g., AECT and AERA). Lin has been invited as an honorary professor at several universities overseas. Lin serves as Director for Texas Center for Educational Technology, and Co-director on the Joint-Lab on Big Data, Little Devices, and Lifelong Learning.

Chapter 8
Virtual School Environments for Neuropsychological Assessment and Training

Thomas D. Parsons, Tyler Duffield, Timothy McMahan, and Unai Diaz-Orueta

Abstract The virtual school environment has been developed and validated by the Computational Neuropsychology and Simulation (CNS) Laboratory of Dr. Thomas Parsons. The overarching goal of the virtual school project is to provide neuropsychological, affective, and social cognitive assessments that are more meaningful for the lives of children. These previously developed and validated virtual reality (VR) simulations of various contexts within the school environment (e.g., classroom, hallway, playground) can be combined and harnessed to gain ecologically valid assessments of children in real-world situations. The virtual school environment generates synthetic surroundings, including a virtual classroom, hallway, and playground via a 360-degree immersive experience. Furthermore, the computational design and administration of the virtual school environment platform allows for simultaneous recording of the child's behavioral and physiological responses. Virtual environments can be used to offer traditional psychometric testing and can collect additional real-time data (e.g., head movements, limb movements that reflect distraction). As such, they have potential to provide greater diagnostic specificity and more useful targets for intervention.

T. D. Parsons (✉)
College of Information, University of North Texas, Computational Neuropsychology and Simulation, Denton, TX, USA
e-mail: Thomas.Parsons@unt.edu; https://cns.unt.edu/

T. Duffield
Oregon Health & Science University, Portland, OR, USA
e-mail: duffielt@ohsu.edu

T. McMahan
University of Texas at Dallas, Richardson, TX, USA
e-mail: Timothy.McMahan@utdallas.edu

U. Diaz-Orueta
Maynooth University, Maynooth, County Kildare, Ireland

© Association for Educational Communications and Technology 2019
T. D. Parsons et al. (eds.), *Mind, Brain and Technology*, Educational Communications and Technology: Issues and Innovations,
https://doi.org/10.1007/978-3-030-02631-8_8

Introduction

Children challenged with congenital neurodevelopmental disorders and acquired brain injuries often have difficulties regulating social attention and emotional reactivity in the dynamic flow of social interactions. Moreover, neurodevelopmental disorders (e.g., autism spectrum disorder, attention-deficit/hyperactivity disorder) are highly comorbid, and their associated attentional difficulties are largely due to frontostriatal brain dysfunction and expressed as executive function deficits. These neurodevelopmental disorders are also a risk factor for acquired brain injury. While there are many established measures of social attention, most fall short of objective and reliable predictions of the child's ability to perform everyday school activities (Parsons, 2014; Parsons & Phillips, 2016). Attentional performances on these tests vary across diagnoses of neurodevelopmental disorders (e.g., autism spectrum disorder, attention-deficit/hyperactivity disorder), and mild-complex traumatic brain injury (mTBI). Comorbidities and overlapping symptoms add additional clinical complications. Since children affected by autism and ADHD often have overlapping symptoms, a pressing need is to better understand the syndrome-specific pattern of attention problems, and related treatment needs, that differentiate children with autism from those affected by ADHD (Parsons, 2014).

Part of this variance across tradition assessments is that they tend to focus upon cold cognitive processes and ignore hot affective processes. Deficits in executive functioning often include both cold cognitive and hot affective challenges that depend upon frontostriatal circuit functioning. Cold executive control found in top-down executive functioning is distinguished from hot affective aspects of executive control found in bottom-up processing (Zelazo & Carlson, 2012). While cold executive functioning tends to be logic-based and free from much affective arousal, hot affective processing occurs with reward and punishment, self-regulation, and decision-making involving personal interpretation (Séguin, Arseneault, & Tremblay, 2007; Chan, Shum, Toulopoulou, & Chen, 2008; Brock, Rimm-Kaufman, Nathanson, & Grimm, 2009).

The cognitive aspects of cold executive functioning and emotional/arousal aspects of hot executive functioning are intrinsically inter-related (Fig. 8.1) making it extremely challenging for clinicians to separate the different functions across these disorders and, as such, have the potential to confound standard neuropsychological test outcomes.

Results of tests generally designed to examine cold executive functioning deficits, such as challenges with planning, topic shifting, and strategy selection, can also be powerfully influenced by broader impairments in hot executive functions including the challenges of motivation, social orienting, self-monitoring, and volitional attention regulation (Parsons, 2015; Parsons, Gaggioli, & Riva, 2017). For instance, cold executive functioning deficits in response to traditional paper-and-pencil testing are confounded by hot executive functioning difficulties elicited by interpersonal interactions between a clinician and a patient. Difficulties with cold executive functioning among individuals with neurodevelopmental disorders are at times (e.g., autism) less likely if participants complete computerized versions of paper-and-pencil tests, removing social interaction from the clinical exam.

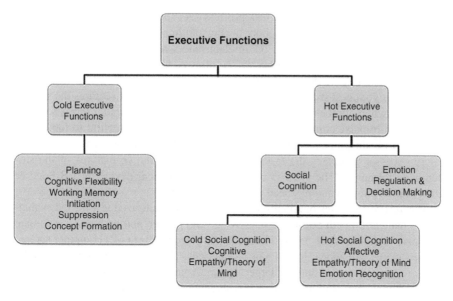

Fig. 8.1 Framework for executive functions taken from Zimmerman, Ownsworth, O'Donovan, Roberts, and Gullo (2016). Reprinted with permission from the publisher

Computer Automated (2D) Assessment of Attentional Processing

The ability to maintain an appropriate level of attention is foundational for education and learning, especially during childhood and school age. Computerized tests have been used to evaluate attention in children, with ADHD as a usual target disorder.

Computerized Continuous Performance Tests

With the aim to study this cold cognitive process separately from other cognitive functions, 2D computerized tests of attention called continuous performance tests (CPT) are often utilized. These tests present a series of stimuli (in a rapid and random way) to students who are instructed to respond. Various CPT paradigms have consistently demonstrated their sensitivity to a variety of both neurological and psychiatric disorders (Riccio, Reynolds, & Lowe, 2001).

A number of CPTS have been developed. Among them, we may find the Gordon Diagnostic System (Gordon, 1983), the Test of Variables of Attention (Greenberg & Waldman, 1993), the Children Sustained Attention Task (Servera & Llabrés, 2004), and the Conners' Continuous Performance Test (Conners, 2004). The Gordon Diagnostic System (GDS; Gordon, 1983) is a CPT that measures impulsivity, inattention, and distractibility. It is a portable microprocessor that administers a series of game-like tasks. The vigilance task proffers data about the ability of a student to focus and sustain attention throughout testing and in absence of feedback. A series of digits, one by one, are shown on an electronic screen. The student is asked to press a button whenever the number "1" is followed by a "9". The system registers correct and incorrect responses, as well as errors when responding to 1/9 combination. For the youngest students, the GDS has a variant that only requires the student to indicate when number "1" appears. The GDS also offers parallel forms for each task and an impulse control test (delayed task) that requires a child to inhibit the answer to obtain points. Each task can be administered in less than 9 min. The microprocessor generates the tasks and registers quantitative features of the student's performance. The GDS is recognized as a medical device by US Food & Drug Administration and has been widely standardized.

The Test of Variables of Attention (TOVA) is a computerized test for the evaluation of inattention with normative data by age and gender, and with an approximate administration time of 21.5 min. The student is placed in front of a computer screen, where squares will appear for 0.1 s in 2-s intervals. The square will illuminate in the upper or bottom part of another larger square. A target stimulus is one that occurs when the upper part is illuminated. A non-target occurs if the illumination appears in the bottom part. Each time the target square appears, the student must press a small switch. Each time the non-target appears, the student must avoid pressing the switch. The TOVA has been used successfully for the diagnosis of ADHD and its subtypes (Forbes, 1998; Llorente et al., 2007; Riccio, Garland, & Cohen, 2007; Wada, Yamashita, Matsuishi, Ohtani, & Kato, 2000; Weyandt, Mitzlaff, & Thomas, 2002).

The Children Sustained Attention Task (CSAT) is a computerized test that can be administered to children from 6 to 11 years old, with a length of 7.5 min. The goal is to assess the ability of sustained attention by means of a vigilance task. The child must press the space bar whenever the sequence "6-3" (a number "6" followed by a "3") appears. According to its authors (Servera & Llabrés, 2004), raw scores of correct answers, reaction times, and commission errors are obtained. Its main problem is the narrow interstimulus interval (only 500 ms), which may misclassify children with low processing speed as ADHD (either inattentive or impulsive) since these children may require a larger interval (up to 1500 ms) to provide an answer.

Finally, the Conners' Continuous Performance Test (Conners, 2004) is another computerized test that requires students to press the space bar (or mouse click) at the appearance of any letter that is not the letter "x". One of its advantages is the normative database that includes 2686 clinical and non-clinical subjects, with large subsamples of individuals with neurological damage. It allows for the comparison of student answers with normative data from the general population, ADHD norms, and brain injury norms. It can be used as a tool to monitor the efficiency of a pharmacological or any other kind of treatment, with high sensitivity (low rate of false positives) and specificity (low rate of false negatives). Errors are divided in two categories: omission and commission errors. Other measures are reaction time for correct answers (as a measure of processing speed; variability in reaction time—variable associated to response consistency and sustainment of vigilance); d' or attentiveness (a kind of quality of attention) which indicates to what extent the person discriminates between target and non-target stimuli; perseverations (indicative of impulsivity, random answers indicative of decline, or very low responses to the previous stimulus that may indicate inattention). Normative data are obtained from the US population. Age groups described in the test manual are a total of 1259 children between 6 and 16 years old, and an ADHD clinical sample in this same age range of 271 children.

Continuous performance tasks offer objective and quantifiable data about the course of an attention or executive control problem (Riccio et al., 2001). Losier, McGrath, and Klein (1996) performed a meta-analysis of 26 studies that measured children with ADHD using different versions of the CPT and confirmed that students with ADHD had greater commissions and omission errors (see Barkley, 1994). Some studies have focused their efforts on investigating which parameters of CPTs correlate with already defined features of ADHD. Epstein et al. (2003), using Conners' CPT, found that omission errors correlate with inattention symptoms described in ADHD; and commission errors with impulsivity symptoms. Moreover, some variables also showed significant relationships with many hyperactivity and impulsivity symptoms. In addition, they found that the reaction time measure acted as a predictor of ADHD symptomatology, showing overall a greater slowness when pressing the button in front of the target stimuli, and evidencing that these children have greater difficulties to differentiate between target and non-target stimuli. Sandford and Turner (1995) found more commission errors when stimuli are presented on an auditory basis, especially in children with ADHD. These findings suggest that tasks of auditory attention can be more sensitive and hence more useful for the identification of sustained attention and executive control problems.

However, a recent study by Zelnik, Bennett-Back, Miari, Goez, and Fattal-Valevski (2012) states that the TOVA and other CPTs are hampered by discrepancies between satisfactory sensitivity indices with a high predictive value, and poor specificities. In other words, the CPT's ability to establish that children without ADHD are actually non-ADHD is poor (for example, in children who show learning difficulties or behavioral disorders). In this sense, relying only on CPT tests can lead to an overdiagnosis and a superfluous use of the term ADHD as a disguise for many conditions that may contribute to a poor school performance.

Computerized Stroop Tests

The Stroop test is another widely used neuropsychological assessment of attention control (Macleod, 1991; 1992). Although there are various iterations of the original Stroop task with varying stimulus presentations across these iterations (e.g., number of items), they all measure freedom from distractibility, selective attention, response conflict, and response inhibition. In a typical Stroop, attentional control is assessed via the presentation of blocks of multiple stimuli on a card (multi-item presentation; Uttl & Graf, 1997). A limitation of this multi-item presentation approach is that it does not allow the neuropsychologist to (a) analyze reaction times, number correct, and/or impact of errors for individual stimuli; or (b) randomize counterbalancing of various trial types (e.g., neutral, interference, cued, facilitated; see Davidson, Zacks, & Williams, 2003; Parsons, Courtney, & Dawson, 2013). Moreover, multi-item presentations may result in confounds from or interactions with visual distractor interference. Also, multi-item presentations expose the participant to all the stimuli at once, which may enhance the training/learning curve resulting in greater practice effects when compared to single item procedures (see Lemay, Bedard, Roulea, & Tremblay, 2004).

Given the limitations of multi-item paper-and-pencil measures, a number of computerized Stroop-like tasks have been developed. Computer automated versions of the Stroop task offer increased standardization of administration and enhanced timing precision. With computerized Stroop assessments, the neuropsychologist has access to response latencies. Moreover, the computerized version can automatically log participant responses.

Often, automatic and controlled responding can function in fluent synchrony, but the two processes can be in conflict based upon task demands or conditions. Thus, Washburn (2016) notes, "tasks like Stroop provide a fertile basis for examining performance under conditions in which the participants' intentions (dictated by instructions or in response to changing task demands) require resisting strong stimulus–response associations that are either naturally prepotent (e.g., because of movement, suddenness, intensity, or novelty) or have been made strong by previous experience" (p. 4).

Studies of inhibition of prepotent responses in individuals with autism typically report unimpaired inhibition. However, when the focus is upon resistance to distractor inhibition, difficulties are apparent. A potential reason for the discrepant findings may be that they reflect performances of individuals with autism in laboratory settings. There is little evidence that these results are generalizable to everyday functioning in real-world environments. An unfortunate limitation of the Stroop task is that it was originally designed as a lab-based measure to examine a cognitive construct (i.e., inhibitory control) in normal populations. It only later began being used clinically in neurologically impaired populations for assessing cognitive constructs that are presumably important to completing real-world activities. However, it has been asserted that current construct-driven tests such as the Stroop, which are neuropsychology's adaptation of outmoded conceptual and experimental frameworks, fail to represent the actual functional capacities inherent within the varying environments found in the real world (Burgess et al., 2006). A number of investigators have argued that performance on traditional neuropsychological construct-driven tests, such as the Stroop or the Wisconsin Card Sorting Test, has little correspondence to activities of daily living (Bottari, Dassa, Rainville, & Dutil, 2009; Manchester, Priestley, & Jackson, 2004; Sbordone, 2008).

Lack of Ecological Validity

A confound for CPTs and Stroop tests is the lack of generalizability to everyday activities. These neuropsychological tests cannot distinguish between hot and cold executive functioning, or break down processing along a temporal continuum, including the domains of context, sequential information processing, and feedback or reinforcement (i.e., the consequences of action). This may be especially true for testing executive function deficits in children with autism because of the social orienting hypothesis of autism. One hallmark of autism is a syndrome-specific difficulty with the tendency to attend to and process social stimuli, such as faces or the direction of eye gaze. Children autism may display confusing commonalities with children affected by other frontostriatal developmental disorders such as ADHD. To resolve this issue, there is a need to develop neuropsychological measures of social orienting executive dysfunction in children with autism.

According to the National Center for Education Statistics (NCES), in the 2007–2008 academic year for public schools in the United States, the average number of hours in the school day was 6.64 and average number of days in the school year was 180. This means that youth attending public school in the United States spend approximately 1200 h in the classroom annually, and approximately over 14,000 h in the classroom by their high school graduation. Thus, assessments are needed that mimic everyday activities.

Studies have found that impairments in either the cold or hot cognitive functions may be related to deficits in everyday decision-making (e.g., school attendance, ability to work, independence at home, and social relations; Chan et al., 2008). Determining a child's functional capabilities requires precise control over the environment and the ability to adjust the potency or frequency of stimuli (White et al., 2014). Given that this control is difficult to ensure in the traditional assessment environment, clinicians often give questionnaires to parents and teachers to get a clear picture of the child's social cognitive functions in everyday activities. Unfortunately, studies indicate that the agreement between parents and teachers is modest. For example, the concordance between parents and teachers on diagnosing ADHD varies from 0.30 to 0.50 depending on the behavioral dimensions being rated (Biederman, Faraone, Milberger, & Doyle, 1993; Mitsis, McKay, Schulz, Newcorn, & Halperin, 2000; de Nijs et al., 2004). Additionally, there is often not a strong overlap between these rating scales and standard tests of cognitive functioning, suggesting that these assessments may be reflective of different aspects of behavior (see Parsons & Phillips, 2016). As a result, parents, teachers, and community interventionists often face clinical assessments that fail to meaningfully align with real-world problems and that do not easily translate into specific intervention/treatment plans.

Neuropsychologists are increasingly interested in ecological validity; that is the degree of relevance or similarity that a test or training system has relative to the real world, and in its value for predicting or improving daily functioning (Chaytor & Schmitter-Edgecombe, 2003; Wilson, 1998). Not only is a classroom likely the most cognitively demanding environment youth interact in, it is also where they spend a significant amount of their young lives. Being able to accurately predict academic performance, as well as potentially remediate and/or improve academic functioning when difficulties exist is important. Educational attainment has been associated with a number of life outcomes, including most notably life expectancy across a number of demographic factors (e.g., race; Kaplan, Howard, Safford, & Howard, 2015). Given all of this data related to the importance of a child's capacity for performing everyday activities, it seems important that neuropsychologists develop assessments with ecological validity in mind.

Potential of Virtual Environments

A potential answer to the limits of ecological validity in traditional neuropsychological assessment is virtual reality. Virtual reality technologies generate full sensory immersion into a synthetic environment, a "feeling of being there" known as "presence." Virtual reality can be used to better predict how the student might respond to real-world difficulties (Parsons et al., 2017; Parsons, 2016). By so doing, VR environments greatly enhance ecological validity. Participants can be immersed into a synthetic world (such as a simulated school environment). VR can capture variations in the performances of real-life tasks via the integration of immersive hardware (e.g., head-mounted displays) with advanced input devices (e.g., eye trackers, gloves, and body trackers). Resulting neuropsychological measurements (e.g., a head turning toward a noise) can target variations in hot and cold executive functioning (Parsons, 2015; Parsons, Gaggioli, & Riva, 2017), such as real-world differences in attention and emotion and specific cognitive domains (Bohil, Alicea, & Biocca, 2011). In addition to these psychometric advances offered by VR technology (i.e., enhanced computational capacities for administration efficiency, stimulus presentation, automated logging of responses, and data analytic processing), the trackers and biometric sensors used in VR might also be employed to overcome communication barriers between the clinician and the patient/participant (Parsons, McMahan, & Kane, 2018; Parsons, Riva, et al., 2017). Reliability of assessment can be enhanced in VR environments by better control of the perceptual environment, more consistent stimulus presentation, and more precise and accurate scoring.

The validity and utility of these VR social attention assessment methods have been demonstrated in studies in which response to distracter conditions differentiated ADHD (Parsons, Bowerly, Buckwalter, & Rizzo, 2007) and autism children (Parsons & Carlew, 2016) from controls on assessments delivered via the virtual classroom environment (Parsons et al., 2007; Duffield, Parsons, Landry, Karam, Otero, & Hall, 2017). Furthermore, individual differences in VR classroom attention performance have been observed to be significantly associated with parent report of ADHD symptoms and allied behavior problems on the Behavioral Assessment System for Children (Adams, Finn, Moes, Flannery, & Rizzo, 2009; Parsons et al., 2007).

Another advantage of VR applications is that they are attractive for participants, including children with autism (Parsons, 2016; Parsons, Carlew, Magtoto, & Stonecipher, 2017). Individuals with autism often prefer tasks administered by a computer to the same tasks administered by humans, and by extension, VR environments may offer an ideal medium for the assessment of autism. Another advantage is that VR provides exactly reproducible sensory stimuli. VR environments allow for controlled presentations of emotionally engaging background narratives to enhance affective experience and social interactions (Parsons, 2015).

Numerous studies now indicate that VR methods are applicable with children with autism. Indeed, they may be especially enjoyable and motivating platforms for children with autism (Parsons, 2016). Children with autism report a sense of presence in VR environments that is comparable to that of typical children and other studies have provided preliminary support for VR based social skills training for individuals with autism (Parsons, 2016) Openness to the virtual classroom environment has been shown in participants with autism comparable to typically developing children (Parsons & Carlew, 2016).

Virtual Classroom Paradigm

One virtual reality-based neuropsychological assessment that is gaining psychometric support is the virtual classroom (Iriarte et al., 2012; Parsons & Rizzo, in press; Rizzo et al., 2006). In the virtual classroom CPT test, participants are instructed to view a series of letters presented on the blackboard and to hit the response button only after viewing the letter "X" preceded by an "A" (i.e., a successive discrimination task) and to withhold their response to any other sequence of letters. Stimuli are presented for 150 ms each, with a fixed interstimulus interval of 1350 ms. There are two 10-min testing conditions, one without distractors and one with distractions (pure auditory, pure visual, and mixed audio-visual distractors). Like the original 2D computerized CPT, a number of virtual reality classroom CPTs have immerged. Various researchers in different countries (and thus languages) have developed their own versions of a virtual classroom environment (with varying attentional tasks). The two main virtual Classrooms that have been validated are ClinicaVR Classroom developed by Digital Media Works (Table 8.1; $N = 749$) and AULA developed by Nesplora (see Table 8.2; $N = 4484$).

As the tables reveal, there is a growing body of literature supporting the virtual classroom CPT for assessment.

Limitations of Traditional Virtual Classroom Assessment Approaches

A limitation of the current virtual classroom CPTs is that they do not tap into the social cognitive processes that are decidedly important for assessing student development. This can be especially limiting when attempting to differentiate between ADHD and autism. Notably, the social orienting deficits of persons with autism and ADHD may limit their capacity for social learning at home and in school and also play a role in their problematic development of social competence and social cognition. Recent research suggests that the social orienting impairments of autism reflect a disturbance of "social executive" functioning that involves frontal motivation, self-monitoring, and volitional attention regulation. Further, deficits appear to be found in temporal/parietal systems that involve orienting and processing information about the behavior of other persons.

A component lacking in the virtual classroom paradigms discussed above is the lack of social interactions between the student and the virtual teacher. The integration of a virtual teacher into a virtual classroom environment allows for a more dynamic assessment of both personal and joint attention. While much of the work discussed

Table 8.1 Digital media works version of the virtual classroom continuous performance test ($N = 749$)

Author(s), year	Research question(s)	Research design	Statistical design	Sample	Age range	Main findings
Parsons et al. (2007)	How does performance vary in a VC between boys with ADHD and boys without ADHD?	Intergroup comparison of participants with ADHD and TDC	ANOVA, Chi-square, regression analysis, Cohen's d	ADHD: $N = 9$ TDC: $N = 10$	8–12	Participants with ADHD exhibited more omission errors, commission errors, and overall body movement than TDC in the VC; participants with ADHD were more affected by distraction than TDC in the VC; VC measures were correlated with traditional ADHD assessment tools, the Behavior Checklist, and flatscreen CPT. No negative side effects were associated with use of the VC
Negut, Jurma, and David (2017)	(1) What is the validity of VC? (2) What is the task difficulty of virtual reality-based measures? (3) What is the effect of auditory distractors on the performance of children with ADHD compared to TDC? and (4) How do the two measures on cognitive absorption compare?	Cross-sectional design. Mean comparison tests	Independent samples t-test, MANCOVA, Cohen's d	ADHD: $N = 33$ TDC: $N = 42$	7–13	VC is effective due to its ability to discriminate between TDC and those with ADHD. Task difficulty is increased with both groups taking longer in virtual reality. Children with ADHD were impacted by auditory distractions, while TDC were not. Measures on cognitive absorption do not differ

Author	Research question	Design	Analysis	Sample	Age	Results
Nolin, Stipanicic, Henry, Joyal, and Allain (2012)	Does VR help identify attention and inhibition deficits in children?	Students participated individually in testing sessions during regular class hours. The order of the traditional and virtual tests was counterbalanced across participants to prevent skewing of the results due to practice or fatigue effects. The data were collected over a period of 5 weeks	ANOVA, ANCOVA	mTBI: $N = 25$ Non-concussed Controls: $N = 25$	12–15	Neuropsychological assessment using VR showed greater sensitivity to the subtle effects of sports concussion than the traditional test, which showed no difference between groups. The results also demonstrated that the sports concussion group reported more symptoms of cybersickness and more intense cybersickness than the control group
Gilboa et al. (2011)	(1) How do children with NF1 compare to TDC when using the VC? (2) Is VR efficient at identifying attention deficits in children?	Cross-sectional design. Mean comparison tests	ANOVA, Chi-square, MANCOVA, Pearson's correlation	NF1: $N = 29$ TDC: $N = 25$	8–16	Significant differences were found between the NF1 and TDC on the number of targets correctly identified (omission errors) and the number of commissions (commission errors) in the VC, with poorer performance by the children with NF1 ($p < 0.005$). Significant correlations were obtained between the number of targets correctly identified, the number of commission errors, and reaction time

(continued)

Table 8.1 (continued)

Author(s), year	Research question(s)	Research design	Statistical design	Sample	Age range	Main findings
Pollak et al. (2009)	How does the performance of both children with ADHD and TDC differ between VR-CPT and TOVA-CPT in recognizing symptoms of ADHD and what are the associated experiences in the VC?	Crossover design	ANOVA, Cohen's *d*	ADHD: N = 20 TDC: N = 17	9–17	Children with ADHD performed worse on all CPTs. The VR-CPT showed similar effect sizes to the TOVA. Subjective feelings of enjoyment were most positive for VR-CPT
Mühlberger et al. (2016)	How does CPT performance vary between children with ADHD who do not take medication, children with ADHD who take medication, and traditionally developing children when using virtual reality?	Cross-sectional study, intergroup comparison between three groups (controls, non- medicated ADHD, and medicated ADHD)	ANOVA, Pearson's correlation, Eta squared	ADHD: Medicated: N = 26 Unmedicated: N = 68 TDC: N = 34	9–14	Children with ADHD had more errors and slower reaction times than TDC. Children with ADHD and no medication had significantly higher reaction times than the other two groups
Pollak, Shomaly, Weiss, Rizzo, and Gross-Tsur (2010)	How does MPH impact performance on CPT, VR-CPT, and TOVA assessments?	Double-blind, placebo controlled, crossover design	ANOVA, Eta squared	ADHD: N = 27 TDC: N = 17	11–17	MPH reduced omission errors to a greater extent on the VR-CPT compared to the no VR-CPT and the TOVA, and decreased other CPT measures on all types of CPT to a similar degree. Children rated the VR-CPT as more enjoyable than the other types of CPT

Bioulac et al. (2012)	How does time impact task completion in a VC between TDC and those with ADHD?	Children with ADHD and TDC were tested at the beginning in the afternoon to try to minimize potential testing effects due to different times of the day. The same physician assessed the children with first the CPT and, after 10 min, the test of the VC	Mann–Whitney U-test, ANOVA, Pearson's correlation	ADHD: $N = 20$ TDC: $N = 16$	7–10	Males with ADHD had a different evolution of performances on this task than TDC. TDC sustained performances over time in the VR task, but patients with ADHD showed a significant performance decrement, with a decrease of correct hits and an increase of reaction time. Worse performance in children with ADHD than in TDC was then observed both in the VC task and in the CPT
Adams et al. (2009)	Is the VR-CPT better able to discern between those with ADHD and those without based upon each participant's distractibility than a standard CPT test without distractions	Both versions of the CPT (with and without the VC) were presented to the participants on a 3D VR dome by Elumens. This provides a field of view (horizontal and vertical) of 140°	Mann–Whitney U-test, Spearman correlation, regression analysis, Cohen's d	ADHD: $N = 19$ TDC: $N = 16$	8–14	While differences between the two groups did not attain statistical significance, there was a strong trend toward a significant difference in percent of targets correctly identified and in number of commission errors. Furthermore, compared to a standard CPT (Vigil), specificity was improved

(continued)

Table 8.1 (continued)

Author(s), year	Research question(s)	Research design	Statistical design	Sample	Age range	Main findings
Gilboa et al. (2015)	(1) What are the symptoms of ABI that can be diagnosed with virtual reality? (2) How accurate is VR? Do severity of injury or other variables impact the accuracy of VR?	Cross-sectional design. The patients underwent the WASI subtests, the TEA-Ch, and the VC assessment and parents answered the CPRS-R:S questionnaire while their child was being tested	T-test, Chi squared, ANOVA, Pearson's correlation	ABI: N = 41 Control: N = 35	8–16	Significant differences were found between the groups regarding the number of targets correctly identified in the VC. Based on the VC results, 45% of the children with ABI suffered marked deficits in sustained attention (lower rates of total correct hits). The concurrent validity of the VC in comparison with neuropsychological tests and a parental questionnaire was sufficient. Attentional performance was found to be related to age, age at injury/diagnosis, and treatment (radiotherapy dose). The VC appears to be a sensitive, playful, and ecologically valid assessment tool for use in the diagnosis of attention deficits among children with ABI
Nolin et al. (2016)	(1) How reliable is VR? (2) How does cybersickness relate to VR? (3) Do gender and age impact performance on the test?	Descriptive study	Bartlett's test, ANOVA	TDC: N = 102 No diagnostic group	7–16	VR is reliable. Cybersickness was not a prevalent issue. Gender has no effect on performance; however, age does have an effect

Parsons and Carlew (2016)	How do individuals with ASD compare to TDC individuals in an advanced VC with real-life distractors?	Study #1: Descriptive study Study #2: Cross-sectional design Mean comparison tests	ANOVA, Chi-square, ANCOVA, Cohen's d	Study 1: TDC: $N = 50$ Study 2: ASD: $N = 8$ TDC: $N = 10$	Study 1: 18–30 Study 2: 18–34	Study #1: VC Bimodal Stroop task may be validly used to examine interference control in a typically developing population. The task elicited an interference effect similar to those found in classic Stroop tasks. Study #2: When under conditions of distraction, individuals with ASD are compromised in their ability to activate external distractor inhibition, though their response time may not suffer
Nolin, Martin, and Bouchard (2009)	How does the performance of children with TBI vary between the traditional CPT and the VR-CPT?	Mean comparison tests with repeated measures were used to compare the output of children with a TBI concerning the number of omissions, the number of commissions, and the reaction time, on the traditional Vigil CPT and the one from the VR-CPT	ANOVA	TBI: $N = 8$ No control group	8–12	The VR-CPT showed much more accurate reports between participants in regard to their TBI through commissions and reaction time measures

(continued)

Table 8.1 (continued)

Author(s), year	Research question(s)	Research design	Statistical design	Sample	Age range	Main findings
Lalonde, Henry, Drouin-Germain, Nolin, and Beauchamp (2013)	What is the relationship between the traditional D-KEFS and BRIEF measures, and the VR-Stroop task?	Descriptive/correlational study. Convergence validity study	Pearson's correlation, regression analysis	TDC: $N = 38$ No diagnostic group	13–17	Performance on the VR-Stroop task correlates with both traditional forms of EF assessment (D-KEFS, BRIEF). In particular, performance on the VR-Stroop task was closely associated with performance on a paper–pencil inhibition task. Furthermore, VR-Stroop performance more accurately reflected everyday behavioral EF than paper–pencil tasks
Nolin et al. (2009)	Can a VR-CPT add value to the assessment of attention in children with TBI?	Mean comparison tests with repeated measures	Paired T-test	TBI: $N = 8$ No control group	8–12	No difference between the two modalities of the CPT was found for omission errors. TBI participants made significantly more commission errors and had longer reaction times in the VR-CPT than in the traditional CPT

ABI acquired brain injury, *ADHD* attention-deficit/hyperactivity disorder, *ANOVA* analysis of variance, *ANCOVA* analysis of covariance, *ASD* autism spectrum disorder, *AULA* Spanish translation of "classroom," *BRIEF* behavior rating inventory of executive functioning, *CPT* continuous performance test, *CPRS-R:S* Connors' parent rating scale, revised; short form, *D-KEFS* Delis–Kaplan executive function system, *DSM-IV* diagnostic and statistical manual, fourth edition, *EDAH* the scale for assessing attention deficit hyperactivity-disorder (English translation), *EEG* electroencephalogram, *EF* executive functioning, *HFASD* high functioning autism spectrum disorder, *I/H* impulsive/hyperactive, *LDX* lisdexamfetamine, *MANCOVA* multivariate analysis of covariance, *MPH* methylphenidate, *NF1* neurofibromatosis type 1, *TBI* traumatic brain injury, *TDC* typically developing controls, *TEA-Ch* test of everyday attention for children, *TOVA* test of variables of attention, *VC* virtual classroom, *VR* virtual reality, *VR-CPT* virtual reality continuous performance test

Table 8.2 AULA Nesplora version of the virtual classroom continuous performance test ($N = 4484$)

Author(s), year	Research question(s)	Research design	Statistical design	Sample	Age range	Main findings
Areces, Rodríguez, García, Cueli, and González-Castro (2018)	Is the AULA Nesplora test effective in discerning between the three major groups of ADHD; I/H, inattentive, and combined?	An ex post facto descriptive-comparative design for four groups, three corresponding to the three types of ADHD presentations and a control group	MANCOVA, Sheffé's test, Cohen's d	Inattentive ADHD: $N = 28$, I/H ADHD: $N = 29$ ADHD combined: $N = 32$ TDC: $N = 28$	5–16	The AULA Nesplora test is able to discriminate between the three major groups of ADHD by recording omissions, response times, and other factors
Díaz-Orueta, Fernández-Fernández, Morillo-Rojas, and Climent (2016)	Is the AULA Nesplora test able to discern between ADHD participants with no medication and those having taken lisdexamfetamine (LDX)?	Pre-experimental design with pre- and post-test conditions and one unique group	Kruskal–Wallis, Wilcoxon	ADHD: $N = 85$ No control group	6–16	The AULA Nesplora test is an effective measure to track the changes derived as an outcome of pharmacological treatment of ADHD with LDX. LDX is an effective drug to treat ADHD
Iriarte et al. (2016)	What will normative data look like for the AULA test?	Normative study to obtain normative data. Single application and processing of data obtained. Descriptive design	Mann–Whitney U-test, Kruskal–Wallis, Wilcoxon	Normative sample $N = 1272$	6–16	Variables provided by AULA were clustered in different categories for their posterior analysis. Differences by age and gender were analyzed, resulting in 14 groups, seven per sex. Differences between visual and auditory attention were also obtained

(continued)

Table 8.2 (continued)

Author(s), year	Research question(s)	Research design	Statistical design	Sample	Age range	Main findings
Díaz-Orueta, García-López, et al. (2014)	How do the AULA Nesplora test and standard CPT compare?	One single measure with AULA and Conners' CPT Convergent validity study between both tests. Comparison of children with ADHD undergoing medical treatment versus those not medicated. Comparison of capacity of AULA and Conners' CPT to differentiate between both groups	Spearman's correlations, Mann–Whitney U-test	ADHD: $N = 57$ No control group	6–16	Both tests showed significant correlations in the measures that were comparable between them. In addition, AULA (but not Conners' CPT) was able to differentiate between ADHD patients with and without pharmacological treatment over a wide range of measures related to inattention, impulsivity, processing speed, motor activity, and quality of attention focus
Rufo-Campos, Cueto, Iriarte, and Rufo-Muñoz (2012)	What is the sensitivity and specificity of AULA to correctly identify ADHD cases and discard non-ADHD individuals?	Cross-sectional, descriptive study	Logistic regression	$N = 124$ $N = 62$ with ADHD $N = 62$ controls	6–16	AULA showed a sensitivity of ADHD detection of 95.2%, and a specificity for discarding non-ADHD cases of 91.9%
Fernández-Fernández and Morillo-Rojas (2012)	What is the test-retest reliability of AULA? Can AULA be used repeatedly without a learning effect?	Mean comparison, intragroup	Wilcoxon	$N = 30$ with ADHD	6–16	A 1-week interval is sufficient for readministration of AULA for treatment monitoring purposes

				N	Age	
Díaz-Orueta, Iriarte, Climent, and Banterla (2012)	How does the testing condition using distractors affect performance in AULA when compared to the absence of distractors?	Mean comparison test	Kruskal–Wallis test	N = 1272	6–16	Results show influence of distractors in both increasing reaction time for providing both correct answers and commission errors, and increasing the time the patients deviate their attention focus
Díaz-Orueta, Cueto, et al. (2014)	What is the factorial validity of AULA? How is the convergent validity between AULA and observational scales like EDAH or DSM-IV ADHD scales?	Cross-sectional, descriptive and correlational study	Factorial validity analysis (Bartlett and Kaiser-Meyer-Olkin), root mean square error of approximation, goodness of fit index, and analysis of similarities	N = 2074 for the factorial analysis N = 188 for the study with EDAH N = 360 for the study with DSM-IV ADHD scales	6–16	Results support the structure of AULA of one single factor that comprises the cognitive variables correlating with ADHD in any of its subtypes. With regard to convergent validity, different nature of AULA as an objective cognitive measure and EDAH and DSM-IV as observational scales suggest they target different aspects or dimensions of patients' behavior and, hence, they may complement each other in the increase of ADHD diagnosis accuracy

(continued)

Table 8.2 (continued)

Author(s), year	Research question(s)	Research design	Statistical design	Sample	Age range	Main findings
Díaz-Orueta, Alonso-Sánchez, and Climent (2014)	What is the convergent validity between AULA and d2 test? Which test is better to differentiate between children with and without reading difficulties?	Cross-sectional, mean comparison study, and convergent validity study	Mann–Whitney U, and analysis of similarities	$N = 60$ (42% female)	6–17	AULA distinguished better than d2 between children with and without reading-writing difficulties (correct visual answers and visual errors: both $U = 166$, $z = -2.08$, $p < 0.05$), and convergent validity analyses showed adequate values for correct answers ($\cos = 0.944$) and concentration indexes ($\cos = 0.929$), while errors seemed to be measured differently in both tests
Zulueta, Iriarte, Díaz-Orueta, and Climent (2013)	What is the convergent validity between AULA and faces test of perception of differences, extended version?	Convergent validity, cross-sectional study	Similarities analysis	$N = 62$ children (26 females and 36 males)	6–16	High significant correlations were observed between test results in faces test of perception of differences (extended version) and AULA with regard to selective and sustained attention, and cognitive impulsivity

| Gutiérrez Maldonado, Letosa Porta, Rus Calafell, and Peñaloza Salazar (2009) | What are the performance differences in the VR-CPT between ADHD and non-ADHD children? | Intergroup comparison after administration of the VR-CPT: 10 diagnosed with ADHD (experimental group), medicated with methylphenidate, and 10 in TDC | Repeated measures ANOVAs, with one inter-variable: group of participants, with two levels (target group and control group) and three intra-variables: block (with six values), sensorial modality (visual and auditory) and distracters (with or without distracters) | ADHD: N = 10 TDC: N = 10 | 6–11 | Differences between groups were expressed in both auditory and visual tasks and became more evident with the presence of distractors |
| Mejías, Redondo, Fernández, and Diaz-Orueta (2016) | Is the pharmacological treatment for ADHD with Methylphenidate effective, as measured with AULA Nesplora? | Pre-experimental design, pre- and post-treatment measures with AULA | Wilcoxon | ADHD = 35 No control group | 6–19 | Attentional performance improves after pharmacological treatment. Patients perform with less omission errors, reaction times are smaller and more stable throughout the whole test administration, and motor activity index is significantly lower |

ABI acquired brain injury, *ADHD* attention-deficit/hyperactivity disorder, *ANOVA* analysis of variance, *ANCOVA* analysis of covariance, *ASD* autism spectrum disorder, *AULA* Spanish translation of "classroom," *BRIEF* behavior rating inventory of executive functioning, *CPT* continuous performance test, *CPRS-R:S* Connors' parent rating scale, revised; short form, *D-KEFS* Delis–Kaplan executive function system, *DSM-IV* diagnostic and statistical manual, fourth edition, *EDAH* the scale for assessing attention deficit hyperactivity-disorder (English translation), *EEG* electroencephalogram, *EF* executive functioning, *HFASD* high functioning autism spectrum disorder, *I/H* impulsive/hyperactive, *LDX* lisdexamfetamine, *MANCOVA* multivariate analysis of covariance, *MPH* methylphenidate, *NF1* neurofibromatosis type 1, *TBI* traumatic brain injury, *TDC* typically developing controls, *TEA-Ch* test of everyday attention for children, *TOVA* test of variables of attention, *VC* virtual classroom, *VR* virtual reality, *VR-CPT* virtual reality continuous performance test thus far has focused on an individual's regulation, control, and management of cognitive processes in isolation of others, persons with developmental disorders may have increased deficits in planning, working memory, attention, problem solving, verbal reasoning, inhibition, mental flexibility, task switching, and initiation and monitoring of actions when interacting in a social environment. Of primary interest is the shared focus (i.e., joint attention) of two or more individuals on an object. Joint attention is achieved when some individual alerts another to an object via eye gaze, pointing, and/or non-verbal indications. As mentioned earlier, children with autism may have deficits in skills related to joint attention: eye gaze; and identifying intention.

Virtual School Environment: Intelligent Virtual Teacher and Students

To make up for deficits in the traditional virtual classroom paradigm, Thomas Parsons has developed a virtual school environment that includes artificially intelligent virtual humans developed in his Computational Neuropsychology and Simulation (CNS) lab at the University of North Texas. The addition of an artificially intelligent virtual human teacher allows for a proscribed set of social stimuli within three school settings: a classroom, a hallway, and a playground. While neuropsychological assessments are administered in the virtual school's classroom in a manner similar to earlier iterations of the virtual classroom paradigm (Iriarte et al., 2012; Parsons & Rizzo, in press), the virtual school environment adds a host of objective measures of each child's response to stimuli: task performance, eye gaze, head movements, and psychophysiology (electrodermal activity, heart rate variability). Moreover, the simulation is expanded to include a virtual hallway and a playground where various social cognitive interactions occur. After the VR experience is completed, the child is asked to relate the story they experienced in the VR setting and what might happen were the story to continue. Behavioral responses are captured with existing technologies (e.g., motion capture, eye tracking, balance recording, heart rate).

Virtual School Battery of Neuropsychological Measures

The virtual school environment develops objective evaluations for a range of discrete social constructs. Parsons and colleagues aim to understand primarily how typical children respond to our VR mechanism and how their responses compare to standardized metrics of social and cognitive ability. The current iteration of the virtual teacher and classroom includes a battery of neuropsychological measures that can be administered with or without social cues from the virtual teacher and/or distractors, such as Go/No-go paradigms (Continuous Performance Test (CPT) and Stroop test). The Virtual school (classroom, hallway, playground) environments may be especially beneficial for the assessment of individuals with neurodevelopmental disorders for a number of reasons, primarily the ambiguity of the literature on frontostriatal functioning highlights the need for more sensitive and specific assessments of executive functioning.

Virtual Human Teacher for Social Orienting

The virtual school environment includes artificially intelligent virtual human teacher and virtual human students that interact with the human participant in a virtual playground, virtual hallway, and virtual classroom settings using a battery of neuropsychological measures that can be administered with or without social cues from the virtual teacher: continuous performance test (CPT), picture naming test, and a Stroop test (Parsons, 2014). The actual virtual environment includes rows of desks, a teacher's desk at the front, a whiteboard across the front wall, a female virtual teacher between her desk and whiteboard, and peers seated "with" the participant in the room. The virtual teacher instructs the participant to look around the room and to point and name the various objects that they observed. Following this 1-min warm-up period, the virtual teacher tells participants that they are going to "play a game." In the virtual environment, participants view a sequence of stimuli (e.g., CPT, Stroop, or pictures) that appear for brief intervals to the left and right of the teacher on the whiteboard. There is a fixed interstimulus interval between the appearance of the stimuli (e.g., CPT, Stroop, or pictures), distractors, and the behavioral cues from the artificially intelligent virtual teacher. The virtual teacher asks participants to depress a button when any of four target stimuli appears behind her. Blocks of stimuli with varying levels of distractors and social cues are presented.

Distracters are presented across the entire presentation series. Some distractors are social (e.g., people moving by outside the classroom), while others are non-social (e.g., cars moving by outside the window). Social and non-social distracters occur with and without social cues from the teacher. A total of 144 stimuli are presented, with 72 targets and 72 non-targets. Participants complete a nondistraction and distraction condition of this task. Within conditions, there are blocks in which the teacher offers visual and verbal cues, as well as blocks where the teacher gives no social cues. Order of distraction and nondistraction, as well as teacher cue and non-cue conditions, are counterbalanced across participants. The duration of each condition is 4.8 min with a 1000 ms interstimulus interval.

This virtual teacher and classroom paradigm yields quantitative measures of: (1) Attention to Task: number of targets correctly noted and average reaction time for correct targets; (2) Teacher-Directed Attention to Task: based on virtual teacher's social cues, assessment of number correct and average reaction times relative to virtual teacher social cues (e.g., teacher looking to the target stimuli, teacher pointing, and teacher stating the need to orient to stimuli) conditions; and (3) Attention to Tasks during Social and Non-Social Distracter: the number of targets correctly noted in Social, Non-Social, and No Distracter conditions and related average reaction times. It is expected that this research paradigm will provide information related to performance with and without social cuing from the artificially intelligent virtual human teacher. The current inclusion of interactive social scenarios promises to greatly extend these results for assessment and training.

Virtual Hallway

The virtual school also includes a virtual hallway that can be used for assessing the child participant's orientation to others and social cognitive processes. The virtual school hallway was developed by Parsons to expand upon research that has been done using virtual characters to examine the roles played by eye gaze in social interactions. Pelphrey and Morris (2006) developed virtual characters that approached the participant and either meet or avoid his or her eyes. While in an MRI scanner, participants viewed these virtual characters, who shifted gaze either toward or away from the participant. In both conditions, the animated gaze evoked activation in the right superior temporal sulcus region. A functional dissociation was found between the superior temporal sulcus and the right fusiform gyrus in which the fusiform gyrus did not differentiate between mutual and averted gaze. This suggests a more direct role of the right fusiform gyrus in face detection, but a more explicit function for the superior temporal sulcus region in gaze comprehension. The behavioral nature of eye-gaze processing deficits in autism, combined with Pelphrey's prior neuroimaging findings, led to the hypothesis that superior temporal sulcus dysfunction might be involved (Pelphrey, Morris, & McCarthy, 2005). To test this, they employed their congruent versus incongruent eye-gaze paradigm in a sample of adult participants with autism and a sample of individuals without autism. Findings revealed that in neurologically normal participants, incongruent gaze shifts evoked more activity in the superior temporal sulcus region, indicating a strong effect of context. Although the superior temporal sulcus region was also activated during observation of gaze shifts in individuals with autism, no difference was found between congruent and incongruent trials. This suggests that activity in these regions was not modulated by the context of the perceived gaze shift. Furthermore, these findings implicate dysfunction in the superior temporal sulcus region as a mechanism contributing to eye-gaze processing deficits in autism (Pelphrey & Morris, 2006).

The virtual school environment hallway paradigm adds context (i.e., a virtual school hallway environment) to the virtual character paradigm. Following the work of Pelphrey and colleagues, the virtual hallway (in the virtual school environment) offers various experimental conditions. In each, participants view a virtual hallway representative of one that might be found in a school environment. A virtual human (male and female versions are available) enters the participant's view by rounding a corner on the far side of the hall. The virtual human walks toward the participant and shifts eye gaze while passing (5.8 s after the onset of the sequence). During the mutual-gaze condition, the virtual human's eyes move toward the participant and remained fixed for 1 s before passing by the participant. During the averted-gaze condition, the virtual human's eyes make a movement of equal magnitude and duration away from the participant before passing by the participant. Prior to the gaze shift, the two conditions are identical. On each trial, the stimulus enters the participant's field of view from either the left or the right and appears to pass by the observer on the left or right, respectively. Four possible stimulus configurations have been developed by crossing the direction of gaze with the side on which the virtual human passes the participant. Hence, averted gaze occurs when the virtual human moves eyes to the right while passing on the right or moving eyes to the left when passing on the left. Mutual gaze occurs when the virtual human moves eyes to the right while passing on the left or moves eyes to the left while passing on the right. Stimuli are counterbalanced so that the virtual human approaches and passes the participant from the left and right sides of the hallway an equal number of times. The mechanical aspects of the gaze shifts are identical across conditions. Only the direction of gaze, and the associated social signal, differs. Participants are instructed to pay attention to the virtual human's eyes as she/he walks down the hallway. Each vignette lasts 7 s, and trials are separated by a 14-s intertrial interval, during which the participant views the virtual school hallway with no virtual human present. Trials are randomized within 7.25-min runs, and each participant completes an average of 8.5 runs.

The behavioral task includes the same two conditions, as well as a third condition in which the passing virtual human does not make a gaze shift. Again, participants view brief scenarios, which are separated by a 3- to 5-s intertrial interval. Participants press buttons to indicate whether the virtual human looks toward or away from them. Participants are instructed to make no response if they do not think the eyes shifted. Across 192 trials, each of the three conditions (mutual gaze, averted gaze, or no gaze) appears 64 times in random order. Trials are presented in four runs lasting 8.87 min each (48 trials per run), and are again counterbalanced so that the virtual human approaches from each side of the hallway an equal number of times.

Virtual Playground

In the virtual school environment, participants also engage in a virtual Cyberball paradigm developed by Dr. Parsons. The virtual playground builds off of 2D (Williams, Cheung, & Choi, 2000) and 3D (Venturini et al., 2016) virtual Cyberball paradigms. The main addition here is the context (a playground) and ability to vary the artificially intelligent virtual human interactions. The task has three players (i.e., two avatar confederates and participants' avatar) in the following conditions: social inclusion (each of three avatars receive 33% of ball tosses), social over-inclusion (percentage of ball tosses to participant is 66%), social exclusion (percentage of ball tosses to participant is below 33% with all demographic variables the same between avatars), and social ostracism (percentage of ball tosses to participant is below 33% with different demographic variables (e.g., skin color or style of clothing) different between confederates and participant) condition designed to elicit out-group status. Participants are randomly assigned to study conditions.

The development of the virtual playground Cyberball platform draws rationale from neuroimaging results for the 2D Cyberball paradigm that revealed significant difference between persons with autism and typically developing participants. Moreover, Cyberball studies have reported less activity during exclusion versus inclusion among participants with autism in brain regions involved in emotion processing, including anterior cingulate cortex and anterior insula. Furthermore, Masten et al. (2011) found less activity during exclusion in regions previously shown to be negatively related to distress during exclusion (i.e., ventrolateral prefrontal cortex, VS). This differential engagement of neural circuitry in response to peer rejection could also be related to peer rejection experiences that adolescents with autism have in their daily lives. They may be more habituated to be rejected by novel groups of peers. Bolling et al. (2011) found that only participants with autism reported an activation to rule violation in bilateral caudate, superior temporal sulcus, and anterior insula. In Krach et al. (2015), only participants with autism showed domain-specific decrements in the neurobiological response of vicarious social pain. McPartland et al. (2011) analyzed temporal dynamics of brain activity associated with social exclusion and reported that in autism there is a dissociation between reported distress and neural responses and differentiation of rejection at an earlier frontal P2 component. The temporal course of the early positivity (P2) indicates a role in more basic cognitive processing, such as visual attention in autism. Lastly, the study using oxytocin administration (Andari, Richard, Leboyer, & Sirigu, 2016) showed that IN-OT helped autism to discriminate between different social contexts and social values associated to faces (Kirsch et al., 2005), by modulating the brain activity of key emotional regions (amygdala and hippocampus). During social reciprocity, OT delivery prompted the activity of anterior OFC in individuals with autism and modulates stress responses as a function of positive social interactions (Chen et al., 2011).

Other studies are emerging that have aimed at evolving the 2D virtual Cyberball paradigm. While some include simple additions like a fourth "neutral" player to verify the level of understanding of exclusion (Van Der Meulen, Van IJzendoorn, & Crone, 2016; Andari et al., 2010), others have evolved Cyberball into a 3D virtual environment (Venturini et al., 2016: Mavromihelaki et al., 2014). In the 3D virtual environment versions of Cyberball, social information about the confederates' avatars can be manipulated to ensure a greater identification with (or differentiation from) the player (Venturini et al., 2016; Bolling et al., 2011). Furthermore, Kassner et al. (2012) created an immersive virtual environment version that places the participant into a virtual and interactive environment. This change induced an effect size medium to large in magnitude of feelings of ostracism. This paradigm could be further implemented by including the variables of gender and age in order to carry out trans-cultural studies.

Immersive 3D Cyberball paradigms may offer enhanced ecological validity to obviate some of the ambiguities found in the literature. While the 2D Cyberball paradigm has been widely used, some of the less robust findings may reflect the fact that 2D versions of the Cyberball task lack the everyday realism and ecological validity that are now available in today's immersive 3D virtual environments. Kassner et al. (2012) proposed an advancement in the Cyberball paradigm, an immersive virtual environment version, in which the participants wear a head-mounted display (HMD), through which the virtual environment was displayed. Results revealed that the more immersive virtual environments induced feelings of ostracism in participants. Data from this study suggest that not only does ostracism in this environment have the same negative effects as in other environments, but these effects are powerful. Other virtual reality desktop versions (Venturini et al., 2016; Mavromihelaki et al., 2014; Bolling et al., 2011) have been developed to allow even greater levels of flexibility for manipulation of social information about the participant's interactions with confederate avatars and virtual humans (Wirth, Feldberg, Schouten, Hooff, & Williams, 2011). The inclusion of virtual humans enhances the Cyberball paradigm because it allows for additional social information such as non-verbal (e.g., eye gaze) information that has been found to convey ostracism (Wirth et al., 2011). Furthermore, the immersive virtual environment Cyberball paradigm offers researchers the ability to control aspects (proxemics and non-verbal communication) of the social context that cannot be accomplished in minimalist ostracism paradigms.

Application of Virtual Classrooms in School Environment

Virtual reality environments are reportedly a valid instructional method that reinforces learning and improves learning retention (Farra, Miller, Timm, & Schafer, 2013; Thorsteinsson & Page, 2008). However, opposing voices like Ellaway (2006) state that educational interventions that diverge from the physical world should be employed with close attention to the ways in which such divergence is helpful and the ways in which it can distract or even detract from the individual's ability to practice. However, many other studies support the idea that simulation used as a teaching strategy eliminates inherent risks in practicing in the healthcare environment. Halvorson, Crittenden, and Pitt (2011) found that a case-based class using a virtual simulated scenario like Second Life (SL) could be held and attended independent of time, distance, and location should the need arise, and supported case teaching in SL as a feasible alternative or supplement to the traditional case teaching and learning approach.

A recent meta-review by Reisoğlu, Topu, Yılmaz, Karakuş Yılmaz, and Göktaş (2017) investigated recent empirical research studies about 3D virtual learning environments. They examined 167 empirical studies involving the utilization of 3D virtual worlds in education. They concluded that 3D virtual learning environments are mainly designed for learning support, simulation, and game, with language learning and science being the most extensively studied topics. Collaborative and exploration-based learning strategies were used most frequently in 3D virtual learning environments. Finally, presence, satisfaction, communication skills, and engagement were found to be the most common emotional and cognitive achievements.

In a very specific experience with Chemistry education, Limniou, Roberts, and Papadopoulos (2008) found that, after the participation in 3D animations, at the 3D VR environment students comprehended the molecules' structure and their changes during a chemical reaction better than during the 2D animations on the computer's desktop, as the limitations of human vision had been overcome. Furthermore, the students were enthusiastic, as they had the feeling that they were inside the chemical reactions and they were facing the 3D molecules as if they were real objects in front of them, thus increasing the feeling of presence and immersion in the VR environment.

Virvou and Katsionis (2008), in relation to the implementation of VR based games in a classroom learning environment, found that, once usability problems are overcome, likeability of the VR game was proportional to the sophistication of the VR environment of the game. They suggested that if VR educational games are designed to reach a high degree of sophistication they will be quite competitive to commercial games of no educational content, and that this would provide the asset of having educational applications that can be equally attractive for the students in the school classroom and at home, increasing their motivation to make better use of both their school time and leisure time to the benefit of educational goals.

Finally, in terms of how to bring VR into educational environments, Fernandez (2017) proposes a six-step methodology to aid adoption of these technologies as basic elements within the regular education: (1) training teachers; (2) developing conceptual prototypes; (3) teamwork involving the teacher, a technical programmer, and an educational architect; (4) and producing the experience, which then provides results in the subsequent two phases wherein (5) teachers are trained to apply augmented- and virtual-reality solutions within their teaching methodology using an available subject-specific experience and then finally (6) implementing the use of the experience in a regular subject with students.

Conclusions

Given the above, it is possible that the virtual school environment can offer an ecologically valid approach to assessments that can meaningfully inform a neuropsychologist's predictive statements about a student's real-world functioning. The differential diagnosis and treatment planning for children with neurodevelopmental disorders that impact the brain's frontostriatal system require assessments that can differentiate the overlapping symptoms. In this chapter we started with a review of 2D computerized CPT assessments of executive functions. Again, although these approaches provide highly systematic control and delivery of performance challenges, they have also been criticized as limited in the area of ecological validity.

We introduced a possible answer to the problems of ecological validity in the form of virtual classroom CPTs. While there is a growing body of literature supporting this approach, we wondered about the lack of artificial intelligence and social interactions in the nonplayer characters (teacher and students) found in these early virtual classroom environments. Perhaps a better approach is found in the virtual school environment and its inclusion of intelligent virtual teachers and interactive virtual students. In the virtual school environment, the child immersed into adaptive and interactive virtual classroom, hallway, and playground environments where she/he interacts with a virtual human teacher. The virtual school environment developed by Parsons at the University of North Texas has combined the attentional assessment found in a virtual classroom environment with virtual human technology. His lab has placed an interactive and intelligent virtual human teacher (as well as students) with verbal and non-verbal receptive and expressive language abilities into the virtual environment to aid in assessment of joint attention. The virtual human teacher acts as a social orienting system that comports well with the social orienting hypothesis of autism. The result is that researchers and clinicians may differentiate attention deficits that exist regardless of social facilitation from those executive functions that may be alleviated by a virtual teacher.

While there is inherent promise in the virtual school environment, not all children will respond to this assessment and treatment modality in the same way. To the extent that our approach is correct, we hope to encourage clinicians and researchers to shift from approaches that assess cold cognitive processing alone to batteries that include assessments of both cold and hot cognitive processes via interactive social simulations.

References

Adams, R., Finn, P., Moes, E., Flannery, K., & Rizzo, A. S. (2009). Distractibility in attention/deficit/hyperactivity disorder (ADHD): The virtual reality classroom. *Child Neuropsychology, 15*(2), 120–135.

Andari, E., Duhamel, J. R., Zalla, T., Herbrecht, E., Leboyer, M., & Sirigu, A. (2010). Promoting social behavior with oxytocin in high-functioning autism spectrum disorders. *Proceedings of the National Academy of Sciences of the United States of America, 107*, 4389–4394.

Andari, E., Richard, N., Leboyer, M., & Sirigu, A. (2016). Adaptive coding of the value of social cues with oxytocin, an fMRI study in autism spectrum disorder. *Cortex, 76*, 79–88.

Areces, D., Rodríguez, C., García, T., Cueli, M., & González-Castro, P. (2018). Efficacy of a continuous performance test based on virtual reality in the diagnosis of ADHD and its clinical presentations. *Journal of Attention Disorders, 22*(11), 1081–1091. https://doi.org/10.1177/1087054716629711

Barkley, R. A. (1994). Can neuropsychological tests help diagnose ADD/ADHD? *The ADHD Report, 2*, 1–3.

Biederman, J., Faraone, S. V., Milberger, S., & Doyle, A. (1993). Diagnoses of attention-deficit hyperactivity disorder from parent reports predict diagnoses based on teacher reports. *Journal of the American Academy of Child & Adolescent Psychiatry, 32*, 315–317.

Bioulac, S., Lallemand, S., Rizzo, A., Philip, P., Fabrigoule, C., & Bouvard, M. P. (2012). Impact of time on task on ADHD patient's performances in a virtual classroom. *European Journal of Paediatric Neurology, 16*(5), 514–521.

Bohil, C. J., Alicea, B., & Biocca, F. A. (2011). Virtual reality in neuroscience research and therapy. *Nature Reviews Neuroscience, 12*, 752–762.

Bolling, D. Z., Pitskel, N. B., Deen, B., Crowley, M. J., Mayes, L. C., & Pelphrey, K. A. (2011). Development of neural systems for processing social exclusion from childhood to adolescence. *Developmental Science, 14*(6), 1431–1444.

Bottari, C., Dassa, C., Rainville, C., & Dutil, E. (2009). The criterion-related validity of the IADL: Profile with measures of executive functions, indices of trauma severity and sociodemographic characteristics. *Brain Injury, 23*, 322–335.

Brock, L. L., Rimm-Kaufman, S. E., Nathanson, L., & Grimm, K. J. (2009). The contributions of 'hot' and 'cool' executive function to children's academic achievement, learning-related behaviors, and engagement in kindergarten. *Early Childhood Research Quarterly, 24*(3), 337–349.

Burgess, P. W., Alderman, N., Forbes, C., Costello, A., Laure, M. C., Dawson, D. R., et al. (2006). The case for the development and use of "ecologically valid" measures of executive function in experimental and clinical neuropsychology. *Journal of the International Neuropsychological Society, 12*(2), 194–209.

Chan, R. C., Shum, D., Toulopoulou, T., & Chen, E. Y. (2008). Assessment of executive functions: Review of instruments and identification of critical issues. *Archives of Clinical Neuropsychology, 23*(2), 201–216.

Chaytor, N., & Schmitter-Edgecombe, M. (2003). The ecological validity of neuropsychological tests: A review of the literature on everyday cognitive skills. *Neuropsychology Review, 13,* 181–197.

Chen, F. S., Kumsta, R., von Dawans, B., Monakhov, M., Ebstein, R. P., & Heinrichs, M. (2011). Common oxytocin receptor gene (OXTR) polymorphism and social support interact to reduce stress in humans. *Proceedings of the National Academy of Sciences, 108*(50), 19937–19942.

Conners, C. K. (2004). *Conners' CPT II: Continuous performance test II.* New York: MHS.

Davidson, D. J., Zacks, R. T., & Williams, C. (2003). Stroop interference, practice, and aging. *Aging, Neuropsychology and Cognition, 10,* 85–98.

de Nijs, P. F., Ferdinand, R. F., de Bruin, E. I., Dekker, M. C. J., van Duijn, C. M., & Verhulst, D. C. (2004). Attention-deficit/hyperactivity disorder (ADHD): Parents' judgment about school, teachers' judgment about home. *European Child & Adolescent Psychiatry, 13,* 315–320.

Díaz-Orueta, U., Alonso-Sánchez, B., & Climent, G. (2014). *AULA versus d2 test of attention: Convergent validity and applicability of virtual reality in the study of reading disorders. Preliminary results.* Poster presented at the 42th Annual Meeting of the International Neuropsychological Society, Seattle, USA, 12–15 February.

Díaz-Orueta, U., Cueto, E., Alonso-Sánchez, B., Crespo-Eguílaz, N., Fernández, M., Otaduy, C., et al. (2014). *AULA VR based attention test: Factorial validity and convergent validity with commonly used ADHD diagnostic tools.* Poster presented at the 9th Conference of the International Test Commission, San Sebastian, Spain, 2–5 July.

Díaz-Orueta, U., Fernández-Fernández, M. A., Morillo-Rojas, M. D., & Climent, G. (2016). Efficacy of lisdexamphetamine to improve the behavioural and cognitive symptoms of attention deficit hyperactivity disorder: Treatment monitored by means of the AULA Nesplora virtual reality test. *Revista de Neurologia, 63*(1), 19–27.

Díaz-Orueta, U., Garcia-López, C., Crespo-Eguílaz, N., Sánchez-Carpintero, R., Climent, G., & Narbona, J. (2014). AULA virtual reality test as an attention measure: Convergent validity with Conners' continuous performance test. *Child Neuropsychology: A Journal on Normal and Abnormal Development in Childhood and Adolescence, 20*(3), 328–342.

Díaz-Orueta, U., Iriarte, Y., Climent, G., & Banterla, F. (2012). AULA: An ecological virtual reality test with distractors for evaluating attention in children and adolescents. *Journal of Virtual Reality, 5,* 1–20.

Duffield, T. C., Parsons, T. D., Landry, A., Karam, S., Otero, T., Mastel, S., & Hall, T. A. (2017). Virtual environments as an assessment modality with pediatric ASD populations: a brief report. *Child Neuropsychology,* 1–8.

Ellaway, R. (2006). eMedical teacher. *Medical Teacher, 28*(8), 751–752.

Epstein, J. N., Erkanli, A., Conners, C. K., Kleric, J., Castello, J. E., & Angold, A. (2003). Relations between continuous performance test performance measures and ADHD behaviors. *Journal of Abnormal Child Psychology, 31*(5), 543–554.

Farra, S., Miller, E., Timm, N., & Schafer, J. (2013). Improved training for disasters using 3-D virtual reality simulation. *Western Journal of Nursing Research, 35*(5), 655–671.

Fernandez, M. (2017). Augmented virtual reality: How to improve education systems. *Higher Learning Research Communications, 7,* 1–15.

Fernández-Fernández, M., & Morillo-Rojas, M. (2012). *Test—Retest validation of AULA Nesplora (virtual reality continuous performance test) for ADHD.* Poster presented at the 2nd International ADHD Conference, Barcelona, Spain, 23–25 May.

Forbes, G. B. (1998). Clinical utility of the test of variables of attention (TOVA) in the diagnosis of attention-deficit/hyperactivity disorder. *Journal of Clinical Psychology, 54,* 461–476.

Gilboa, Y., Kerrouche, B., Longaud-Vales, A., Kieffer, V., Tiberghien, A., Aligon, D., et al. (2015). Describing the attention profile of children and adolescents with acquired brain injury using the Virtual Classroom. *Brain Injury, 29*(13–14), 1691–1700.

Gilboa, Y., Rosenblum, S., Fattal-Valevski, A., Toledano-Alhadef, H., Rizzo, A. S., & Josman, N. (2011). Using a Virtual Classroom environment to describe the attention deficits profile of children with Neurofibromatosis type 1. *Research in Developmental Disabilities, 32*(6), 2608–2613.

Gordon, M. (1983). The Gordon Diagnostic System (GDS) The Standard in Computerized Assessment of Attention and Self Control (online). Retrieved September 25, 2014, from http://www.devdis.com/gds.html (online).

Greenberg, L. M., & Waldman, I. D. (1993). Developmental normative data on the Test of Variables of Attention (TOVA). *Journal of Child Psychology and Psychiatry, 34*, 1019–1030.

Gutiérrez Maldonado, J., Letosa Porta, A., Rus Calafell, M., & Peñaloza Salazar, C. (2009). The assessment of Attention Deficit Hyperactivity Disorder in children using continuous performance tasks in virtual environments. *Anuario de Psicología, 40*(2), 211–222.

Halvorson, W., Crittenden, V. L., & Pitt, L. (2011). Teaching cases in a virtual environment: When the traditional case classroom is problematic. *Decision Sciences Journal of Innovative Education, 9*(3), 485–492.

Iriarte, Y., Díaz-Orueta, U., Cueto, E., Irazustabarrena, P., Banterla, F., & Climent, G. (2016). AULA—Advanced virtual reality tool for the assessment of attention: Normative study in Spain. *Journal of Attention Disorders, 20*(6), 542–568.

Kaplan, R. M., Howard, V. J., Safford, M. M., & Howard, G. (2015). Educational attainment and longevity: results from the REGARDS US national cohort study of blacks and whites. *Annals of epidemiology, 25*(5), 323–328.

Kassner, M. P., Wesselmann, E. D., Law, A. T., & Williams, K. D. (2012). Virtually ostracized: Studying ostracism in immersive virtual environments. *Cyberpsychology, Behavior, and Social Networking, 15*(8), 399–403.

Kirsch, P., Esslinger, C., Chen, Q., Mier, D., Lis, S., Siddhanti, S., et al. (2005). Oxytocin modulates neural circuitry for social cognition and fear in humans. *Journal of Neuroscience, 25*(49), 11489–11493.

Krach, S., Kamp-Becker, I., Einhäuser, W., Sommer, J., Frässle, S., Jansen, A., et al. (2015). Evidence from pupillometry and fMRI indicates reduced neural response during vicarious social pain but not physical pain in autism. *Human Brain Mapping, 14*, 4730–4744.

Lalonde, G., Henry, M., Drouin-Germain, A., Nolin, P., & Beauchamp, M. H. (2013). Assessment of executive function in adolescence: A comparison of traditional and virtual reality tools. *Journal of Neuroscience Methods, 219*(1), 76–82.

Lemay, S., Bedard, M. A., Roulea, I., & Tremblay, P. L. G. (2004). Practice effect and test–retest reliability of attentional and executive tests in middle-aged to elderly subjects. *The Clinical Neuropsychologist, 18*, 284–302.

Limniou, M., Roberts, D., & Papadopoulos, N. (2008). Full immersive virtual environment CAVETM in chemistry education. *Computers & Education, 51*(2), 584–593.

Llorente, A. M., Voigt, R., Jensen, C. L., Fraley, J. K., Heird, W. C., & Rennie, K. M. (2007). The test of variables of attention (TOVA): Internal consistency (Q(1) vs Q(2) and Q(3) vs Q(4)) in children with attention deficit/hyperactivity disorder [ADHD]. *Child Neuropsychology, 3*, 1–9.

Losier, B. J., McGrath, P. J., & Klein, R. M. (1996). Error patterns on the continuous performance test in non-medicated and medicated samples of children with and without ADHD: A meta-analytic review. *Journal of Child Psychology and Psychiatry, 37*, 971–987.

MacLeod, C. M. (1991). Half a century of research on the Stroop effect: an integrative review. *Psychological Bulletin, 109*(2), 163– 203.

MacLeod, C. M. (1992). The Stroop task: The "gold standard" of attentional measures. *Journal of Experimental Psychology: General, 121*(1), 12–14.

Manchester, D., Priestley, N., & Jackson, H. (2004). The assessment of executive functions: Coming out of the office. *Brain Injury, 18*(11), 1067–1081.

Masten, C. L., Colich, N. L., Rudie, J. D., Bookheimer, S. Y., Eisenberger, N. I., & Dapretto, M. (2011). An fMRI investigation of responses to peer rejection in adolescents with autism spectrum disorders. *Developmental Cognitive Neuroscience, 1*(3), 260–270.

Mavromihelaki, E., Eccles, J., Harrison, N., Grice-Jackson, T., Ward, J., Critchley, H., et al. (2014). *Cyberball3D+: A 3D serious game for fMRI investigating social exclusion and empathy*. 6th International Conference on Games and Virtual Worlds for Serious Applications: VS-GAMES 2014.

McPartland, J. C., Crowley, M. J., Perszyk, D. R., Naples, A., Mukerji, C. E., Wu, J., et al. (2011). Temporal dynamics reveal atypical brain response to social exclusion in autism. *Developmental Cognitive Neuroscience, 1*(3), 271–279.

Mejías, M., Redondo, M., Fernández, M., & Diaz-Orueta, U. (2016). *Eficacia del metilfenidato de liberación prolongada en la mejora sintomática cognitiva y conductual del TDAH monitorizado a través de AULA Nesplora*. XX Congreso Anual de la Academia Iberoamericana de Neurología Pediátrica (AINP), Madrid, Spain, 8th–10th September.

Mitsis, E. M., McKay, K. E., Schulz, K. P., Newcorn, J. H., & Halperin, J. M. (2000). Parent-teacher concordance for DSM–IV attention-deficit/hyperactivity disorder in a clinic-referred sample. *Journal of the American Academy of Child & Adolescent Psychiatry, 39*, 308–313.

Mühlberger, A., Jekel, K., Probst, T., Schecklmann, M., Conzelmann, A., Andreatta, M., et al. (2016). The influence of methylphenidate on hyperactivity and attention deficits in children with ADHD: A virtual classroom test. *Journal of Attention Disorders*, 1087054716647480.

Neguţ, A., Jurma, A. M., & David, D. (2017). Virtual-reality-based attention assessment of ADHD: ClinicaVR: Classroom-CPT versus a traditional continuous performance test. *Child Neuropsychology, 23*(6), 692–712.

Nolin, P., Martin, C., & Bouchard, S. (2009). Assessment of inhibition deficits with the virtual classroom in children with traumatic brain injury: A pilot-study. *Studies in Health Technology and Informatics, 144*, 240–242.

Nolin, P., Stipanicic, A., Henry, M., Joyal, C. C., & Allain, P. (2012). Virtual reality as a screening tool for sports concussion in adolescents. *Brain Injury, 26*(13–14), 1564–1573.

Nolin, P., Stipanicic, A., Henry, M., Lachapelle, Y., Lussier-Desrochers, D., Rizzo, A., et al. (2016). ClinicaVR: Classroom-CPT: A virtual reality tool for assessing attention and inhibition in children and adolescents. *Computers in Human Behavior, 59*, 327–333.

Parsons, T. D. (2014). Virtual teacher and classroom for assessment of neurodevelopmental disorders. In S. Brahnam & L. C. Jain (Eds.), *Serious games, alternative realities, and play therapy* (pp. 121–137). Heidelberg: Springer.

Parsons, T. D. (2015). Virtual reality for enhanced ecological validity and experimental control in the clinical, affective and social neurosciences. *Frontiers in Human Neuroscience, 9*, 660.

Parsons, S. (2016). Authenticity in virtual reality for assessment and intervention in autism: A conceptual review. *Educational Research Review, 19*, 138–157.

Parsons, T. D., Bowerly, T., Buckwalter, J. G., & Rizzo, A. A. (2007). A controlled clinical comparison of attention performance in children with ADHD in a virtual reality classroom compared to standard neuropsychological methods. *Child Neuropsychology, 13*, 363–381.

Parsons, T. D., & Carlew, A. R. (2016). Bimodal virtual reality Stroop for assessing distractor inhibition in autism Spectrum disorders. *Journal of Autism and Developmental Disorders, 46*(4), 1255–1267.

Parsons, T. D., Carlew, A. R., Magtoto, J., & Stonecipher, K. (2017). The potential of function-led virtual environments for ecologically valid measures of executive function in experimental and clinical neuropsychology. *Neuropsychological Rehabilitation, 37*(5), 777–807.

Parsons, T. D., Courtney, C., & Dawson, M. (2013). Virtual reality Stroop task for assessment of supervisory attentional processing. *Journal of Clinical and Experimental Neuropsychology, 35*, 812–826.

Parsons, T. D., Gaggioli, A., & Riva, G. (2017). Virtual environments in social neuroscience. *Brain Sciences, 7*(42), 1–21.

Parsons, T. D., & Phillips, A. (2016). Virtual reality for psychological assessment in clinical practice. *Practice Innovations, 1*, 197–217.

Parsons, T. D., Riva, G., Parsons, S., Mantovani, F., Newbutt, N., Lin, L., et al. (2017). Virtual reality in pediatric psychology: Benefits, challenges, and future directions. *Pediatrics, 140*, 86–91.

Parsons, T.D., McMahan, T., & Kane, R. (2018). Practice Parameters Facilitating Adoption of Advanced Technologies for Enhancing Neuropsychological Assessment Paradigms. The Clinical Neuropsychologist, 32, 16–41.

Parsons, T. D., & Rizzo, A. A. (in press). A virtual classroom for ecologically valid assessment of attention-deficit/hyperactivity disorder. In P. Sharkey (Ed.), *Virtual reality technologies for health and clinical applications: Psychological and neurocognitive interventions.* Heidelberg: Springer.

Pelphrey, K. A., & Morris, J. P. (2006). Brain mechanisms for interpreting the actions of others from biological-motion cues. *Current Directions in Psychological Science, 15*(3), 136–140.

Pelphrey, K. A., Morris, J. P., & McCarthy, G. (2005). Neural basis of eye gaze processing deficits in autism. *Brain, 128*(5), 1038–1048.

Pollak, Y., Shomaly, H. B., Weiss, P. L., Rizzo, A. A., & Gross-Tsur, V. (2010). Methylphenidate effect in children with ADHD can be measured by an ecologically valid continuous performance test embedded in virtual reality. *CNS Spectrums, 15*(2), 125–130.

Pollak, Y., Weiss, P. L., Rizzo, A. A., Weizer, M., Shriki, L., Shalev, R. S., et al. (2009). The utility of a continuous performance test embedded in virtual reality in measuring ADHD-related deficits. *Journal of Developmental & Behavioral Pediatrics, 30*(1), 2–6.

Reisoğlu, I., Topu, B., Yılmaz, R., Karakuş Yılmaz, T., & Göktaş, Y. (2017). 3D virtual learning environments in education: A meta-review. *Asia Pacific Education Review, 18*(1), 81–100.

Riccio, C. A., Garland, B. H., & Cohen, M. J. (2007). Relations between the test of variables of attention (TOVA) and the Children's Memory Scale (CMS). *Journal of Attention Disorders, 11*, 167–171.

Riccio, C. A., Reynolds, C. R., & Lowe, P. (2001). *Clinical applications of continuous performance tests.* New York: Wiley.

Rizzo, A. A., Bowerly, T., Buckwalter, J. G., Limchuk, D., Mitura, R., & Parsons, T. D. (2006). A virtual reality scenario for all seasons: The virtual classroom. *CNS Spectrums, 11*, 35–44.

Rufo-Campos, M., Cueto, E., Iriarte, Y., & Rufo-Muñoz, M. (2012). *Sensitivity study of a new diagnostic method for ADHD: Aula Nesplora.* Paper presented at the XXXVI Annual Meeting of the Spanish Society of Pediatric Neurology, Santander, Spain, 31st May–2nd June.

Sandford, J. A., & Turner, A. (1995). *Manual for the integrated visual and auditory (IVA) continuous performance test.* Richmond, VA: BrainTrain.

Sbordone, R. J. (2008). Ecological validity of neuropsychological testing: Critical issues. In A. M. Horton Jr. & D. Wedding (Eds.), *The neuropsychology handbook* (pp. 367–394). New York, NY: Springer.

Séguin, J. R., Arseneault, L., & Tremblay, R. E. (2007). The contribution of "cool" and "hot" components of decision-making in adolescence: Implications for developmental psychopathology. *Cognitive Development, 22*(4), 530–543.

Servera, M., & Llabrés, J. (2004). *CSAT: Children sustained attention task [Book in Spanish].* Madrid: TEA.

Thorsteinsson, G., & Page, T. (2008). Innovative technology education using a virtual reality learning environment. *Pedagogy Studies (Pedagogika), 90*, 26–35.

U.S. Department of Education, National Center for Education Statistics, Schools and Staffing Survey (SASS). "Public School Data File," 2007–2008.

Uttl, B., & Graf, P. (1997). Color–Word Stroop test performance across the adult life span. *Journal of Clinical and Experimental Neuropsychology, 19*, 405–420.

Van Der Meulen, M., Van IJzendoorn, M. H., & Crone, E. A. (2016). Neural correlates of prosocial behavior: Compensating social exclusion in a four-player cyberball game. *PLoS One, 11*(7), 1–13.

Venturini, E., Riva, P., Serpetti, F., Romero, L., Pallavincini, F., Mantovani, F., et al. (2016). A comparison of 3D versus 2D virtual environments on the feelings of social exclusion, inclusion and over-inclusion. *Annual Review of CyberTherapy and Telemedicine, 14*, 89–94.

Virvou, M., & Katsionis, G. (2008). On the usability and likeability of virtual reality games for education: The case of VR-ENGAGE. *Computers and Education, 50*(1), 154–178.

Wada, N., Yamashita, Y., Matsuishi, T., Ohtani, Y., & Kato, H. (2000). The test of variables of attention (TOVA) is useful in the diagnosis of Japanese male children with attention deficit hyperactivity disorder. *Brain Development, 22*, 378–382.

Washburn, D. A. (2016). The Stroop effect at 80: The competition between stimulus control and cognitive control. *Journal of the Experimental Analysis of Behavior, 105*(1), 3–13.

Weyandt, L. L., Mitzlaff, L., & Thomas, L. (2002). The relationship between intelligence and performance on the test of variables of attention (TOVA). *Journal of Learning Disabilities, 35*, 114–120.

White, S. W., Richey, J. A., Gracanin, D., Bell, M. A., LaConte, S., Coffman, M., et al. (2014). The promise of neurotechnology in clinical translational science. *Clinical Psychological Science, 3*(5), 797–815.

Williams, K. D., Cheung, C. K. T., & Choi, W. (2000). CyberOstracism: Effects of being ignored over the Internet. *Journal of Personality and Social Psychology, 79*, 748–762.

Wilson, B. A. (1998). Cognitive rehabilitation: How it is and how it should be. *Journal of the International Neuropsychological Society, 3*, 487–496.

Wirth, J., Feldberg, F., Schouten, A. P., Hooff, B., & Williams, K. D. (2011). Using virtual game environments to study group behavior. In A. Hollingshead & M. Scott Poole (Eds.), *Research methods for studying groups and teams: A guide to approaches, tools and technologies* (pp. 1–24). New York, NY: Routledge.

Zelazo, P. D., & Carlson, S. M. (2012). Hot and cool executive function in childhood and adolescence: Development and plasticity. *Child Development Perspectives, 6*(4), 354–360.

Zelnik, N., Bennett-Back, O., Miari, W., Goez, H. R., & Fattal-Valevski, A. (2012). Is the test of variables of attention reliable for the diagnosis of attention-deficit hyperactivity disorder (ADHD)? *Journal of Child Neurology, 27*, 703. https://doi.org/10.1177/0883073811423821. Published online, 28th February 2012.

Zimmerman, D. L., Ownsworth, T., O'Donovan, A., Roberts, J., & Gullo, M. J. (2016). Independence of hot and cold executive function deficits in high-functioning adults with autism spectrum disorder. *Frontiers in Human Neuroscience, 10*, 24.

Zulueta, A., Iriarte, Y., Díaz-Orueta, U., & Climent, G. (2013). Aula Nesplora: Progress in assessing attention processes—A convergent validity study with the Faces—Perception of Differences Test (extended version). *ISEP Science, 4*, 3–10.

Thomas D. Parsons is Director of the NetDragon Digital Research Centre and the Computational Neuropsychology and Simulation (CNS) laboratory at the University of North Texas. His work integrates neuropsychology, psychophysiology, and simulation technologies for novel assessment, modeling, and training of neurocognitive and affective processes. He is a leading scientist in this area and he has been PI of 17 funded projects during his career and an investigator on an additional 13 funded projects (over $15 million in funding). In addition to his patents for eHarmony.com's Matching System (U.S. Patent Nos. 2004/6735568; 2014/0180942 A1), he has invented and validated virtual reality-based assessments (including the virtual school environment) of attention, spatial abilities, memory, and executive functions. He uses neural networks and machine learning to model mechanisms underlying reinforcement learning, decision-making, working memory, and inhibitory control. In addition to his five books, he has over 200 publications in peer reviewed journals and book chapters. His contributions to neuropsychology were recognized when he received the 2013 National Academy of Neuropsychology Early Career Achievement award. In 2014, he was awarded Fellow status in the National Academy of Neuropsychology.

Tyler Duffield, Ph.D., received his clinical psychology degree with a neuropsychology emphasis from Brigham Young University. During that time he worked in the Brain Imaging and Behavior Lab and the Utah Neuroimaging Project under the mentorship of Erin Bigler, Ph.D., primarily conducting structural imaging post-processing to be integrated and examined with neuropsychological performances. Dr. Duffield has a clinical background with neurodevelopmental and TBI populations in rehabilitation settings, and most recently working in the concussion clinic in sports medicine at OHSU. Dr. Duffield's research interests continue to involve innovative technologies, now primarily virtual reality paradigms.

Timothy McMahan, Ph.D., received his doctoral degree in Computer Science from the University of North Texas. He also completed a postdoctoral fellowship with Dr. Thomas Parsons in Computational Neuropsychology. He has a comprehensive background in Computer science and neurogaming. His expertise include videogame design and programming, machine learning, artificial intelligence, databases, and security. He has significant experience in the development of virtual reality applications using a multitude of human–computer interfaces and related devices. He has produced cutting edge research in neurogaming and brain–computer interfaces where he was able to program a system that successfully detects changes in users' neurocognitive and affective states while immersed in videogames. This also included the development and validation of new methods for assessing user experience and interactions with video games.

Unai Diaz-Orueta, Ph.D., received his Psychology Ph.D. from the University of Deusto, Spain in 2006. Since 2000, he worked as a clinical psychologist in a variety of settings, including the Crownsville Hospital Center, Crownsville, Maryland (USA, 2000–2001), Hospital Psiquiátrico de Bermeo, (Spain, 2001–2002), La Loma Geriatric Residence (Spain, 2003–2005), and Zutitu Ltd (2005–2006). His doctoral dissertation, "Effects of psychological intervention in cognitive decline of residentialized elderly people," was published by UMI Dissertation Publishing, Ann Arbor, MI (USA). Additionally, his experience includes teaching courses and workshops in maintenance of cognitive functions, well-being, and laugh-therapy for elderly people at IPACE Ltd, Vitoria (Spain, 2007–2008). From 2008 to 2012, he worked as a research psychologist at Fundación INGEMA, in several projects related to aging and physical disability. From May 2012 to December 2015, he worked as a researcher and then as R+D+I Director of Nesplora S.L. (Donostia-San Sebastian, Spain), and since May 2014, as a Collaborator Professor for the Neuropsychology and Education Master's Degree of the UNIR university (Spain). Since February 2016, he works as Marie Sklodowska-Curie Actions Postdoctoral Research Fellow in Dublin City University (Dublin, Ireland) on the EC funded project "E-SPACE: European Standardised Process Approach to Cognitive Evaluation in older people."

Part III
Policies and Praxes

Chapter 9
Implications of Social Neuroscience for Learning Technology Research and Development

Nancy W. Y. Law and Haley W. C. Tsang

Abstract Neuroscientific research has unequivocally pointed to the deeply social nature of human learning. Learning at the cognitive behavioral level is underpinned by neurophysiological changes in brain structure and connectivity across different parts of the brain as the learner interacts with others and the environment. Studies of epigenetic processes show that learning is dynamic, requiring learner engagement and contingent feedback. Agency, contingency and appropriate feedback are also keys to learning effectiveness at higher cognitive levels. The field of instructional design has traditionally focused on supporting the instructor, built on a model of *learning as receiving instructions*. Based on learning outcomes that are important for learners in the twenty-first century (communication, collaboration, creativity, critical thinking, and global competence), this model of learning support is outdated and irrelevant. This chapter begins with a review of key research directions in the deployment of technology-enhanced learning for infants and children based on neuroscience research, with a focus on social robots and serious games. It then reviews the challenges in the assessment and provision of learning support for collaborative problem-solving. The chapter ends by identifying some research directions for interdisciplinary collaboration among researchers in learning/instructional design and the science of learning that will help to advance theory and educational practice in collaborative problem-solving.

Introduction

What is the meaning of learning, and how do human beings develop? How a researcher in learning design and technology answers the above question, determines to a large extent the focus and direction of his/her research. Piaget (1970) made important contributions to our understanding of learning by demonstrating that learners are not *tabula rasa* to be filled with knowledge in classrooms, and that

N. W. Y. Law (✉) · H. W. C. Tsang
Faculty of Education, The University of Hong Kong, Pokfulam, Hong Kong
e-mail: nlaw@hku.hk; haleywct@connect.hku.hk; http://web.edu.hku.hk/staff/academic/nlaw

© Association for Educational Communications and Technology 2019
T. D. Parsons et al. (eds.), *Mind, Brain and Technology*, Educational Communications and Technology: Issues and Innovations,
https://doi.org/10.1007/978-3-030-02631-8_9

they learn through constructing their own understanding based on prior experiences and interactions with the external environment.

A more recent classic work by Thelen and Smith (1994) put forward a dynamic systems approach to understanding human development developed by connecting dynamic systems theory to developmental psychology and neuroscience theories and empirical findings. This work demonstrates that complex forms of behavior are constructed through individuals' explorations of the social and physical world in their everyday life. For example, an infant develops the ability to reach from flapping his arms and learns to walk from kicking his legs. Further, there is no single causality for change, and any developmental progression would involve a multitude of changes involving perceptual, biochemical, physiological, neurological, cognitive, and social processes as the person acts and interacts with the surrounding physical and social environment. Designs and technologies for learning need to be underpinned by an understanding of how children's everyday activities contribute to their developmental change. Further the authenticity of the learning environment and task design are also of paramount importance in influencing the achievement of the targeted learning outcomes.

The escalating speed of technological development is both empowering and challenging our society in fundamental ways. The invention of the Internet and digital communication technologies have in particular brought almost instantaneous connection to people separated at vast distances at a very low or no additional cost. New media technologies such as virtual reality and augmented reality have created new modalities of experience and interaction that aim to provide alternative reality for learning, entertainment and productivity in formal, informal and workplace settings. How do these changes affect the cognitive, social and emotional development of human beings?

At the societal level, the changes brought about by an increasingly connected and globalizing world impacts the twenty-first century learning priorities. Lifelong learning for decent work and for social and civic life is an important focus in the United Nations Sustainable Development Goals 2030 for quality education (UNESCO, 2017). Worldwide, many research and development projects have been conducted and policy documents published on this theme. While the details of the recommendations vary, there is broad consensus that problem-solving, collaboration, and communication for lifelong-learning are key competencies for the twenty-first century (e.g., Trilling & Fadel, 2012). This has brought about, among other concerns, great interest in the learning and assessment of collaborative problem-solving (CPS) among the broad education community (researchers, practitioners, publishers of educational resources, policy makers) and beyond.

How does the pervasive use of technology change the human brain? How can technology be leveraged to enhance learning? Given the deeply social nature of learning as identified by research in the science of learning (which will be briefly reviewed in the next section), and the importance of collaborative problem-solving as an important twenty-first century human capacity, this chapter provides an overview of the implications of neuroscience research for learning technology design and development with a focus on collaborative problem-solving.

Social Neuroscience and Learning Technology

Few studies have investigated the importance of social interactions in learning (de Greeff & Belpaeme, 2015). Social neuroscience, an emerging discipline that studies the social dimension of learning from neurophysiological, psychological, and other perspectives (Blakemore, Winston, & Frith, 2004), seeks to understand the processes and mechanisms going on inside different regions of the brain when a person learns and interacts in social contexts (Meltzoff et al., 2009). Social neuroscience moves beyond neurophysiological studies of isolated individuals to investigate the effects of different factors, including complex social stimuli on a person's learning in social situations. People's thoughts, feelings, beliefs, and relationships to others during social interactions have mutual impact on each other's neurophysiological and cognitive processes, which are also contingent upon the nature of the social interactions involved (Singer, 2012). A comprehensive review of literature shows that infant and young children up to 3 years old rarely learn from televised screens independent of the mediation of an adult (Richert, Robb, & Smith, 2011). A recent study on early language learning carried out by Roseberry, Hirsh-Pasek, and Golinkoff (2014) found that toddlers between 24 and 30 months only learned novel verbs through social interactions in the form of live interactions or via video chat. These findings are very important for the design of technology-mediated learning. Social neuroscientific studies of brain mechanisms involved in the close coupling between individuals during social interaction has the potential to provide a neurological basis for enhanced learning through social interactions (Blakemore, 2012).

Social Robots and Learning

Though social neuroscience is still a young field, it has already contributed to the design of learning technologies. One area of impact is in the development of social robots, which are robots programmed to interact with people, environment, and other robots according to social and cultural norms, with the ability to (a) move and detect the presence of persons or objects by vision, touch, sound, and other means, (b) engage in conversations, (c) acknowledge receipt of external stimuli, invitations, or changes, (d) express and perceive emotions, and (e) recognize and perform gestures (Li, Cabibihan, & Tan, 2011).

Results from studies of intervention involving social robots in language learning for infants and toddlers have been particularly encouraging. Movellan et al. (2009) show that toddlers in an early education center learning target words from a fully autonomous robot for 2 weeks show a 27% improvement compared to matched control words. Robots providing personalized affective feedback as learning companions to preschool second language learners invoke significantly higher valence from the children than non-personalizing robots (Gordon et al., 2016). In an innovative study of teaching sign language to deaf and hearing 6–12 month old infants using a robot and a virtual human avatar, Scassellati et al. (2018) were able to demonstrate that such a system can gain and direct the infants' attention to the linguistic content of sign language, maintaining their engagement and producing signs taught by the avatar.

Beyond language learning, Park et al. (2017) show that when children play a puzzle-solving game with social robots as a peer, those playing with robots that are programmed with behavior indicative of a growth mindset report a stronger growth mindset and demonstrated greater perseverance when encountering challenging tasks than those who played with robots with neutral mindsets. With emerging advances in social neuroscience, the potential of social robots as an emerging form of learning technology will increase as we gain deeper understanding of the brain mechanisms underpinning socially contingent interactions and learning, and develop more sophisticated ways of detecting and guiding socially contingent behavior.

Collaborative Serious Games

While there are burgeoning interests in the deployment of social robots to support learning, ongoing research in this area has been largely confined to studies involving children below the age of 7.[1] This is possibly because the range, flexibility, and sophistication in the robot's responses are relatively limited in their ability to sustain engagement for older children and adults. For the latter group, collaborative learning by means of multiplayer serious games can provide engaging opportunities for socially oriented learning that foster the development of "soft skills" such as communication, collaboration, critical thinking and creativity that are considered important for the twenty-first century (Wendel et al., 2010).

Engagement, interactivity, real-time response and feedback, and immersion are hallmarks of video games, offering rich, playful human-machine interfaces to scaffold social interactions (Griffiths, 2002). Well-designed video games can serve as powerful teaching tools (Bavelier et al., 2011). Game mechanics such as the setting of difficulty levels and rewards play an important role in giving learners a strong sense of accomplishment or status to drive their engagement (Phillips & Popović, 2012). In addition to the possibility of providing fast, informative and pertinent feedback contingent to the learners' actions, multiplayer game environments can afford interactions with non-player characters (NPC) and virtual objects in addition to interactions with other learners (Dickey, 2007).

Gee (2011) differentiates between two kinds of serious games: problem games and world games. The former focuses on a particular type of problems and often focuses on the learning of specific knowledge and/or skills. The latter provides a

---

[1] Social robots deployed for use by adults are primarily for therapeutic purposes in the service of senior adults.

simulated environment for the learners to explore complex real world problems. Examples include games such as *Quest Atlantis* (Barab et al., 2007) and the commercial game *Civilization*. The learner's actions and interactions with other players and NPCs are crucial to the learning process. In fact, as Gee (2011) and other learning games scholars (e.g., Barab et al., 2007) point out, the learning afforded by games, particularly in the case of world games, does not only come from the game as software but from the whole system of social interactions that the players engage in, often referred to as the "meta-game." Hence, serious games have the potential of providing a safe environment for learners to experience and learn about concepts, issues, and skills that cannot be adequately learned without understanding the complexity of the targeted social systems and the social interactions within them.

CPS: The Assessment Challenge

Socially organized learning, or learning that leverages the innate human preference for social interactions, can be deployed to achieve different kinds of learning outcome goals. In this chapter, we focus on collaborative problem-solving (CPS), which is a core twenty-first century capability that helps develop effective pedagogical strategies and learning technologies. In this section, we begin with a discussion of the challenge of assessing CPS and the role that learning technologies can play in its assessment. This will help to provide a clear conceptual anchor in defining the learning outcome that is being targeted.

Efforts to address the challenge of assessing CPS only started in the twenty-first century. Internationally, there are two well-known and widely recognized collaborative problem-solving (CPS) skills frameworks in education, the ATC21S (Assessment and Teaching of 21st Century Skills) for 11–15-year-old students, and PISA (Programme for International Student Assessment) for 15-year-old students. A brief description for these technology-based assessment frameworks and their implementation is given below.

The ATC21S Assessment Framework and Implementation

The ATC21S assessment framework comprises a three-level hierarchy of component skills (Hesse et al., 2015). At the top level are social process skills and cognitive process skills. "Social process" refers to skills required in carrying out inter-personal communication, interaction and coordination, and is further differentiated into (1) participation skills (in action, interaction and task completion), (2) perspective taking skills (to achieve adaptive responsiveness and audience awareness), and (3) social regulation skills (for negotiation, self-evaluation, transactive memory and responsible initiative). "Cognitive process" refers to skills in reasoning and managing the fine details of tasks, from identifying and defining the problem to planning, executing, reporting, monitoring and reflecting during the problem-solving process. The cognitive process skills can be further differentiated into task regulation skills (comprising problem analysis, goal setting, resource management, flexibility and ambiguity, information collection, and systematicity); and learning and knowledge-building skills (comprising the skills to represent and formulate relationships, to formulate and execute rules, and to formulate and evaluate hypothesis). Table 9.1 provides a summary of the complete list of the skills at all three levels.

In ATC21S, the CPS assessment consists of a number of tasks to be completed by two students who collaborate online to solve problems together, communicating via a chat box (Care et al., 2015). The tasks are designed so that they cannot be solved alone but would have to depend on information from or coordination with the other for task completion, thus requiring collaboration. The cognitive and collaborative levels vary from task to task.

The user-end technology required to carry out the ATC21S assessment is relatively simple compared to popular video games with instant messaging clients, and far less complex than those used in multi-player video games serving hundreds of users playing and communicating with each other at the same time.

Table 9.1 The ATC21S CPS Assessment Framework (Hesse, Care, Buder, Sassenberg, & Griffin, 2015, pp. 41–52)

The ATC21S CPS assessment framework		
Level 1	Level 2	Level 3
(1) Social process skills	(i) Participation skills	(a) Action
		(b) Interaction
		(c) Task completion/perseverance
	(ii) Perspective taking skills	(a) Adaptive responsiveness
		(b) Audience awareness (mutual modelling)
	(iii) Social regulation skills	(a) Negotiation
		(b) Self-evaluation (Metamemory)
		(c) Transactive memory
		(d) Responsibility initiative
(2) Cognitive process skills	(i) Task regulation skills	(a) Problem analysis
		(b) Goal setting
		(c) Resource management
		(d) Flexibility and ambiguity
		(e) Information collection
		(f) Systematicity
	(ii) Learning and knowledge building skills	(a) Relationships (representations and formulations)
		(b) Rules: "If…then"
		(c) Hypothesis "what if…" (reflection and monitoring)

The PISA 2015 Assessment of CPS

The Programme for International Student Assessment (PISA) is a triennial international survey conducted by OECD to evaluate education systems worldwide by testing the skills and knowledge of 15-year-old students. PISA introduced CPS assessment for the first time in 2015, which is also the first large scale international comparative assessment of CPS (OECD, 2017).

The PISA CPS assessment framework is similar to that of the ATC21S, but with a simpler structure, also with two dimensions: the cognitive and collaborative processes needed respectively for CPS. The framework further defines four cognitive processes (exploring and understanding, representing and formulating, planning and executing, and monitoring and reflecting) and three collaborative processes (maintaining shared understanding, taking action to solve the problem, and maintaining team organization) respectively, thus forming a 4 × 3 matrix (see Table 9.2). Each CPS task in PISA 2015 can be identified as requiring one of three collaborative problem-solving competences in the accomplishment of one of four problem-solving steps.

Unlike the ATC21S assessment in which pairs of students collaborate, students taking part in the PISA 2015 CPS assessment only "collaborate" with computer agents. Each CPS task is comprised of several items, with each corresponding to an

Table 9.2 PISA 2015 CPS Assessment Framework (Source: OECD, 2017, p. 50)

Problem-solving process	Collaborative problem-solving competencies		
	(1) Establishing and maintaining shared understanding	(2) Taking appropriate action to solve the problem	(3) Establishing and maintaining team organization
(a) Exploring and understanding.	(a1) Discovering perspectives and abilities of team members	(a2) Discovering the type of collaborative interaction to solve the problem, along with goals	(a3) Understanding roles to solve the problem
(b) Representing and formulating	(b1) Building a shared representation and negotiating the meaning of the problem (common ground)	(b2) Identifying and describing tasks to be completed	(b3) Describing roles and team organization (communication protocol/ rules of engagement)
(c) Planning and executing	(c1) Communicating with team members about the actions to be/being performed	(c2) Enacting plans	(c3) Following rules of engagement, (e.g., prompting other team members to perform their tasks)
(d) Monitoring and reflecting	(d1) Monitoring and repairing the shared understanding	(d2) Monitoring results of actions and evaluating success in solving the problem	(d3) Monitoring, providing feedback and adapting the team organization and roles

action a student could choose in the problem-solving process as a result of interacting with and collecting information from the computer agents.

The Challenge of Assessing CPS and Neuroscience Research

As can be seen from the above descriptions, ATC21S and PISA 2015 represent two very different approaches to how collaboration is organized in assessing CPS. In both cases, the CPS outcome to be measured is an attribute of the individual. In the case of PISA 2015, the human subject involved in the assessment is an individual, engaging in human to computer agent interaction (H2A). This setting ensures that all subjects are exposed to the same assessment conditions and hence the results are comparable. However, the validity of this form of assessment has been challenged (Griffin, Care, & Harding, 2015) in demonstrating that students in these H2A settings have similar experiences as in real life collaboration situations, and that the assessment results do predict their CPS performance in real life.

In the case of ATC21S, the assessment engages human-to-human (H2H) interactions in dyads. It also faces validity challenges, as there cannot be "standardized humans" in the assessment setting. ATC21S has established that there is no difference in the measured performance at an aggregate level whether the students are assigned to role A or role B in the task context. This same result is obtained whether the task is symmetrical or asymmetrical (i.e. whether the task measures the same indicator for both roles or otherwise). On the other hand, whether differences in the abilities of the collaborating dyad will affect their individual performance has yet to be investigated (Griffin et al., 2015)

The dilemmas and challenges to assessing CPS are unlikely to be resolved through studies within the confines of the psychometrics and assessment research. There is inadequate understanding about cognitive, metacognitive, and social affective functioning in CPS contexts, which also limits our ability to provide learning technology support for CPS. Interdisciplinary research involving neuroscientific methods to study CPS will provide an important, missing piece of the puzzle for us to seek a deeper understanding of the processes and mechanisms involved in collaborative problem-solving contexts, which will contribute to the development of better learning and assessment technologies. This is explored further in the next section.

CPS: The Learning Challenge

How does a person's perception and understanding about the social world develop? What is the developmental trajectory for a child to learn to collaborate with others? Studies show that young children can move beyond an egocentric world view and exhibit an awareness of the different perspectives taken by others. Rather than a

Piagetian stage model of egocentrism, Donaldson (1978) shows that even very young children can "decentre" and communicate with others if given the right context. What is needed for a person to advance from perspective taking to becoming a collaborator in problem-solving?

In the ATC21S framework, the social process skills (participation, perspective taking, social regulation) are considered separately from the cognitive process skills involved in the problem-solving process. These two sets of skills can be reported separately or as a single dimension for each member of the dyad. The data analysis and interpretation are based on well-established psychometric principles grounded on behavioral data gathered through the assessment tasks, and the assessment results can be presented as a progression from novice to expert performance. However, from a learning perspective, there remains a problem of whether the cognitive and social neural processes are independent of each other. The statistical distribution of item difficulties and students' scores does not reveal how an individual necessarily progresses in CPS, or what might be the obstacles to CPS advancement or how the individual could be helped to make progress in CPS.

The PISA 2015 CPS assessment also has no explicit discussion about the independence of the collaborative and problem-solving processes. However, if we inspect its assessment framework, there is an important difference in the underpinning assumption about the relationship between the social and cognitive dimensions in a collaborative problem-solving situation which is much more intertwined. First of all, in the definition of the social dimension, PISA does not use labels that construe social processes as generic across different types of tasks, but rather refer to the dimension as collaborative problem-solving competences. The three competencies under this dimension are more specific for solving problems when working with others. The matrix in Table 9.2 guides the design of CPS assessment items. There is no assumption that *Discovering perspectives and abilities of team members* is the same competence as *Communicating with team members about the actions to be/being performed*, even though both belong to the broad category of *Establishing and maintaining shared understanding* of collaborative problem-solving competence. However, there is also no assumption that these competencies are exercised separately in the CPS process (OECD, 2017).

Despite the differences in the framing of the ATC21S and PISA 2015 CPS frameworks, the statistical analysis to arrive at a description of the CPS achievement progression in terms of what students at different positions of the achievement ladder can perform is similar. While it would be instructive to see how the same individuals' performance on the two assessments may triangulate, the mapping of behavioral performance per se does not address the issue of how people learn to collaborate to solve problems effectively. There is a need for inquiry that connects behavioral observations with social neuroscientific inquiry in order for us to better understand how CPS competence develops, and whether identifiable developmental trajectories/pathways can be delineated. We illustrate further in this section how neuroscientific explorations in conjunction with behavioral observations would contribute much to our understanding of key questions related to CPS development.

How Does the Social Brain Develop?

In assessments of CPS, we may try to "control" who the assessee interacts with, as in PISA 2015, or assume that the achievement results would not be affected by the ability or behavior of the collaborator. However, in learning and in actual work situations, whether the collaborators know each other and if so their pre-existing relationships, and the attributes of the team members matter. Recent advances in social cognition and neuroscientific research (Fiske & Taylor, 2013) have shed light on how our understanding of self and others develops from early infancy (e.g., Rochat, 2014). However, investigations must provide better scientific grounding for the design of learning activities and learning technologies. Specifically, we need to understand whether people's perception and interaction with others under the following situations differ, and if there is a developmental trajectory with regard to differences in response:

1. Interacting with familiar individuals vs. strangers
2. Interacting with perceived authority figures (e.g., parents) vs. lower status figures (e.g., younger infants)
3. Interacting face-to-face vs. via different media (e.g., voice only or video) vs. via avatars
4. Interacting with one other person vs. a group of people

Supplementing cognitive behavioral studies to address the above questions with studies of neural activities over time with varying contextual conditions along the above four dimensions will provide us with a better understanding of how maturation in social cognition can be facilitated. Dimension (3), establishing and maintaining team organization, is especially important in authentic everyday workplace CPS contexts in which people often switch back and forth between the physical and virtual world, alone or interacting and collaborating with others. How does this capability develop through life, from childhood to adulthood, and how does this interact with the digital interactions and environment of the learner?

What Are the Conditions Underpinning Productive CPS?

One of the reasons that people engage in social interactions is to be better able to solve problems. Jonassen (2000) put forward a taxonomy of problem types and argues that there are different cognitive and affective requirements for solving different types of problems. Further, individual attributes of the problem-solver, such as familiarity with the problem type, domain knowledge, skill level, cognitive controls, metacognitive skills, epistemological beliefs, and affective and cognitive characteristics, make a difference in the problem-solving process and outcomes. If individual attributes influence the outcome of his/her problem-solving, clearly these characteristics of the interacting dyad or group will affect the process and outcomes in CPS contexts. However, examining combinations of individual attributes of collaborators may not be the most expedient approach. It is well accepted that the outcome of collaboration achieved by a well-functioning group often exceeds the sum of what can be achieved by individual group members (OECD, 2017). The implication from this observation is that the CPS capacity of a group can only be assessed at the group level. Many researchers in the field of collaborative learning have also focused their studies at the group or community level (Hmelo-Silver, 2013).

What happens when people interact to solve a problem? Studies in the learning sciences have shown that groups that achieve successful CPS outcomes are characterized by joint attention and mutuality of exchanges (Barron, 2000). Neural and body movement synchrony have been observed to increase after cooperative social interaction. Studies of neurophysiologic patterns of teams when they engage in solving time-critical problems collaboratively find that the differences in these patterns reflect the teams' efficiency (Stevens et al., 2009). These findings show strong corroborations between observed behavior and patterns of interpersonal neural activity during social interactions and CPS. On the other hand, from a learning and learning technology design perspective, there is a need for such research to be extended to reveal why some groups can successfully develop productive neurophysiologic collaboration patterns while others do not, and even more importantly, what conditions bring about these different patterns.

Learning Technology Research and Development for CPS

Earlier in this chapter, we review briefly two emerging learning technologies, namely social robots and serious games. The former is a technological approach to leverage the affordance of social interactions to support learning, while the latter provides a simulated learning environment to scaffold learning involving complex social contexts and interactions. Serious games are particularly relevant as a technologically mediated environment for the learning and assessment of CPS as these have two potential advantages: motivating engagement and simulating authenticity.

Games for Motivating Engagement and Attentional Focus

Studies have shown that dopamine release is increased significantly during game play, particularly in areas of the brain connected to learning and rewards (Koepp et al., 1998). Dopamine is a neurotransmitter that helps to control the brain's responses to reward and pleasure, and is hence strongly related to reward-motivated behavior such as addiction, pleasure, and learning. Studies further show that uncertainty, difficulty, or challenges in a game increases the dopaminergic activity, producing immersive effects on players (Murad, 2017).

Another "counterintuitive" finding about game play is that some video games may in fact enhance players' attentional focus. Using fMRI (functional Magnetic Resonance Imaging), Bavelier et al. (2012) found that the area of the brain connected with attention allocation is less active in gamers than non-gamers during pattern recognition tasks. One interpretation of this finding is that gamers are less affected by outside interferences and thus able to allocate attentional resources more efficiently.

Serious Games Simulating Authentic Contexts for Learning

One challenge in fostering problem-solving capacities in educational settings is the lack of an authentic context for students to practice. Hence, laboratory work, problem-based learning and field experience are valued pedagogical approaches to provide learning environments and contexts that are close to the real world situations targeted for learning. However, such real world settings may not always be feasible and mistakes can be costly. In a virtual environment, a learner's actions, behaviors, and thoughts are embedded in human-to-human and human-to-object interactions in the learning process, which may provide authentic, near real-life experiences (Nicaise, Gibney, & Crane, 2000; Pearce, 2016).

In a comprehensive review of studies on serious games and learning outcomes related to twenty-first century skills, Romero, Usart, and Ott (2015) found that all analyzed studies reported collaboration, teamwork, communication, social skills and digital competence as observed outcomes, and most also included creativity, critical thinking, and problem-solving. The review also shows strong associations between some game characteristics and twenty-first century outcomes: collaboration with teamwork and communication outcomes, complex collaboration with the ability to manage and solve conflicts, the need to exercise strategy and tactics with the demonstration of critical thinking and self-direction. One important advantage of game play is the possibility of programming realistic and authentic consequences of learners' actions, including socially oriented ones, without causing actual harm or damages. Opportunities to learn from mistakes or failures through games are educationally valuable for the players (Charsky, 2010).

One advantage of learning through virtual worlds is that different levels of authenticity can be provided as environments for individual or collaborative problem-solving (Chang et al., 2010; Huang, Rauch, & Liaw, 2010). Virtual environments in serious games can be more versatile and richer in features and functionalities (e.g., assigning players to a specific task) than are real-world contexts, and may serve as valuable pedagogical settings for fostering CPS competences.

Looking into the Future

In this chapter, we highlight the importance of social interactions in learning and development, and identify CPS as a focal challenge for education and hence also for learning technology research and development. We review research in social neuroscience and the potential it holds for the development of learning technology to support socially contextualized learning. This is followed by a review of the challenges encountered in the assessment and learning of CPS, and how neuroscientific methods may contribute to addressing these challenges.

In the context of learning technologies that support CPS, we suggest that serious games may offer the greatest learning potential through engaging and authentic environments that can be flexibly manipulated to suit problem and learner requirements. Here, in this final section, we wish to posit that serious games also provide a suitable environment for us to conduct research to address the assessment and learning challenges identified.

As identified earlier in this chapter, observation and behavioral data collected during the CPS process and the outcome indicators may not reflect developmental progress of individuals or groups as these only provide population descriptions of behavior and performance. Further, such data are prone to idiosyncratic variations due to specific settings and tasks. On the other hand, changes at the neurophysiological level are likely to be more gradual and hence reflect more fundamental, developmental changes. By designing studies that balance observational and behavioral data on CPS process and outcomes with neurophysiological and neuropsychological data, the research community can deepen the understanding of CPS competency development.

The study of CPS requires research environments that allow for easy manipulation of study conditions and data collection. Serious games offer multiple advantages for studying CPS. First of all, players are likely to be motivated to spend a long time on the games (if designed appropriately to engage learners), affording extended observations of changes in behavior and outcomes. Newer technologies, including 3D virtualization, simulation, VR, and AR, offer further opportunities for the design of engaging/authentic elements into the game design (Bavelier & Davidson, 2013). Further, the versatility of the online environment can be used to manipulate different research conditions for data collection. Hence, it is possible to design studies to address questions related to *how the social brain develops* and *the conditions underpinning productive CPS*. Further, the automatic online data collection afforded on serious games platforms makes it possible for massive amounts of data to be collected without much human intervention. Data mining, as well as more conventional analytical methods, may be employed in the research.

We started this chapter by referring to research that points to the dynamic nature of the brain and cognitive development. The brain is constructed dynamically over time by continuous interactions between biology and experience. Hence, feedback is an important component in the design of learning technologies. A further advantage of using serious games in CPS research is that in-game assessments can be designed to be utilized for the provision of feedback to learners. The subsequent impact of the feedback over time can also be studied. In other words, in-game assessment in serious games can be used as formative assessment in cycles of teach-assess-inform (students) during the learning process. In the ideal case, the players do not perceive that they are being assessed and the formative assessment and feedback become embedded into the game mechanics (Phillips & Popović, 2012), thus reducing the pressure and negative emotions often associated with formal assessment.

Acknowledgements The authors wish to acknowledge that this work is funded by the Research Grants Council of the HKSAR Government, #T44-707/16/N, under the Theme Based Research Scheme.

References

Barab, S., Dodge, T., Tuzun, H., Job-Sluder, K., Carteaux Jr., R., Gilbertson, J., et al. (2007). The Quest Atlantis Project: A socially-responsive play space for learning. In B. E. Shelton & D. Wiley (Eds.), *The design and use of simulation computer games in education* (pp. 159–186). Rotterdam, The Netherlands: Sense Publishers.

Barron, B. (2000). Achieving coordination in collaborative problem-solving groups. *The Journal of the Learning Sciences, 9*(4), 403–436. https://doi.org/10.1207/S15327809JLS0904_2

Bavelier, D., Achtman, R. L., Mani, M., & Föcker, J. (2012). Neural bases of selective attention in action video game players. *Vision Research, 61*, 132–143. https://doi.org/10.1016/j.visres.2011.08.007

Bavelier, D., & Davidson, R. J. (2013). Games to do you good. *Nature, 494*, 425. https://doi.org/10.1038/494425a

Bavelier, D., Green, C. S., Han, D. H., Renshaw, P. F., Merzenich, M. M., & Gentile, D. A. (2011). Brains on video games. *Nature Reviews Neuroscience, 12*, 763. https://doi.org/10.1038/nrn3135

Blakemore, S.-J. (2012). Development of the social brain in adolescence. *Journal of the Royal Society of Medicine, 105*(3), 111–116. https://doi.org/10.1258/jrsm.2011.110221

Blakemore, S.-J., Winston, J., & Frith, U. (2004). Social cognitive neuroscience: Where are we heading? *Trends in Cognitive Sciences, 8*(5), 216–222. https://doi.org/10.1016/j.tics.2004.03.012

Care, E., Griffin, P., Scoular, C., Awwal, N., & Zoanetti, N. (2015). Collaborative problem solving tasks. In P. Griffin & E. Care (Eds.), *Assessment and teaching of 21st century skills: Methods and approach* (pp. 85–104). Dordrecht: Springer.

Chang, C.-W., Lee, J.-H., Wang, C.-Y., & Chen, G.-D. (2010). Improving the authentic learning experience by integrating robots into the mixed-reality environment. *Computers & Education, 55*(4), 1572–1578. https://doi.org/10.1016/j.compedu.2010.06.023

Charsky, D. (2010). From edutainment to serious games: A change in the use of game characteristics. *Games and Culture, 5*(2), 177–198. https://doi.org/10.1177/1555412009354727

de Greeff, J., & Belpaeme, T. (2015). Why robots should be social: Enhancing machine learning through social human-robot interaction. *PLOS One, 10*(9), e0138061. https://doi.org/10.1371/journal.pone.0138061

Dickey, M. D. (2007). Game design and learning: A conjectural analysis of how massively multiple online role-playing games (MMORPGs) foster intrinsic motivation. *Educational Technology Research and Development, 55*(3), 253–273.

Donaldson, M. (Ed.). (1978). *Children's minds*. Glasgow: Fontana/Collins.

Fiske, S. T., & Taylor, S. E. (Eds.). (2013). *Social cognition: From brains to culture*. Thousand Oaks, CA: Sage.

Gee, J. P. (2011). Reflections on empirical evidence on games and learning. In J. D. Fletcher & S. Tobias (Eds.), *Computer games and instruction* (pp. 223–232). Charlotte, NC: IAP.

Gordon, G., Spaulding, S., Westlund, J. K., Lee, J. J., Plummer, L., Martinez, M., et al. (2016). *Affective personalization of a social robot tutor for children's second language skills.* Paper presented at the 13th AAAI Conference on Artificial Intelligence.

Griffin, P., Care, E., & Harding, S. (2015). Task characteristics and calibration. In P. Griffin & E. Care (Eds.), *Assessment and teaching of 21st century skills: Methods and approach.* Dordrecht: Springer.

Griffiths, M. D. (2002). The educational benefits of videogames. *Education and Health, 20*(3), 47–51.

Hesse, F., Care, E., Buder, J., Sassenberg, K., & Griffin, P. (2015). A framework for teachable collaborative problem solving skills. In P. Griffin & E. Care (Eds.), *Assessment and teaching of 21st century skills* (pp. 37–56). Dordrecht: Springer.

Hmelo-Silver, C. E. (Ed.). (2013). *The international handbook of collaborative learning.* New York: Routledge.

Huang, H.-M., Rauch, U., & Liaw, S.-S. (2010). Investigating learners' attitudes toward virtual reality learning environments: Based on a constructivist approach. *Computers & Education, 55*(3), 1171–1182. https://doi.org/10.1016/j.compedu.2010.05.014

Jonassen, D. H. (2000). Toward a design theory of problem solving. *Educational Technology Research and Development, 48*(4), 63–85. https://doi.org/10.1007/BF02300500

Koepp, M. J., Gunn, R. N., Lawrence, A. D., Cunningham, V. J., Dagher, A., Jones, T., et al. (1998). Evidence for striatal dopamine release during a video game. *Nature, 393*, 266. https://doi.org/10.1038/30498

Li, H., Cabibihan, J.-J., & Tan, Y. K. (2011). Towards an effective design of social robots. *International Journal of Social Robotics, 3*(4), 333–335. https://doi.org/10.1007/s12369-011-0121-z

Meltzoff, A. N., Kuhl, P. K., Movellan, J., & Sejnowski, T. J. (2009). Foundations for a new science of learning. *Science, 325*(5938), 284–288.

Movellan, J. R., Eckhardt, M., Virnes, M., & Rodriguez, A. (2009). *Sociable robot improves toddler vocabulary skills.* Paper presented at the 2009 4th ACM/IEEE International Conference on Human-Robot Interaction (HRI).

Murad, S. S. (2017). Brain involvement in the use of games in nursing education. *Journal of Nursing Education and Practice, 7*(6), 90. https://doi.org/10.5430/jnep.v7n6p90

Nicaise, M., Gibney, T., & Crane, M. (2000). Toward an understanding of authentic learning: Student perceptions of an authentic classroom. *Journal of Science Education and Technology, 9*(1), 79–94. https://doi.org/10.1023/A:1009477008671

OECD (Ed.). (2017). *PISA 2015 Results (Volume V): Collaborative Problem Solving.* Paris: PISA, OECD Publishing.

Park, H. W., Rosenberg-Kima, R., Rosenberg, M., Gordon, G., & Breazeal, C. (2017). *Growing growth mindset with a social robot peer.* Paper presented at the Proceedings of the 2017 ACM/IEEE International Conference on Human-Robot Interaction.

Pearce, S. (2016). Authentic learning: What, why and how? e-Teaching, 10.

Phillips, V., & Popović, Z. (2012). More than child's play: Games have potential learning and assessment tools. *Phi Delta Kappan, 94*(2), 26–30. https://doi.org/10.1177/003172171209400207

Piaget, J. (1970). *Genetic epistemology* (Woodbridge lectures; no. 8). New York: Columbia University Press.

Richert, R. A., Robb, M. B., & Smith, E. I. (2011). Media as social partners: The social nature of young children's learning from screen media. *Child Development, 82*(1), 82–95. https://doi.org/10.1111/j.1467-8624.2010.01542.x

Rochat, P. (Ed.). (2014). *Early social cognition: Understanding others in the first months of life.* Hove: Psychology Press.

Romero, M., Usart, M., & Ott, M. (2015). Can serious games contribute to developing and sustaining 21st century skills? *Games and Culture, 10*(2), 148–177. https://doi.org/10.1177/1555412014548919

Roseberry, S., Hirsh-Pasek, K., & Golinkoff, R. M. (2014). Skype me! Socially contingent interactions help toddlers learn language. *Child Development, 85*(3), 956–970. https://doi.org/10.1111/cdev.12166

Scassellati, B., Brawer, J., Tsui, K., Nasihati Gilani, S., Malzkuhn, M., Manini, B., et al.(2018). *Teaching Language to Deaf Infants with a Robot and a Virtual Human.* Paper presented at the 2018 CHI Conference on Human Factors in Computing Systems.

Singer, T. (2012). The past, present and future of social neuroscience: A European perspective. *NeuroImage, 61*(2), 437–449.

Stevens, R. H., Galloway, T., Berka, C., & Sprang, M. (2009). Can neurophysiologic synchronies provide a platform for adapting team performance? In *International Conference on Foundations of Augmented Cognition* (pp. 658–667). Berlin: Springer.

Thelen, E., & Smith, L. B. (Eds.). (1994). *A dynamic systems approach to the development of cognition and action.* Cambridge, MA: The MIT Press.

Trilling, B., & Fadel, C. (Eds.). (2012). *21st century skills: Learning for life in our times.* New York: John Wiley & Sons.

UNESCO. (2017). *Education for sustainable development goals: Learning objectives* (pp. 62). Paris: UNESCO.

Wendel, V., Hertin, F., Göbel, S., & Steinmetz, R. (2010). *Collaborative learning by means of multiplayer serious games.* Paper presented at the International Conference on Web-Based Learning.

Nancy W. Y. Law   is a professor in the Division of Information Technology in Education, Faculty of Education at the University of Hong Kong. She served as the Founding Director for the Centre for Information Technology in Education (CITE) for 15 years from 1998. Her research interests include international comparative studies of technology-enabled learning innovations, models of ICT integration in schools and change leadership, computer supported collaborative learning, the use of expressive and exploratory computer-based learning environments, learning design, and learning analytics. She has served on a number of policy advisory boards/working groups related to ICT in education for the University of Hong Kong, the Hong Kong government, and other community groups. She has also been contributing as expert/consultant to the European Commission, UNESCO, and OECD on various aspects of technology-enhanced learning.

Haley W. C. Tsang   is currently a Ph.D. student in the Division of Information and Technology Studies at the Faculty of Education of The University of Hong Kong. She holds an M.Phil. degree and a double degree in business administration (marketing) and engineering. She was an active member of a team which designed and implemented an international award-winning cloud-based Personal Learning Environment & Network (PLE&N) to support social and lifelong learning in higher education. She was also the winner of the "Best Paper and Presentation" in a recent European conference. In her undergraduate years, she obtained several scholarships and was listed on the Dean's Honours List of Outstanding Students. Her current research interests include collaborative problem-solving and serious games.

Chapter 10
Cross-Sectional Studies Investigating the Impacts of Background Sounds on Cognitive Task Performance

Deborah Cockerham, Lin Lin, Zhengsi Chang, and Mike Schellen

Abstract This chapter synthesizes findings from a series of five studies examining the impacts of different background sounds on cognitive task performance. Four out of the five studies compared background sounds of silence, white noise (rain), calm music without lyrics (Rachmaninoff's "Vocalize, Op. 34"), and fast, energetic music without lyrics (Benny Goodman's "Sing, Sing, Sing"). The other study examined task performance under different musical tempos (fast, slow) and pitches (high, low). Cognitive load and academic domain (arithmetic, language, spatial) varied between studies. Findings indicated that, in general, the participants performed better on lower cognitive load tasks while listening to fast music. Performance on tasks with higher cognitive loads did not vary significantly by different listening backgrounds. Implications and future directions are discussed.

Introduction

As the ease of accessing media increases, new technologies are creating a world in which we are surrounded by never-ending sounds. Background music streams constantly into stores, restaurants, museums, and doctors' offices; and, when music is not in the environment, individuals often choose to hear their preferred music through personal devices. Over 75% of Americans report listening to music for over 25 h per

D. Cockerham
Department of Learning Technologies, Fort Worth Museum of Science and History,
University of North Texas, Fort Worth, TX, USA
e-mail: deborahcockerham@my.unt.edu

L. Lin (✉) · M. Schellen
University of North Texas, Denton, TX, USA
e-mail: Lin.Lin@unt.edu

Z. Chang
University of Texas at Dallas, Denton, TX, USA
e-mail: zhengsi.chang@utdallas.edu

© Association for Educational Communications and Technology 2019
T. D. Parsons et al. (eds.), *Mind, Brain and Technology*, Educational
Communications and Technology: Issues and Innovations,
https://doi.org/10.1007/978-3-030-02631-8_10

week (Nielsen.com, 2015). The ubiquity of this ever-present soundscape contrasts sharply against the eerie silence of many classrooms, and parents and children often debate the benefits of listening to music while studying or doing homework.

While humans have always engaged in multitasking (e.g., talking while walking), the ability to acquire new information when distracted by other activities or sounds may be limited (Poldrack & Foerde, 2008). The desire to media multitask, fueled by 24/7 access to media, is in direct conflict with the goal of accomplishing the primary task. McLuhan (2002) maintained that media creates both extensions and amputations of ourselves, adding benefits and drawbacks to our lives. How does the never-ending auditory stimulation affect task performance or learning in and outside classrooms?

In a series of studies, we investigated the impact of the technology-generated listening environment upon task accuracy. Our first study found that participants were significantly more productive on a simple math task when listening to fast, energetic music than when listening to calm music, rain sounds, or working in silence. When we increased the participants' cognitive load, little difference was seen between the four conditions, but a closer investigation into specific musical elements associated fast tempo with increased productivity. Findings support the duplex-mechanism theory (Hughes, Vachon, & Jones, 2007), and suggest that the ability to screen out irrelevant sounds may be more controllable through greater top-down task engagement. In addition, increased media stimulation may be impacting our motivation and affect as it changes our attentional needs. In this chapter, we first provide an overview of literature that has provided theoretical frameworks for our studies. We then briefly discuss each of the five studies we conducted in sequence. Based on findings of the five studies, we discuss implications and future studies.

Literature and Theoretical Framework

Task Productivity While Listening to Background Music

Studies focused on background music have investigated the impact of media-based music upon a variety of actions, from online shopping (Ding & Lin, 2012) to bullying (Ziv & Dolev, 2013) to perception of crying faces (Hanser, Mark, Zijlstra, & Vingerhoets, 2015). Studies have shown that background music can change our food preferences (Fiegel, Meullenet, Harrington, Humble, & Seo, 2014), that people drink water faster while listening to fast music (McElrea & Standing, 1992, cited in Thompson, Schellenberg, & Letnic, 2012), and that individuals turn the steering wheel more frequently when listening to fast music (Konz & McDougal, 1968, cited in Thompson et al., 2012).

While all of these studies show the impact of background music in daily activities, studies with cognitive tasks have shown conflicting results. Avila, Furnham, and McClelland (2011) examined the impact of familiar music presented both with and without vocals upon three types of cognitive tasks: verbal, numerical, and logic.

Results varied between tasks, with the numerical task showing no influence of music, the logic task showing stronger performance with music, and the verbal task hindered by both instrumental and vocal music. Other research (Jäncke & Sandmann, 2010) investigated verbal tasks in four different conditions: fast tempo, out of tune; fast tempo, in tune; slow tempo, out of tune; and slow tempo, in tune. Authors found no musical influence on verbal learning from any of the listening conditions. In an earlier study, Salamé and Baddeley (1989) found that background music, particularly vocal music, can disrupt verbal memory.

Arousal-Mood Hypothesis

Differences in task performance while listening to background music have often been attributed to the emotions experienced when listening to the music. The arousal-mood hypothesis (Husain, Thompson, & Schellenberg, 2002) suggests that music's impact upon arousal, or alertness, and mood, or the feeling of emotion, may be the reason that task performance differs when background music is playing (Schellenberg, Nakata, Hunter, & Tamoto, 2007). The effect of music upon arousal and mood is often considered in the design of studies that investigate music's impact upon an individual's task performance. When Jäncke, Brügger, Brummer, Scherrer, and Alahmadi (2014) investigated the impact of background music upon verbal learning, authors included only music rated with an emotionally positive valence. In this way, they reasoned, learning would be supported with positive emotions. Moreno and Mayer (2000) hypothesized that the positive emotions elicited by music would strengthen memory performance.

In a series of four studies conducted by Lonsdale and North (2011), researchers concluded that most people listen to music for one of three reasons: to regulate mood, to prevent boredom, or to pass time. Each of these factors supports the arousal-mood hypothesis.

The Role of Attention

Posner and Rothbart (2007) highlight three different brain networks involved in attention: alerting (noticing the stimulus), orienting (determining which sensory information to process), and the executive network (monitoring and resolving conflicts between thoughts, feelings, and behaviors). Each of these networks takes place in different neural areas. The alerting system primarily activates the thalamus and other cortical areas, the orienting network is focused in parietal areas, and the executive network centers on the frontal lobes.

Many studies indicate that, although each sensory system (e.g., vision or hearing) is processed in separate neural structures, attending to any of them requires use of the same attentional network (Petersen & Posner, 2012, cited in Rothbart & Posner, 2015).

Thus, listening to music appears to activate the same brain network as looking at this page. Because of this, performance in one of the two tasks is lowered as the brain directs attention towards the other task (Lin, Cockerham, Chang, & Natividad, 2015).

One of the first models of selective attention, the filter theory of attention (Broadbent, 1958), theorizes that, when two incoming stimuli are presented at the same time, they both gain pre-attentive access to a sensory buffer. One of the inputs is allowed entrance, based on physical features such as color, pitch, or location. The other is held briefly in the buffer for later processing. In this way, the brain's attentional store is not overloaded beyond its limited capacity.

Kahneman (1973) builds upon this theory, suggesting that attention can vary in both quantity and intensity. His measurements of effort, based upon an individual's electrodermal response and the size to which the pupils of his eyes are dilated, led him to assert that a familiar task or stimulus requires less neural processing than a novel or unanticipated task or stimulus. Kahneman also noted that a person's ability to sustain attention wanes with time. Based on these observations, Kahneman proposed that humans have a limit on their attentional capacity. His capacity model of attention (Kahneman, 1973) suggests that the most important activity or stimulus will receive the majority of the attention, and other tasks will receive any "leftover" attention as it becomes available.

Chou (2011) suggests that Kahneman's theory applies even when a task is relegated to a secondary status (e.g., lack of awareness that music is playing in the background). His attention drainage effect claims that attention can be "drained" as the background sounds demand attentional resources, resulting in poorer task performance. An individual may have enough attentional resources to complete a simple task while listening to music, but may not have enough to meet the needs of a higher cognitive task.

Auditory Distractions

The human brain is constantly bombarded by sensory stimuli. Because it could be easily overwhelmed by the abundance of sensory information, it must work to balance priority stimuli with inputs that may not be relevant to its goals. Many distracting stimuli can be limited through voluntary actions: closing our eyes can limit incoming visual input, shutting our mouths can prevent unwanted tastes, and pulling our hands away can thwart the sense of touch. But, unlike the other senses, the auditory sense cannot be limited voluntarily. Auditory input can enter the brain without consent, and this permeability appears to be a protective mechanism to alert us to dangers in the environment (Hughes, Hurlstone, Marsh, Vachon, & Jones, 2013). However, permeability may also result in distractibility as irrelevant auditory stimuli move our attention away from the goal.

The brain compensates for the inability to passively filter by actively filtering consistent sounds, as in repeated syllables or monotones (Elliott, 2002; Rinne, Särkkä, Degerman, Schröger, & Alho, 2006). For example, the ticking of a grandfather clock may not be noticed after a time, or a person who lives near a train track eventually may not "hear" the train going past his house. In contrast, auditory stimuli that varies, or is relevant (e.g., a person's name or someone yelling, "Fire!"), cannot be ignored and becomes an auditory distraction.

In their duplex-mechanism theory, Hughes et al. (2007) propose two potential causes for auditory distractions. *Interference-by-process* occurs when the neural resources required by the task are the same as those required by the auditory sounds. In this case, the cause of the distraction is task-related. When the auditory distraction interrupts the activity, but uses different neural structures, *attentional capture* occurs. During attentional capture, the ability to screen out irrelevant sounds is more controllable through greater top-down task engagement (Sörqvist, 2010). According to this theory, the higher the cognitive load, the more we can ignore auditory distractions (Hughes et al., 2007).

Our Studies

Figure 10.1 below provides an overview of the five studies conducted by our team over a period of 3 years.

All five studies were approved in accordance with the ethical standards of the Institutional Review Board and were conducted at the Research and Learning Center (RLC) of the Fort Worth (TX) Museum of Science and History. The RLC engages museum guests in the scientific discovery process by bringing researchers into the museum to conduct research studies. Families often come to the museum together, which provides the researchers with opportunities to recruit participants of various ages. In total, over 1000 individuals aged 5 years to over 70 years old participated in the studies.

Two sets of background sounds were used in the five studies. The first, second, fourth, and fifth studies use the following set of background sounds:

1. Silence
2. White noise: sounds of rain, accessed through Simply Rain app
3. Fast, energetic dance music with no lyrics ("Sing, Sing, Sing" by Benny Goodman)
4. Calm classical music with no lyrics ("Vocalize, Op. 34" by Sergei Rachminoff)

The third study used the following set of background sounds:

1. High (pitch), fast (tempo) music
2. High (pitch), slow (tempo) music
3. Low (pitch), fast (tempo) music
4. Low (pitch), slow (tempo) music

Based on the results of our first study, we set out in two directions: (1) We increased the level of cognitive load for the task, moving from a math task with a low cognitive load to more cognitively challenging tasks that involved skills from other

Basic listening set: Music listening set:

  1. Silence   1. High, fast music

  2. White noise   2. High, slow music

  3. Fast dance music   3. Low, fast music

  4. Slow classical music   4. Low, slow music

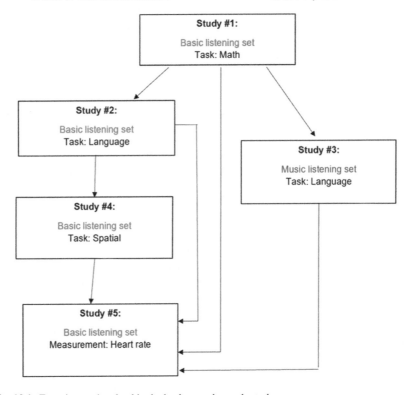

Fig. 10.1 Experiments involved in the background sounds study

academic areas (language and spatial). (2) We looked at specific musical elements (pitch and tempo) to try to determine which elements might be most supportive of task productivity. Thus, the music for the music listening set examined task performance while listening to music with high pitch, low pitch, fast tempo, and slow tempo. For both background sound sets, the sequence of the listening conditions was alternated to account for factors such as familiarity with the task and fatigue. Before completing the task, participants in each study completed a demographic survey that measured age, gender, musical experience, and online habits.

Study #1

Participants 511 museum guests (289 f, 222 m, ages 6–77) participated in the study.

Materials Participants completed a simple math task (See Fig. 10.2) with a low cognitive load. The sound environment was the basic listening set. Participants also completed a brief demographic survey.

Design and procedure A repeated-measures design was used, in which all participants completed the task during each of the four sound conditions. For each condition, participants were asked to answer as many single-digit math questions as possible within 1 minute.

Results Repeated-measures ANOVA indicated that participants were significantly more productive when listening to fast, energetic dance music than when listening to white noise or to silence. See Fig. 10.3.

Study #2

Participants A total of 217 museum guests (127 f, 90 m, ages 7–72; $M = 29.1$; $SD = 18.6$) participated in the experiment.

Materials Two versions of worksheets (four worksheets per version) were prepared. The children's version, designed for ages 7–12, contained a list of randomly placed words from two categories, and adult worksheets contained words from three categories (See Fig. 10.4) Words in each category were taken from wordlists in Enchanted Learning Educational website (Col & Spector, 2015). Cognitive load for the task was high, and the basic listening set was used.

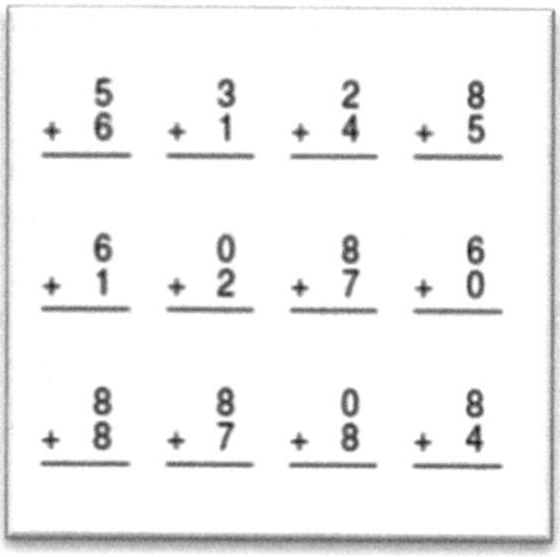

Fig. 10.2 Sample of math task

$$
\begin{array}{cccc}
5 & 3 & 2 & 8 \\
+\,6 & +\,1 & +\,4 & +\,5 \\
\hline
\end{array}
$$

$$
\begin{array}{cccc}
6 & 0 & 8 & 6 \\
+\,1 & +\,2 & +\,7 & +\,0 \\
\hline
\end{array}
$$

$$
\begin{array}{cccc}
8 & 8 & 0 & 8 \\
+\,8 & +\,7 & +\,8 & +\,4 \\
\hline
\end{array}
$$

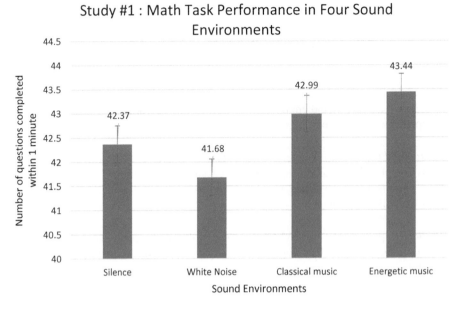

Fig. 10.3 Results of experiment #1 (math task, basic listening set)

Design and procedure. A repeated-measures design was used, in which all participants completed the task during each of the four sound conditions. For each condition, participants were asked to categorize as many words as possible within
1 minute.

Results. Repeated-measures ANOVA indicated no significant differences between
sound environments, $F(3, 645) = 1.715$, $p = 0.163$, partial $\eta^2 = 0.008$. See Fig. 10.5.

Study #3

Participants A total of 231 museum guests (183 f, 48 m, ages 8–75; $M = 28.25$;
$SD = 18.98$) participated in the experiment.

Methods This task used the same worksheets as those in Experiment #2. Again, the
cognitive load was high. In this study, the music listening set was used.

Design and procedure A repeated-measures design was used, in which all participants completed the task during each of the four music conditions. For each condition, participants were asked to categorize as many words as possible within
1 minute.

```
┌─────────────────────────────────────────────────────────────────────┐
│  T = Transportation and Vehicles                                     │
│  O = Occupations and Jobs                                            │
│  B = Buildings and Other Structures                                  │
│  ─────────────────────────────                                       │
│                                                                       │
│   canoe_____          attorney_____         airplane_____            │
│   rancher_____        office_____           bowling alley_____       │
│   retailer_____       shelter_____          subway_____              │
│   bridge_____         automobile_____       taxi_____                │
│   chemist_____        fire engine_____      athlete_____             │
│   police car_____     nurse_____            cashier_____             │
│   cart_____           tower_____            college_____             │
│   monorail_____       rowboat_____          stable_____              │
│   detective_____      motorcycle_____       rocket_____              │
│   igloo_____          helicopter_____       log cabin_____           │
│   arena_____          programmer_____       sled_____                │
│   doorman_____        painter_____          barber_____              │
│   forklift_____       mall_____             teacher_____             │
│   apartment_____      warehouse_____        ship_____                │
│   builder_____        sailor_____           stroller_____            │
│   custodian_____      baker_____            house_____               │
│   driver_____         hot air balloon_____  hotel_____               │
│   prison_____         wagon_____            duplex_____              │
│   dump truck_____     lighthouse_____       palace_____              │
│   school bus_____     farm_____             elevator_____            │
│   cop_____            artist_____           unicycle_____            │
│   chef_____           school_____           dentist_____             │
└─────────────────────────────────────────────────────────────────────┘
```

Fig. 10.4   Adult language categorization task

Results   Task scores were significantly stronger while listening to fast than to slow music, but little difference was seen between high and low pitch (Fig. 10.6).

Study #4

Participants   135 museum guests (72 f, 63 m, ages 9–66; $M = 29.17$; $SD = 13.44$) participated in the study.

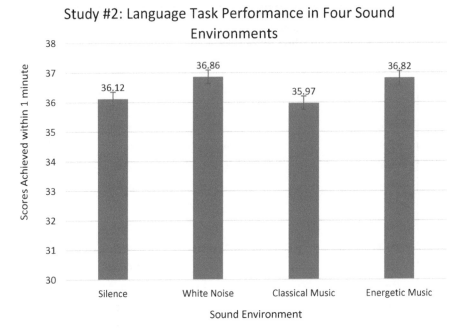

Fig. 10.5 Results of experiment #2 (language study, basic listening set)

Materials For each of the four sound environments, participants completed a different nine-block design from the Kohs block design test (Kohs, 1920; See Fig. 10.7). In the Kohs task, a person must look at a picture of a design and then arrange colored cubes to reproduce the design. The cognitive load was high, and the basic listening set was used.

Design and procedure Each participant was given nine blocks and was given time to practice with each of two block designs before the testing began. During the testing, the block arrangement task changed with each sound condition. All block arrangements were comparable in skill level and complexity. Time to successfully complete each block arrangement task was recorded, and background sounds continued to play until the participant completed the design.

Results Repeated-measures ANOVA indicated no significant differences between listening environments. However, participants generally completed the task in the shortest length of time when listening to the fast, energetic music. See Fig. 10.8.

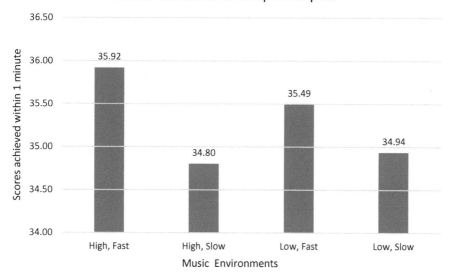

Fig. 10.6   Results of experiment #3 (language study, music listening set)

Fig. 10.7   Kohs block
design test

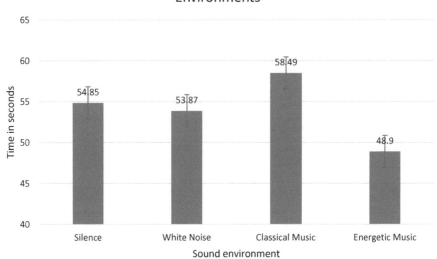

Fig. 10.8 Results of experiment #4 (spatial task, basic listening set)

Study #5

Participants A total of 101 museum guests (56 f, 45 m, ages 8–75; $M = 29.17$; $SD = 13.44$) participated in the study.

Materials Heart rate was measured using a heart rate monitor.

Design and procedure Participants put on earphones and a heart rate monitor. After sitting quietly and listening to the sound environment for 30 s, the individual's heart rate was measured. Participants alternated between left and right arms for the different measures.

Results No significant difference was seen in between listening environments. See Fig. 10.9 (Table 10.1).

Discussions and Future Directions

The main goal of the background sounds studies was to explore the impacts of the sound environment upon academic task performance. Studies #1, #2, and #4 examined the effect of the same set of sound environments on three tasks with complexity ranging from simple to high and across three cognitive domains. Results suggested that participants generally achieved more correct answers for the low cognitive task during the fast music condition. Although not significant, heart rate also measured slightly higher when listening to fast music than to the other basic listening set sounds.

Task performance was based upon number of correct task answers, but speed was also a factor in achieving a high score. The faster the participants worked, the more correct answers they achieved. As was seen in the Kämpfe, Sedlmeier, and Renkewitz (2011) meta-analysis, faster tempo music seemed to support faster behavior, leading to stronger academic task performance. Findings also support the arousal-mood hypothesis (Husain et al., 2002), suggesting that fast music, which increases arousal,

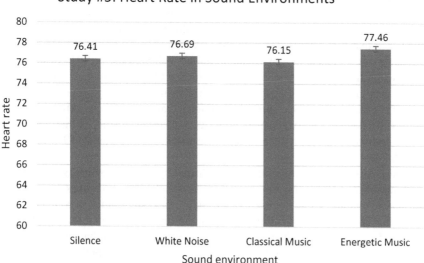

Fig. 10.9 Results of experiment #6 (heart rate, basic listening set)

Table 10.1 Summary of the five studies

Studies	Task	Number of participants	Findings	Notes
Study 1	Single-digit math addition	511 (289 f, 222 m)	Significantly higher scores in fast, energetic music	Basic listening set
Study 2	Language task	217 (127 f, 90 m)	No significant difference	Basic listening set
Study 3	Language task	231 (183 f, 48 m)	Significant main effect of tempo	Music listening set
Study 4	Spatial task	135 (72 f, 63 m)	No significant difference	Basic listening set
Study 5	Heart rate	98 (56 f, 44 m)	No significant difference	Basic listening set

can support positive emotional states and may lead to stronger task performance on tasks with either low cognitive or high cognitive demands.

To explore the potential impact of arousal level as proposed by the arousal-mood hypothesis, we also conducted Experiment #6. The results from this study showed no significant difference in heart rate due to listening environments. One explanation could be that, as opposed to previous experiments, in Study #5, participants were not asked to perform a cognitive task, but sat quietly while listening to music. This different experiment setting may result in different motivation and task engagement.

Studies #1 and #3 together shed some insights into the impact of musical elements on cognitive task performance. In these studies, fast tempo enhanced task performance, whereas pitch did not appear to influence the performance.

In contrast, higher cognitive language task performance on the basic listening set varied little when listening to white noise and to all other sound environments, including silence. Similar task performance during all four sound environments suggested that participants' focus on the task may have supported abilities to filter out irrelevant sounds in the environment. In line with Sörqvist's (2010) postulation, tasks with higher cognitive loads appear to reduce the power of the sound environment to capture attention. Background music or white noise may provide a distracting effect because of our limited attentional capacity (Chou, 2011), but the duplex-mechanism theory (Hughes et al., 2007) further postulates that our attentional systems may not find the need to respond when surrounded by continual sound.

Many participants commented on the "irritating" or "annoying" sound of the continual rain, and others expressed their personal likes or dislikes for specific musical selections. These comments and study results suggest the need to consider individual preferences in determining optimum learning environments, as indicated by a study in which participants were asked to select their own background music (Cassidy & MacDonald, 2009). In this study, researchers hypothesized that the stronger task performance of participants when self-selected music was playing was due to increased emotional and attentional engagement. In our media-saturated society, supporting an individual in defining and differentiating his own "pleasant" sounds (e.g., sounds of nature or preferred music) and "irritating" sounds (e.g., construction site noise) may enhance his learning capacity.

With the ubiquity of music in our everyday environments, habituation may be a factor in our abilities to screen out background sounds. Media usage can stimulate our "positive reward systems," leading to a desire for increased media usage (Levitin, 2014). As one young adult commented, "I couldn't focus at all when no sound was playing! Without added sounds, I was very distracted."

Background music or white noise may be novel the first time a person hears it, but it quickly becomes commonplace when presented in the everyday environment. As the listener habituates to the sound, the impact of the sound weakens to the point where it may not be noticed at all (Gluck, Mercado, & Myers, 2007). Perhaps, in our media-saturated world, music and white noise are losing their novelty and relevance. Increasing amounts of media stimulation in our everyday environments may build not only a desire, but also a need for media input in order to maintain focus.

Despite the increasing number of studies investigating sound effect on work and study, there is still lack of agreement. In their review, Kämpfe et al. (2011) noted the inconsistent and even contradictory findings across early studies investigating the impact of background sound upon task performance. One reason behind the mixed results was the large variety of cognitive tasks that were utilized in these studies. Kämpfe et al. (2011) argued that the studies they included in the review involved various cognitive processes (e.g., math, reading, memory) and, therefore, the results from these studies were by nature not comparable. To see trends shared by studies using similar tasks, they assigned those studies into groups based on three domains: motor, cognition, and emotion. However, the new groups, as the authors admitted, are still unsatisfyingly broad, with heterogeneous tasks in each group. At the end, they suggest that comparable studies using the same sound conditions or cognitive tasks will reduce the heterogeneity in the field and help us progressively build up a more systematic understanding of the effects of background sound upon cognitive task performance.

Our study took the initiative to meet this need by using the same set of sound conditions every time a different task was used. Thus, we gradually increased the complexity of the task from simple single-digit addition to language categorization to spatial task. By comparing the results from these studies, we may obtain insights into how the type of listening environment works in conjunction with the type of task work to affect our performance.

We live in a sound-filled world. Man-made sounds are now considered a pollutant raising international concerns (Radford, Kerridge, & Simpson, 2014). As people consciously or unconsciously struggle to escape aural distractions, they often turn to the ever-present media to find soothing background music or white noise. Others, holding on to the "Mozart effect" idea (Rauscher, Shaw, & Ky, 1993), continue to look for the ideal music or sound to support cognitive skill development. In determining the optimal learning environment, classroom teachers and instructional designers may need to consider the abundance of music in our everyday lives, since silence is becoming an unnatural sound environment in our society. Media and music are involved in much of the iGeneration's daily lives (Rosen, 2010), and today's students may need the extra stimulation that music provides in order to maintain focus on academic tasks. The productivity of today's students and workers may depend upon the addition of music to the environment.

Acknowledgements The authors wish to thank our research assistants and volunteers, Claire Nicolas, Katie Hervey, Lauren Nolan, Tori Short, Charlie Metcalf, Tasneem Alqahtani, Alshaima Almarwai, Ken Cockerham, Maria Balduf, Joanne Wu, and Will Whitaker, for their assistance with conducting the study and organizing data. We also wish to thank the Research and Learning Center at the Fort Worth Museum of Science and History for their hospitality and continued support.

References

Avila, C., Furnham, A., & McClelland, A. (2011). The influence of distracting familiar vocal music on cognitive performance of introverts and extraverts. *Psychology of Music, 40*(1), 84–93.

Broadbent, D. (1958). *Perception and Communication*. London: Pergamon Press.

Cassidy, G., & MacDonald, R. (2009). The effects of music choice on task performance: A study of the impact of self-selected and experimenter-selected music on driving game performance and experience. *Musicae Scientiae, 13*(2), 357–386.

Chou, P. T. M. (2011). Attention drainage effect: How background music effects concentration in Taiwanese college students. *Journal of the Scholarship of Teaching and Learning, 10*(1), 36–46.

Col, J., & Spector, M. (2015). Word categories. In *Enchanted learning*. Retrieved October 2015, from http://www.EnchantedLearning.com

Ding, C., & Lin, C. (2012). *Electronic commerce research and applications* (Vol. 11, Issue 3, pp. 299–307). ISSN 1567–4223.

Elliott, E. M. (2002). The irrelevant-speech effect and children: Theoretical implications of developmental change. *Memory & Cognition, 30*(3), 478–487.

Fiegel, A., Meullenet, J. F., Harrington, R. J., Humble, R., & Seo, H. S. (2014). Background music genre can modulate flavor pleasantness and overall impression of food stimuli. *Appetite, 76*, 144–152.

Gluck, M. A., Mercado, E., & Myers, C. E. (2007). *Learning and memory: From brain to behavior*. New York: Worth Publishers.

Hanser, W. E., Mark, R. E., Zijlstra, W. P., & Vingerhoets, A. J. (2015). The effects of background music on the evaluation of crying faces. *Psychology of Music, 43*, 75–85.

Hughes, R. W., Hurlstone, M. J., Marsh, J. E., Vachon, F., & Jones, D. M. (2013). Cognitive control of auditory distraction: impact of task difficulty, foreknowledge, and working memory capacity supports duplex-mechanism account. *Journal of Experimental Psychology: Human Perception and Performance, 39*(2), 539–553.

Hughes, R. W., Vachon, F., & Jones, D. M. (2007). Disruption of short-term memory by changing and deviant sounds: Support for a duplex-mechanism account of auditory distraction. *Journal of Experimental Psychology: Learning, Memory, and Cognition, 33*(6), 1050–1061.

Husain, G., Thompson, W. F., & Schellenberg, E. G. (2002). Effects of musical tempo and mode on arousal, mood, and spatial abilities. *Music Perception: An Interdisciplinary Journal, 20*(2), 151–171.

Jäncke, L., Brügger, E., Brummer, M., Scherrer, S., & Alahmadi, N. (2014). Verbal learning in the context of background music: No influence of vocals and instrumentals on verbal learning. *Behavioral and Brain Functions, 10*(10), 5.

Jäncke, L., & Sandmann, P. (2010). Music listening while you learn: No influence of background music on verbal learning. *Behavioral and Brain Functions, 6*(1), 3.

Kahneman, D. (1973). *Attention and effort* (Vol. 1063, p. 246). Englewood Cliffs, NJ: Prentice-Hall.

Kämpfe, J., Sedlmeier, P., & Renkewitz, F. (2011). The impact of background music on adult listeners: A meta-analysis. *Psychology of Music, 39*(4), 424–448.

Kohs, Samuel C. (1920). Kohs Block Design Test. In *Stoelting Co*. Retrieved July 20, 2017, from https://www.stoeltingco.com/kohs-block-design-test-3496.html

Konz, S., & McDougal, D. (1968). The effect of background music on the control activity of an automobile driver. *Human Factors: The Journal of the Human Factors and Ergonomics Society, 10*(3), 233–243.

Levitin, D. J. (2014). *The organized mind: Thinking straight in the age of information overload*. New York: Penguin.

Lin, L., Cockerham, D., Chang, Z., & Natividad, G. (2015). Task speed and accuracy decrease when multitasking. *Technology, Knowledge and Learning, 21*(307), 1–17.

Lonsdale, A. J., & North, A. C. (2011). Why do we listen to music? A uses and gratifications analysis. *British Journal of Psychology, 102*(1), 108–134. https://doi.org/10.1348/00712610/x50683

McElrea, H., & Standing, L. (1992). Fast music causes fast drinking. *Perceptual and Motor Skills, 75*(2), 362–362.

McLuhan, M. (2002). *Understanding media: The extensions of man* (10th ed.). Cambridge, MA: MIT Press.

Moreno, R., & Mayer, R. E. (2000). A coherence effect in multimedia learning: The case for minimizing irrelevant sounds in the design of multimedia instructional messages. *Journal of Educational Psychology, 92*(1), 117.

Nielsen.com. (2015). Everyone listens to music, but how we listen is changing. In *Nielsen Newswire*. Retrieved July 14, 2017, from http://www.nielsen.com/us/en/insights/news/2015/everyone-listens-to-music-but-how-we-listen-is-changing.html

Petersen, S. E., & Posner, M. I. (2012). The attention system of the human brain: 20 years after. *Annual Review of Neuroscience, 35*, 73–89.

Poldrack, R. A., & Foerde, K. (2008). Category learning and the memory systems debate. *Neuroscience & Biobehavioral Reviews, 32*(2), 197–205.

Posner, M. I., & Rothbart, M. K. (2007). Research on attention networks as a model for the integration of psychological science. *Annual Review of Psychology, 58*, 1–23.

Radford, A. N., Kerridge, E., & Simpson, S. D. (2014). Acoustic communication in a noisy world: Can fish compete with anthropogenic noise? *Behavioral Ecology, 25*(5), 1022–1010.

Rauscher, F. H., Shaw, G. L., & Ky, C. N. (1993). Music and spatial task performance. *Nature, 365*(6447), 611–611.

Rinne, T., Särkkä, A., Degerman, A., Schröger, E., & Alho, K. (2006). Two separate mechanisms underlie auditory change detection and involuntary control of attention. *Brain Research, 1077*(1), 135–143.

Rosen, L. D. (2010). *Rewired: Understanding the iGeneration and the way they learn*. New York: Macmillan.

Rothbart, M. K., & Posner, M. I. (2015). The developing brain in a multitasking world. *Developmental Review, 35*, 42–63.

Salamé, P., & Baddeley, A. (1989). Effects of background music on phonological short-term memory. *The Quarterly Journal of Experimental Psychology, 41*(1), 107–122.

Schellenberg, E. G., Nakata, T., Hunter, P. G., & Tamoto, S. (2007). Exposure to music and cognitive performance: Tests of children and adults. *Psychology of Music, 35*(1), 5–19.

Sörqvist, P. (2010). High working memory capacity attenuates the deviation effect but not the changing-state effect: Further support for the duplex-mechanism account of auditory distraction. *Memory & Cognition, 38*(5), 651–658.

Thompson, W. F., Schellenberg, E. G., & Letnic, A. K. (2012). Fast and loud background music disrupts reading comprehension. *Psychology of Music, 40*(6), 700–708.

Ziv, N., & Dolev, E. (2013). The effect of background music on bullying: A pilot study. *Children & Schools, 35*(2), 83–90.

Deborah Cockerham Managing Director of the Research and Learning Center at the Fort Worth Museum of Science and History, Deborah Cockerham also serves as Visiting Research Scholar at Texas Christian University's Center for Science Communication. In these roles, she works to strengthen interdisciplinary communication and build connections between research scientists and the public, and has supported multiple research university collaborations in public education and communication. In earlier work as a learning disabilities specialist, she taught children and adolescents with a variety of learning and attentional differences. Her work with students who have attention deficit hyperactivity (ADHD) and/or autism spectrum disorder (ASD) has focused on social learning, based on connections between communication skills and the fine arts. Cockerham's research takes place at the intersection of learning technologies, psychology, education, and communication. Recent investigations include EEG studies on ASD interpretation of nonverbal emotional cues, and behavioral studies focused on media multitasking and mobile technology. She is a graduate of the University of Texas at Arlington's Masters of Mind, Brain, and Education. Through her work and studies, Cockerham focuses on developing community-based collaborations that build skills for lifelong learning.

Lin Lin is a Professor of Learning Technologies at the University of North Texas (UNT). Lin's research looks into interactions between mind, brain, and technology in smart learning environments. Specially, she has conducted research on (1) media multitasking; (2) learning in online/blended/virtual reality environments; and (3) Computer-supported Collaborative Learning (CSCL). Lin is the Editor-in-chief for the development section of *Educational Technology Research and Development*, one of the most respected journals in the field. She is also Associate Editor for the *International Journal of Smart Technology and Learning* (IJSmartTL) as well as serving on the several other journal editorial boards. Lin has played leadership roles in several professional organizations (e.g., AECT and AERA). Lin has been invited as an honorary professor at several universities overseas. Lin serves as Director for Texas Center for Educational Technology, and Co-director on the Joint-Lab on Big Data, Little Devices, and Life-long Learning.

Zhengsi Chang is a third year PhD student of the Psychological Sciences at the University of Texas at Dallas. Her current research work includes the use of Virtual Reality (VR) technologies in psychological and clinical studies. She is currently writing articles on the design of VR based tasks and protocols for assessment and intervention. She is also participating in a project on VR based rehabilitation program for veterans surviving Traumatic Brain Injury (TBI). In addition, she is also interested in studying human reasoning in VR environments.

Mike Schellen is a PhD student in Learning Technologies within the College of Information at the University of North Texas. Mike's research interests include the effects of educational technologies on cognition and critical thinking. Current research includes the study of immersive technologies including virtual reality. Mike's professional background is in corporate learning, with emphases on learning facilitation, instructional design, and learning leadership.

Chapter 11
Neuroethics in Educational Technology: Keeping the Brain in Mind When Developing Frameworks for Ethical Decision-Making

Thomas D. Parsons

> *"It just doesn't matter whether the data are stored somewhere inside the biological organism or stored in the external world. What matters is how information is poised for retrieval and for immediate use as and when required."*
>
> Clark (2003), p. 69

Abstract Cyberlearning involves the convergence of psychology, education, learning technologies, computer science, engineering, and information science. Given the similar rate of advances in the educational neuroscience over the past couple decades, there is a growing interest in interaction between neuroscience and education. While cyberlearning has called attention to the stimulating potential that these new technologies (and the research behind them) have to offer, less emphasis has been placed upon the moral and ethical issues that may result from the widespread use of the learning technologies and neuroscience. This chapter aims to offer a first attempt at discussing some of the ethical issues inherent in brain-based cyberlearning research and practice.

Introduction

Cyberlearning is a recent branch of educational psychology that has increased in importance as new technologies have been developed and proliferate our classrooms (Montfort & Brown, 2013). The National Science Foundation has developed

T. D. Parsons (✉)
College of Information, University of North Texas, Computational Neuropsychology and Simulation, Denton, TX, USA
e-mail: Thomas.Parsons@unt.edu; https://cns.unt.edu/

© Association for Educational Communications and Technology 2019
T. D. Parsons et al. (eds.), *Mind, Brain and Technology*, Educational Communications and Technology: Issues and Innovations, https://doi.org/10.1007/978-3-030-02631-8_11

cyberlearning programs to fund exploratory and synergistic research projects that emphasize learning technologies for education and re-education of learners of all ages in science, technology, engineering, and mathematics. Cyberlearning involves the convergence of psychology, education, learning technologies, computer science, engineering, and information science. Given the similar rate of advances in the educational neuroscience over the past couple decades, there is a growing interest in interaction between neuroscience and education (Stein & Fischer, 2011). There are now dozens of laboratories around the world that have converged to investigate education questions using both cyberlearning and neuroscience approaches. Technological advances surround education, and educators regularly connect or disconnect from others via multifarious digital venues. While cyberlearning has called attention to the stimulating potential that these new technologies (and the research behind them) have to offer, less emphasis has been placed upon the moral and ethical issues that may result from the widespread use of the learning technologies and neuroscience. This chapter aims to offer a first attempt at discussing some of the ethical issues inherent in brain-based cyberlearning research and practice. It is important to note that this discussion will need to be expanded to include a wider sociocultural discourse. Brain-based learning technologies have the potential for both positive and negative change of not only understandings of humanity in general, but also specific and contextualized notions of personhood, free will, conscious experience, authenticity, and relatedness to others.

Ethics in Educational Technology

While most brain-based educational technologists are not philosophers, and few have extensive experience as ethicists, they often deal with moral issues and dilemmas. These range from the daily awareness of distributive justice as they consider the imbalanced allocation of technologies in schools to discussing and balancing the complex issues involved in educational neuroscience research with learning technologies. These situations are often challenging and some quite perplexing. In general, training in ethical issues typically involves a handful of courses (perhaps only one course) emphasizing codes of conduct and ethical principles developed initially by Beauchamp and Childress (2001). The content may include a discussion of the Nuremburg Code (Allied Control Council, 1949), the World Medical Association's Declaration of Helsinki (1964), and the Belmont Report (1978). From the Belmont report (i.e., Ethical Principles and Guidelines for the Protection of Human Subjects Research), we find three principles that provide the foundation for many current ethical guidelines for behavioral research: respect for persons, beneficence, and justice (Office for Human Research Protections [OHRP], 1979). While there is some terminological variation used in these guidelines and codes, they include the following ethical principles: autonomy (i.e., free will or agency); beneficence (i.e., mercy, kindness, and charity); nonmaleficence (i.e., do no harm); and justice (i.e., fair distribution of benefits and burdens).

Attempts have been made by the Association for Educational Communications and Technology (AECT) to define ethical research and practice: "Educational technology is the study and ethical practice of facilitating learning and improving performance by creating, using, and managing appropriate technological processes and resources" (Januszewski & Molenda, 2007, p. 1). Furthermore, AECT's TechTrends offers a column on various aspects of normative and applied ethics in educational technology (see for example Yeaman, 2016). Michael Spector (2005) proposed an Educratic Oath for educators that included: (1) restraining from acts that impair learning/instruction; (2) encouraging acts that improve learning/instruction; (3) acting in an evidence-based manner; (4) disseminating instruction principles; and (5) respecting individual rights.

Given that the Educratic Oath was not widely embraced, Spector (2015, 2016; Spector, Merrill, Elen, & Bishop, 2013) moved from principles to more general explication of values. Specifically, Spector (2016) argued for approaching ethical issues in the use of educational technologies to include five interrelating dimensions: values, principles, persons, context (e.g., school), and technologies. In addition to Spector's five ethical areas, a brain-based cyberlearning approach to ethics needs to take seriously the advances in cognitive, affective, and social neuroscience that have the potential to revolutionize educational assessments (Parsons, 2015; Parsons, Gaggliolo, & Riva, 2017) and training using technology-rich environments (Immordino-Yang & Singh, 2011).

Perspectives from the Neurosciences on Cyberlearning Technologies

In the past decade, there has been a rapid increase in research from the neurosciences that relates the human brain's neural mechanisms to the Internet (Montag & Reuter, 2017), social media (Meshi, Tamir, & Heekeren, 2015), virtual reality (Bohil, Alicea, & Biocca, 2011; Parsons et al., 2017; Parsons, Rizzo, Rogers, & York, 2009), and related technologies (Kane & Parsons, 2017; Parsons, 2016, 2017). To encourage the inclusion of research advances in cognitive, affective, and social neuroscience in the cyberpsychology domain, Parsons's (2017) proposed a framework for combining neuroscience and cyberlearning for the study of social, cognitive, and affective processes and the neural systems that support them. Following Parsons's brain-based cyberpsychology approach, a cyberlearning approach that draws from the neurosciences can be understood as (1) the neurocognitive, affective, and social aspects of students interacting with technology and (2) affective computing aspects of students interacting with devices/systems that incorporate computation. As such, a brain-based cyberlearning approach will be interested in both the ways in which educators and students make use of devices and the neurocognitive processes, motivations, intentions, behavioral outcomes, and effects of online and offline use of technology.

What are some key themes that have emerged from the neurosciences for a brain-based cyberlearning? First, there is emerging research that supports the long-held view of educators that thinking and learning are concurrently cognitive and affective processes that occur in social and cultural contexts (Fischer & Bidell, 2006; Frith & Frith, 2007; Mitchell, 2008). In the same way that affective neuroscientific evidence links student's bodies and minds in processes of emotion, social neuroscientific evidence links students' self-perceptions to the understanding of others (Immordino-Yang, 2008; Uddin, Iacoboni, Lange, & Keenan, 2007). The interactions between students and others results in a social extension of their cognitive processes. Likewise, the interactions among students, smart classrooms, and cyberlearning technologies serve to extend their cognitive processes. While students and educators behave in accordance with subjective goals and interests that develop over time as they interact socially, the values, judgments, and calculations made by technologies represent the data, algorithms, and system constraints that programmed by their developers (Immordino-Yang & Singh, 2011). Given that the parameters governing these calculations are often decided outside of interactions with the student (either beforehand or during postprocessing), there are concerns about the potential ethical implications of using these technologies.

Advances in cyberlearning technologies have heightened our awareness of the impact technologies have on the structure and function of the student's brain. Along with these rapid developments is an increased need to grapple with the ethical implications of cyberlearning tools and discoveries. Although several reviews have been written to synthesize the growing literature on neuroscience and ethics in general (Clausen & Levy, 2015; Farah, 2012; Illes, 2017; Racine & Aspler, 2017), there is a dearth of discussion related to the ethical implications of brain-based cyberlearning research, theory, and praxes. A brain-based cyberlearning framework will evolve at the interface of the neurosciences, education, and technologies of the extended mind. Educational theories and praxes are being and will continue to be transformed by the neurosciences. The ethical issues facing a rapidly developing brain-based cyberlearning fall under at least two distinct types: (1) those inherited from other areas of ethics (e.g., neuroethics; Lalancette & Campbell, 2012) and (2) those that are unique to or generated by the field of cyberlearning and other more general areas of concern to mind, brain, and educational technologies (Stein & Fischer, 2011).

Extended Cognition

An additional component for our understanding of cognitive, affective, and social processes for cyberlearning is the notion that technology is an extension of our cognitive processes (Parsons, 2015, 2017). It is becoming increasingly apparent that the educational technologies used in schools have the potential to extend a child's cognitive processes beyond the embodied cognition of their forebears (Parsons et al., 2017). Andy Clark and David Chalmers (1998) developed an "extended mind" theory, in which cognitive processes are understood as going beyond wetware (i.e., child's brain) to educational software and hardware used by the child's brain. This perspective allows for an understanding of the child's cognition as processed in a system coupled with the child's environment.

Clark and Chalmers describe the extended mind in terms of an extended cognitive system that includes both brain-based cognitive processes and external objects (e.g., technologies like tablets, iPads, smartphones) that serve to accomplish functions that would otherwise be attained via the action of brain-based cognitive processes acting internally to the human (Clark, 2008; Clark & Chalmers, 1998). They make use of a "parity principle" that states:

> If, as we confront some task, a part of the world functions as a process which, were it to go on in the head, we would have no hesitation in recognizing as part of the cognitive process, then that part of the world is (so we claim) part of the cognitive process. (Clark & Chalmers, 1998, p. 8)

From the parity principle, one can argue that if a process that happens in the classroom (external world) would readily be classified as part of the cognitive toolkit when it goes on in the student's head, then it is, at least for that point in time, part of the cognitive process. Using the parity principle as a guide, Clark and Chalmers present a thought experiment using fictional characters Inga and Otto to demonstrate the parity principle. Both Inga and Otto are navigating to a museum. Inga can navigate via recall of directions from her internal brain-based memory processes. Otto, on the other hand, has Alzheimer's disease. This requires Otto to depend on directions found in a notebook, which serves as an external navigation aide to his internal brain-based memory processes. Such extended mental processing can be understood as information-processing loops that spread beyond the neural. Clark and Chalmers assert the equivalence of neuronal memory and paper memory as information storage strategies in the case of Otto and Inga.

Paul Smart (2012) has applied the idea of extended cognitive processes to the specific sociotechnical context of the Web. The result is a "Web-extended mind," in which the Internet serves as a mechanism that realizes human mental states and processes. Various examples can be found in the ways in which students regularly enhance their cognitive performance with various technologies (e.g., tablets and iPads). Students are able to store their memories using technologies. While a student may not be able to remember what the average daytime temperature in the winter is near the poles on Mars, the student, plus her technology, can recall that it can get down to $-195°F$ ($-125°C$).

The potential for the extended cognitive processing perspective seems even more apparent with the advent of mobile technologies. Although early iterations of the Internet were bounded by wires, later iterations only had to be near a router. Today, with the influx and expansion of tablets and iPads in the classroom, the vast information base of the Internet is available to the student. The number of tablets and Smartphones found in schools are quickly approaching the point where billions of students will have access. Moreover, the technological assets of tablets and iPads offer several improvements to deliberations on externalization. Early metaphors emphasized external memory storage, iPads, and tablets connected to the Internet extend beyond memory assistants to robust mobile computation devices. In fact, mobile technologies connected to the Internet allow teachers and cyberlearning researchers to investigate the interactions of students as they participate with a global workspace and connected knowledgebases. Furthermore, access to the Internet may allow for interactive possibilities a paradigm shift in how we see student learning and the ways in which we understand the nature of students cognitive and epistemic competences.

It is important to consider the circumstances under which a device qualifies as a technology of the student's extended mind. First, it is helpful to explore what is meant by the word "mind." While a fully nuanced account of the term "mind" is beyond the scope of this chapter, a few words of clarification will be helpful to situate the notion of technology of the student's extended mind in context. While the term mind is used liberally in this chapter, it is not with the intent of slipping into some version of substance dualism (i.e., there is brain-stuff and mind-stuff). Instead, a specific distinction is made between brain and mind, in which the brain is understood as a thing while the mind is understood as a concept. The aim here is to keep from mixing these ontological levels in a way that so often ends in muddling the relation between brain and mind. A way of considering this issue is to consider the mind as representing the full set of cognitive resources that the student deploys in the service of thinking. Thinking can be understood as reflective, algorithmic, and autonomous thinking (Stanovich, 2009). This approach comports well with the extended mind hypothesis because the idea of a "full set of cognitive resources" allows for additional contributions (in addition to the brain) to conceptions of mental processing. The extension of mental processes outside of the brain (e.g., technologies of the student's extended mind) means that mental processes cannot be fully reduced to brain processes (Levy, 2007a; Nagel, Hrincu, & Reiner, 2016; Reiner & Nagel, 2017).

Technologies of the Student's Extended Mind

What sorts of devices can be considered technologies of the student's extended mind? One thing to keep in mind when answering this question is that not every algorithmic function performed by devices (external to the student's brain) should be understood as a technology of the student's extended mind. Instead, it is preferable to conceptualize technologies of the student's extended mind as a fairly continuous interface between brain and algorithm in which the student perceives the algorithm as being an actual extension of her mind. For example, consider an updated version of context-based learning games like the ones developed by the MIT Media Lab in the early 2000s (Klopfer, Perry, Squire, Jan, & Steinkuehler, 2005; Mystery at the Museum, 2003). In Mystery at the Museum, the student take part in an indoor augmented reality simulation that is enacted through the Boston Museum of Science. The background narrative includes a burglary that occurred in a science museum, and the students are instructed to apprehend the burglar by playing the role of a biologist, technologist, or detective so that they can ascertain what was stolen and what methods were used during the robbery. Mystery at the Museum was implemented using Wi-Fi for short-range information acquisition and communication. For our updated version, we could have the students use the Global Positioning System (GPS) in a tablet. Visualize a 13-year-old boy Tommy who has been instructed on how to enter exhibits into the search engine of a tablet application that will show him the best route to destinations for the context-based learning game quest. Once he arrives at the destination, the augmented reality enabled tablet can be used interactively by Tommy to learn about science and to solve the mysteries of the fictional burglary. This tablet application is particularly helpful because it allows Tommy to not get lost, as many of the game destinations lead him to visit parts of the museum with which he was unfamiliar. Tommy has heard stories from his classmates that they are not sure that the GPS interface for the museum always leads to the right place. As a result, Tommy remains alert to his environment so that he can be sure that he makes it to quest destinations in the museum without problem.

Is Tommy's GPS functioning as a technology of the student's extended mind? While it is undoubtedly performing computations that are external to Tommy's brain, the GPS in Tommy's tablet is probably better considered as cognitive assistance. Why is this the case? The answer is that neither the algorithmic calculations nor Tommy's use of them are integrated with Tommy's cognitive processes. Now consider a different scenario in which Tommy has taken part in the context-based learning game several times over the course of a month. Even though he now has slightly more knowledge of the museum, he always uses the GPS in his tablet to navigate through the museum, and it has not failed him. At this point, when he enters an exhibit into the tablet application's search interface and the route is presented on the tablet screen, he automatically follows it to the destination suggested by his tablet. The GPS is beginning to function as a technology of the student's extended mind because Tommy has integrated its algorithmic output into the working of his mind.

Neuroethical Issues for Technologies Extending the Student's Mind

What are the potential ethical implications of Tommy using a technology that extends his cognitive processes beyond his brain? One place to look for brain-based ethics is the relatively new discipline of neuroethics. Today, many ethical discussions about brain and technology interfaces are being discussed as neuroethical musings about the nature of the brain and the ways in which persons interact with technologies to make decisions. The discipline of neuroethics is often understood as twofold, with both the neuroscience of ethics and the ethics of neuroscience as two domains on inquiry. Herein, the main concern is the neuroscience of ethics and investigations of the digital self, values, beliefs, and motivations. While neuroethical issues for technologies of the extended mind have been discussed by a number of neuroethicists (see for example Heersmink, 2017; Heersmink & Carter, 2017; Levy, 2007a, 2007b, 2011; Nagel et al., 2016; Reiner & Nagel, 2017), they were first introduced in Neil Levy's (2007a) paper that argued for the substantial implications of the extended mind hypothesis for neuroethics. From a neuroethical perspective, Levy argues that the parity principle (if a cognitive process that happens in the classroom would readily be classified as part of the cognitive toolkit when it goes on in the student's head, then it is, at least for that point in time, part of the cognitive process) found in the extended mind hypothesis can be extended to an ethical parity principle for neuroethics.

> Neuroethics focuses ethical thought on the physical substrate subserving cognition, but if we accept that this substrate includes not only brains, but also material culture, and even social structures, we see that neuroethical concern should extend far more widely than has previously been recognized. In light of the extended mind thesis, a great many questions that are not usually seen as falling within its purview—questions about social policy, about technology, about food and even about entertainment—can be seen to be neuroethical issues. (Levy, 2007a, b)

Levy offers two moral principles for neuroethics labeled as versions of the ethical parity principle that can be used for discussion of moral concerns about neurological modification and enhancement: (1) Strong ethical parity: given that the mind extends into the external environment (e.g., classroom), adjustments of external props (e.g., iPad; tablets; smartphones) used for cognitive processes have ceteris paribus (i.e., all other things being equal) ethical parity with changes in the brain; and (2) Weak ethical parity: changes of external props have ceteris paribus ethical parity with changes in the brain, to the exact extent to which a person's explanations for deciding that brain changes are problematic can be transferred to changes of the environment in which it is embedded. Support for Levy's ethical parity principle is drawn from Clark and Chalmers's view that "in some cases interfering with someone's environment will have the same moral significance as interfering with their person."

Reiner and Nagel (2017, see also Nagel et al. (2016)) agree with Levy and present three issues have particular import for further discussion: (1) threats to autonomy from manipulations of technologies of a person's extended mind; (2) threats to privacy by examinations technologies of a person's extended mind; and (3) cognitive enhancements via technologies extending a person's mind. In the following, there is a discussion of Reiner and Nagel's manuscript as it applies to technologies extending the student's mind. A fundamental feature of their first issue, autonomy, is that the autonomous student should not be unduly influenced when making decisions. It is important to note that decisions made by students are guided frequently by the contribution of others (e.g., teachers, peers, caregivers) and/or the books and materials that they read, as well as their physical environment (e.g., classroom, playground). As a result, some have updated traditional notions of autonomy (Beauchamp and Childress (2001) to relational autonomy (Christman, 2004;

Mackenzie, 2010; Nedelsky, 1989). In the same way that establishing what influences are due and undue in the context of others can be a difficult task, so too can it be difficult to determine the influence of technologies that extend the student's mind. Prior to this, it is worth considering Reiner and Nagel's (2017) explication of the general features of algorithms that could impact the degree to which a influences are considered to be violations of autonomy. Nagel et al. (2016) argue for three important factors: (1) the algorithm's persuasiveness in decision-making; (2) the gravity of the decision; and (3) the algorithm's ability to identify the student's preferences.

In terms of persuasiveness of technologies, violations to autonomy are apparent when decision-making is influenced (Verbeek, 2006, 2009). If the student is still able to participate thoughtfully in decision-making and can reflect on the situation, then the impact of the technology will not be considered to be a violation of autonomy because there is no impediment to self-regulation. For their next factor, the gravity (i.e., seriousness) of the decision is relative to the level of potential harm or benefit a student may experience that may result from a given decision. Hence, the lower the assumed potential costs or benefits, the lower the apparent seriousness of the decision. Finally, their third factor, ability to learn about student preferences is important. If a technology simply executes a set of preprogrammed directives, then there is less concern. On the other hand, if the technology can monitor and learn from student behaviors and preferences, then there is increased possibility that an autonomy infraction may occur. Given these factors, an extension of the GPS example (see above) can be offered to illustrate the relevant issues for a student.

An illustrative example of the neuroethical concerns for technologies of the student's extended mind may begin with the GPS application for the museum on Tommy's tablet described above. Recall that Tommy's initial use of the GPS application involved vigilant attention to both the application and the environment to make sure that he could trust the functioning of the application and not get lost. Here the tablet application is not functioning as a technology of the student's extended mind because, while it is performing computations that are external to Tommy's brain, the GPS in Tommy's tablet is probably better considered as cognitive assistance.

Consider another situation, in which Tommy has been using the tablet application for a couple weeks, and the relationship between Tommy and the tablet app has grown more intimate—Tommy now integrates its algorithmic output into the working of his mind while traveling both inside the museum and around his neighborhood (e.g., to and from school, as well as to and from the locations of various extracurricular activities). Tommy is continuing his training in the museum and while working on an assignment that requires that he travel to an exhibit, he hears alerts from the tablet as he passes a sign advertising the museum's constellation of eateries (on the first floor, right across from the Museum Store); and alerts chime again when the museum's eateries are just up ahead.

Here, the situation has changed as the algorithms have learned Tommy's preferences and are attempting to influence his actions. Moreover, the algorithm from the tablet GPS application may increase its level of suggestion by "asking" Tommy whether he would like to take a moment to get something to eat, or perhaps shop in the museum store (right across from the museum's eateries). While Tommy may recognize that he needs to complete his assignment (continue his quest to solve the fictional burglary mysteries), he reasons that little harm would come from stopping to get something to eat and perusing the gift shop. Here, one finds a clear effect of the technology on Tommy that was influential enough to cause an alteration of his second-order desires to complete his assignment. Most likely, parents and teachers (as well as ethicists) would view this as undue influence. While the influence is relatively trivial, this scenario reflects a violation of autonomy.

This violation becomes much more pronounced when one considers the fact that the very same algorithm that has become an extension of Tommy's mind is also an extension of the mind of the corporate entity that designed the tablet application. Perhaps the corporate entity was paid by vendors at the Café and Museum store for directing Tommy to them. Such potential conflicts of interest muddy the ethical waters when attempting to ascertain the extent to which a technology of the student's extended mind has resulted in a violation of autonomy.

Cognitive Enhancement

Another area of concern for cyberlearning ethics is the issue of using advanced technologies to enhance cognitive abilities (Farah et al., 2004; Lalancette & Campbell, 2012; Parens, 2000). Developments in scientific knowledge are promising to enhance students' cognitive performance, memory, and/or or productivity through new applications of neuropharmaceuticals and/or possible technological advances (Forlini, Gauthier, & Racine, 2013). Cognitive enhancement refers to the capability of achieving psychological enhancements beyond what is needed to maintain or restore good health, such as modifications to memory and/or executive functions (Farah et al., 2004; Juengst, 1998). As a result, the widespread use of cognitive enhancers has led some to conclude that cognitive enhancement is now a socially accepted practice (Berg, Mehlman, Rubin, & Kodish, 2009; Farah et al., 2004; Singh & Kelleher, 2010), there are increasing calls for discussions of the ethical issues surrounding the use of biomedical techniques to enhance cognition (Gaucher, Payot, & Racine, 2013).

Students are increasingly using prescription drugs to cognitively enhance their academic performance (Howard-Jones, 2010; Maher, 2008; Poulin, 2001; Wilens et al., 2008). The so-called "smart pills" are nootropics (i.e., neuropharmaceuticals) that were originally established to treat neurodevelopmental and other brain-based disorders. These nootropics have started making their way into schools because healthy (typically developing) students believe that they can use them to enhance memory (piracetam), wakefulness (modafinil), and attention (methylphenidate/Ritalin).

In an article exploring the ethics implications of cognitive enhancements in students, Singh and Kelleher (2010) urged professional medical associations to establish policy statements related to bringing neuroenhancement into primary care. One example can be seen in the American Academy of Neurology's recently development and publishing of a position statement regarding the ethics of pediatric enhancement within the patient–parent–physician relationship (Graf et al., 2013). The decision of the statement was that physicians should not prescribe cognitive enhancers to children or adolescents. They based their decision on the fiduciary responsibility of physicians toward their pediatric patients.

An obvious ethical challenge to education is that the non-clinical use of nootropics is a lifestyle choice made in response to performance pressures in a competitive environment (Racine & Illes, 2008). Illes (2006) described four main ethical challenges related to the use of nootropic: safety, coercion, distributive justice, and personhood. From this, questions emerge: Does greater effort confer "dignity"? Is the student the same person when on Ritalin? Moreover, there seems to be a coercive factor in teachers' preference for enhanced children because they tend to be more receptive to learning and interactions. That said, the restriction of nootropics could be viewed as coercive when the restriction limits freedom of choice about whether or not to enhance. A further issue is distributive justice because unfairness results between haves and have-nots. The inequities in society, from private tutoring to technological access, it is not an issue specific to nootropics until the question of cheating is added. Is enhancement in itself a form of cheating? Discussions of cheating include issues of fairness and carries de facto moral wrongness when understood as the infringement upon implicit rules and/or the access to inequitable benefits (Lalancette & Campbell, 2012).

Conclusions

The challenges of applying neuroscientific findings to learning technologies are numerous, but have a common denominator: the framework supporting a brain-based cyberlearning has to be well defined and explicit. Attempts have been made by the Association for Educational Communications and Technology to define ethical research and practice. Moreover, attempts have been made to present a framework for approaching ethical issues in the use of educational technologies (Spector, 2016). Herein, there has been a discussion of the ways in which such frameworks can be extended to develop a brain-based cyberlearning approach to ethics that emphasizes the advances in cognitive, affective, and social neuroscience.

Extending the framework to some extent involves the recognition that our mental states are constituted by our neurocognitive and affective states and a shifting collection of external resources and scaffolding. Our understanding of what constitutes a person is partially a function of the student's environment, inasmuch as the student's capacities are dependent on features of her context. Moreover, a student's identity is largely a product of social relations to others.

Following the extended mind thesis, there is a strong prima facie case for ethical concerns accompanying various means of enhancing cognitive performance. While some approaches to learning technologies emphasize ethical principles, neuroethics focuses on the neural substrates subserving cognitive processes. Herein, the emphasis has been upon combining these approaches via an argument that mental processes include not only brains, but also learning technologies, and even classroom social structures. This allows for the ethical concerns of educational technologists, educational neuroscientists, and neuroethicists to extend far more widely than has previously been recognized. Given the extended mind thesis, a number of ethical concerns about using educational technologies can be seen to be neuroethical issues. In making decisions about how educators structure classroom environments and employ educational technologies, decisions can be made about the ways in which technologies of the extended mind are employed, and such decisions must be informed by neuroethical thinking.

References

Allied Control Council. (1949). *Trials of War Criminals Before the Nuernberg Military Tribunals Under Control Council Law No. 10*. Washington, DC: US Government Printing Office.

Beauchamp, T. L., & Childress, J. F. (2001). *Principles of biomedical ethics*. New York: Oxford University Press.

Berg, J. W., Mehlman, M. J., Rubin, D. B., & Kodish, E. (2009). Making all the children above average: Ethical and regulatory concerns for pediatricians in pediatric enhancement research. *Clinical Pediatrics, 48*(5), 472–480.

Bohil, C. J., Alicea, B., & Biocca, F. A. (2011). Virtual reality in neuroscience research and therapy. *Nature Reviews Neuroscience, 12*(12), 752–762.

Christman, J. (2004). Relational autonomy, liberal individualism, and the social constitution of selves. *Philosophical Studies, 117*(1), 143–164.

Clark, A. J. (2003). *Natural-born cyborgs: Minds, technologies and the future of human intelligence*. Oxford: Oxford University Press.

Clark, A. (2008). *Supersizing the mind: Embodiment, action, and cognitive extension*. Oxford: Oxford University Press.

Clark, A., & Chalmers, D. (1998). The extended mind. *Analysis, 58*(1), 7–19.

Clausen, J., & Levy, N. (Eds.). (2015). *Handbook of neuroethics*. Dordrecht: Springer.

Farah, M. J. (2012). Neuroethics: The ethical, legal, and societal impact of neuroscience. *Annual Review of Psychology, 63*, 571–591.

Farah, M. J., Illes, J., Cook-Deegan, R., Gardner, H., Kandel, E., King, P., et al. (2004). Neurocognitive enhancement: What can we do and what should we do? *Nature Reviews Neuroscience, 5*(5), 421–425.

Fischer, K. W., & Bidell, T. (2006). Dynamic development of action and thought. In W. Damon & R. Lerner (Eds.), *Handbook of child psychology, Vol. 1: Theoretical models of human development* (6th ed., pp. 313–399). Hoboken: Wiley.

Forlini, C., Gauthier, S., & Racine, E. (2013). Should physicians prescribe cognitive enhancers to healthy individuals? *Canadian Medical Association Journal, 185*(12), 1047–1050.

Frith, C. D., & Frith, U. (2007). Social cognition in humans. *Current Biology, 17*(16), R724–R732.

Gaucher, N., Payot, A., & Racine, E. (2013). Cognitive enhancement in children and adolescents: Is it in their best interests? *Acta Paediatrica, 102*(12), 1118–1124.

Graf, W. D., Nagel, S. K., Epstein, L. G., Miller, G., Nass, R., & Larriviere, D. (2013). Pediatric neuroenhancement Ethical, legal, social, and neurodevelopmental implications. *Neurology, 80*(13), 1251–1260.

Heersmink, R. (2017). Extended mind and cognitive enhancement: Moral aspects of cognitive artifacts. *Phenomenology and the Cognitive Sciences, 16*(1), 17–32.

Heersmink, R., & Carter, J. A. (2017). The philosophy of memory technologies: Metaphysics, knowledge, and values. *Memory Studies*. https://doi.org/10.1177/1750698017703810

Howard-Jones, P. (2010). *Introducing neuroeducational research: Neuroscience, education and the brain from contexts to practice*. New York: Routledge.

Illes, J. (2006). *Neuroethics: Defining the issues in theory, practice, and policy. Oxford*. New York: Oxford University Press.

Illes, J. (Ed.). (2017). *Neuroethics: Anticipating the future*. Oxford: Oxford University Press.

Immordino-Yang, M. H. (2008). The smoke around mirror neurons: Goals as sociocultural and emotional organizers of perception and action in learning. *Mind, Brain, and Education, 2*(2), 67–73.

Immordino-Yang, M. H., & Singh, V. (2011). Perspectives from social and affective neuroscience on the design of digital learning technologies. In R. A. Calvo & S. K. D'Mello (Eds.), *New perspectives on affect and learning technologies* (pp. 233–241). New York: Springer.

Januszewski, A., & Molenda, M. (Eds.). (2007). *Educational technology: A definition with commentary* (2nd ed.). New York: Routledge.

Juengst, E. (1998). What does enhancement mean? In E. Parens (Ed.), *Enhancing human traits: Ethical and social implications* (pp. 29–47). Washington, DC: Georgetown University Press.

Kane, R. L., & Parsons, T. D. (Eds.). (2017). *The role of technology in clinical neuropsychology*. Oxford: Oxford University Press.

Klopfer, E., Perry, J., Squire, K., Jan, M. F., & Steinkuehler, C. (2005, May). Mystery at the museum: a collaborative game for museum education. In *Proceedings of the 2005 Conference on Computer Support for Collaborative Learning: Learning 2005: The Next 10 Years!* (pp. 316–320). International Society of the Learning Sciences.

Lalancette, H., & Campbell, S. R. (2012). Educational neuroscience: Neuroethical considerations. *International Journal of Environmental and Science Education, 7*(1), 37–52.

Levy, N. (2007a). Rethinking neuroethics in the light of the extended mind thesis. *American Journal of Bioethics, 7*(9), 3–11.

Levy, N. (2007b). *Neuroethics: Challenges for the 21th century*. Cambridge, MA: Cambridge University Press.

Levy, N. (2011). Neuroethics and the extended mind. In J. Illes & B. J. Sahakian (Eds.), *Oxford handbook of neuroethics* (pp. 285–294). Oxford: Oxford University Press.

Mackenzie, C. (2010). Imagining oneself otherwise. In C. Mackenzie & N. Stoljar (Eds.), *Relational autonomy: Feminist perspectives on autonomy, agency, and the social self* (pp. 124–150). New York: Oxford University Press.

Maher, B. (2008). Poll results: Look who's doping: In January, Nature launched an informal survey into readers' use of cognition-enhancing drugs. Brendan Maher has waded through the results and found large-scale use and a mix of attitudes towards the drugs. *Nature, 452*(7188), 674–676.

Meshi, D., Tamir, D. I., & Heekeren, H. R. (2015). The emerging neuroscience of social media. *Trends in Cognitive Sciences, 19*(12), 771–782.

Mitchell, J. P. (2008). Contributions of functional neuroimaging to the study of social cognition. *Current Directions in Psychological Science, 17*(2), 142–146.

Montag, C., & Reuter, M. (Eds.). (2017). *Internet addiction: Neuroscientific approaches and therapeutical implications including smartphone addiction*. Berlin: Springer.

Montfort, D. B., & Brown, S. (2013). What do we mean by cyberlearning: Characterizing a socially constructed definition with experts and practitioners. *Journal of Science Education and Technology, 22*(1), 90–102.

Mystery at the Museum. (2003). [*Computer software*]. Cambridge, MA: MIT Teacher Education Program & The Education Arcade. Retrieved March 17, 2013, from http://education.mit.edu/ar/matm.html

Nagel, S. K., Hrincu, V., & Reiner, P. B. (2016, May 13–14). *Algorithm anxiety—do decision-making algorithms pose a threat to autonomy?* Presented at 2016 IEEE International Symposium on Ethics in Engineering, Science and Technology, Vancouver, BC.

National Commission for the Protection of Human Subjects of Biomedical and Behavioral Research. (1978). *The Belmont Report: Ethical principles and guidelines for the protection of human subjects of research-the National Commission for the Protection of Human Subjects of Biomedical and Behavioral Research.* US Government Printing Office.

Nedelsky, J. (1989). Reconceiving autonomy: Sources, thoughts and possibilities. *Yale Journal of Law and Feminism, 1*(1), 5.

Office for Human Research Protections [OHRP]. (1979). *The Belmont Report: Ethical principles and guidelines for the protection of human subjects of research.* Retrieved from http://www.hhs.gov/ohrp/humansubjects/guidance/belmont.html

Parens, E. (Ed.). (2000). *Enhancing human traits: Ethical and social implications.* Washington, DC: Georgetown University Press.

Parsons, T. D. (2015). Virtual reality for enhanced ecological validity and experimental control in the clinical, affective, and social neurosciences. *Frontiers in Human Neuroscience, 9,* 660.

Parsons, T. D. (2016). *Clinical neuropsychology and technology: What's new and how we can use it.* Berlin: Springer.

Parsons, T. D. (2017). *Cyberpsychology and the brain: The interaction of neuroscience and affective computing.* Cambridge: Cambridge University Press.

Parsons, T.D., Gaggioli, A., & Riva, G. (2017). Virtual environments in social neuroscience. *Brain Sciences, 7*(42), 1–21.

Parsons, T. D., Riva, G., Parsons, S., Mantovani, F., Newbutt, N., Lin, L., et al. (2017). Virtual reality in pediatric psychology: Benefits, challenges, and future directions. *Pediatrics, 140,* 86–91.

Parsons, T. D., Rizzo, A. A., Rogers, S. A., & York, P. (2009). Virtual reality in pediatric rehabilitation: A review. *Developmental Neurorehabilitation, 12,* 224–238.

Poulin, C. (2001). Medical and nonmedical stimulant use among adolescents: From sanctioned to unsanctioned use. *Canadian Medical Association Journal, 165*(8), 1039–1044.

Racine, E., & Aspler, J. (Eds.). (2017). *Debates about neuroethics: Perspectives on its development, focus, and future.* Berlin: Springer.

Racine, E., & Illes, J. (2008). Neuroethics. In P. Singer & A. Viens (Eds.), *Cambridge textbook of bioethics* (pp. 495–504). Cambridge, MA: Cambridge University Press.

Reiner, P. B., & Nagel, S. K. (2017). Technologies of the extended mind: Defining the issues. In J. Illes & S. Hossain (Eds.), *Neuroethics: Anticipating the future* (pp. 108–122). Oxford: Oxford University Press.

Singh, I., & Kelleher, K. J. (2010). Neuroenhancement in young people: Proposal for research, policy, and clinical management. *AJOB Neuroscience, 1*(1), 3–16.

Smart, P. R. (2012). The web-extended mind. *Metaphilosophy, 43*(4), 446–463.

Spector, J. M. (2005). Innovations in instructional technology: An introduction to this volume. In J. M. Spector, C. Ohrazda, A. Van Schaack, & D. A. Wiley (Eds.), *Innovations in instructional technology: Essays in honor of M. David Merrill* (pp. xxxi–xxxvi). Mahwah: Erlbaum.

Spector, J. M. (2015). *Foundations of educational technology: Integrative approaches and interdisciplinary perspectives* (2nd ed.). New York: Routledge.

Spector, J. M. (2016). Ethics in educational technology: Towards a framework for ethical decision making in and for the discipline. *Educational Technology Research and Development, 64*(5), 1003–1011.

Spector, J. M., Merrill, M. D., Elen, J., & Bishop, M. J. (Eds.). (2013). *Handbook of research on educational communications and technology* (4th ed.). New York: Springer.

Stanovich, K. E. (2009). Distinguishing the reflective, algorithmic, and autonomous minds: Is it time for a tri-process theory. In J. Evans & K. Frankish (Eds.), *In two minds: Dual processes and beyond* (pp. 55–88). Oxford: Oxford University Press.

Stein, Z., & Fischer, K. W. (2011). Directions for mind, brain, and education: Methods, models, and morality. *Educational Philosophy and Theory, 43*(1), 56–66.

Uddin, L. Q., Iacoboni, M., Lange, C., & Keenan, J. P. (2007). The self and social cognition: The role of cortical midline structures and mirror neurons. *Trends in Cognitive Sciences, 11*(4), 153–157.

Verbeek, P.-P. (2006). Persuasive technology and moral responsibility toward an ethical framework for persuasive technologies. *Persuasive, 6*, 1–15.

Verbeek, P.-P. (2009). Ambient intelligence and persuasive technology: The blurring boundaries between human and technology. *NanoEthics, 3*(3), 231–242.

Wilens, T. E., Adler, L. A., Adams, J., Sgambati, S., Rotrosen, J., Sawtelle, R., et al. (2008). Misuse and diversion of stimulants prescribed for ADHD: A systematic review of the literature. *Journal of the American Academy of Child & Adolescent Psychiatry, 47*(1), 21–31.

World Medical Association. (1964). *World Medical Association Declaration of Helsinki - ethical principles for medical research involving human subjects.* Ferney-Voltaire: World Medical Association.

Yeaman, A. R. J. (2016). Competence and circumstance. *TechTrends, 60,* 195–196.

Thomas D. Parsons   is Director of the NetDragon Digital Research Centre and the Computational Neuropsychology and Simulation (CNS) laboratory at the University of North Texas. His work integrates neuropsychology, psychophysiology, and simulation technologies for novel assessment, modeling, and training of neurocognitive and affective processes. He is a leading scientist in this area, and he has been PI of 17 funded projects during his career and an investigator on an additional 13 funded projects (over $15 million in funding). In addition to his patents for eHarmony.com's Matching System (U.S. Patent Nos. 2004/6735568; 2014/0180942 A1), he has invented and validated virtual reality-based assessments (including the Virtual School Environment) of attention, spatial abilities, memory, and executive functions. He uses neural networks and machine learning to model mechanisms underlying reinforcement learning, decision-making, working memory, and inhibitory control. In addition to his five books, he has over 200 publications in peer-reviewed journals and book chapters. His contributions to neuropsychology were recognized when he received the 2013 National Academy of Neuropsychology Early Career Achievement award. In 2014, he was awarded Fellow status in the National Academy of Neuropsychology.

Author Index

© Association for Educational Communications and Technology 2019
T. D. Parsons et al. (eds.), *Mind, Brain and Technology*, Educational
Communications and Technology: Issues and Innovations,
https://doi.org/10.1007/978-3-030-02631-8

Subject Index